THE FELLOWSHIP OF

The key to understanding the context of the Church within divine providence

{Revised July 2018}

Richard L. Barker

*Unto me who is the most inferior of all the saints was this grace granted that I should proclaim to the nations the unsearchable riches of Christ so as to enlighten everyone regarding the **fellowship of the secret hidden in God through the ages**, who created all things through Jesus Christ – that through the Church should now be made known to the sovereignties and authorities in the heavens, the multi-faceted nature of God's wisdom according to the purpose of the ages made in Christ Jesus our Lord.*

PUBLISHED BY:

Richard L. Barker on Amazon

The Fellowship of the Secret

Copyright 2017 ISBN 9781545319260

by Richard L. Barker

A re-edited version of the e-book originally published by Matador under the title "Saul of Tarsus and the Fellowship of the Secret" in March 2015.

Table of Contents

Introduction

This book resulted from an extraordinary spiritual experience I encountered a few summers ago in which I came to understand the Bible in quite a new way. The writings of the apostle Paul are the focus of my synopsis, starting with the passage in Ephesians from which the book's title is derived. Some English language Bibles translate the phrase "fellowship of the mystery" whilst others utilize a textual variant which reads in the Greek *"oikonomia"* (administration or dispensation) rather than *"koinonia"* (fellowship) - either of which will suffice given that Paul is here referring to the Church, being both a community or fellowship but also an administration pertaining to the gospel age. I will show that it was the unforetold nature and racial make-up of this sacred assembly that led to Saul of Tarsus being called "out due of time" as the thirteenth faithful apostle, Matthias having replaced Judas Iscariot to make up the twelve. That was so that Paul might *"enlighten everyone concerning the fellowship pertaining to the secret (plan) known only to God who had created all things through Jesus Christ; (this mystery or secret) having been hidden through the ages from the authorities of Heaven is brought to light through the Church, so revealing the multi-faceted nature of God's wisdom regarding His purpose for the ages which He accomplished in Christ* (Eph3:9-11). God's secret plan, a mystery from our perspective, was revealed to Paul and somewhat cryptically by him; its meaning obscured further by some spurious translations such that its significance has largely been hidden from the Church, in accordance I believe with divine intentions for her pathway of discovery. Once Paul's meaning here is grasped and taken together with its related passage in Romans (ch11 vv11-15), one's understanding of divine providence is transformed as one comes to appreciate that the exclusive Covenants of Promise pertaining to Israel and the Church are just a part of a broader, more inclusive redemptive strategy.

In terms of prophecy, what I refer to in shorthand as "the fellowship of the secret" explains why the expectations of the Old Testament prophets and even some of Jesus's prophetic statements in the Gospels are neither being fulfilled in reality nor "realized within the spiritual sphere by the Church", apart from in a certain dual perspective sense that I explain in my opening chapter, by which I mean that what had been anticipated for the Temple but not fulfilled there, will be, or has already been paralleled within Church history. Other matters such as any applicable geopolitical considerations pertaining to the Jewish apocalypse and Israel's status as the "children of the Kingdom" are not currently being fulfilled, rather placed on hold until in Paul's words *"the fullness of the Gentiles has come in"* (Rom11:25). That is referring to the time when Christ shall come in glory to herald what Scripture variously describes as "the renaissance" (Mt19:28), the liberation of the created order (Rom8:19-23) or "the restoration of all things" (Acts3:21). Traditionally many understand the Parousia to be the end of the space-time universe when Christians (and some might add faithful Jews) are transported to Heaven and everyone else is effectively consigned to the cosmic wastepaper basket. Their understanding of the Good News, and in the past my understanding, was that only the members of the exclusive Covenants of Promise were the people that God intended to reconcile to Himself and bring into His Kingdom. The bulk of humanity, as the most influential theologian of the first Christian millennium Augustine of Hippo made a point of emphasizing, were destined for eternal punishment in accordance with God's good pleasure: *"Many more are left under punishment than are delivered from it, in order that it may thus be shown what was due to all"* [A].

Many Christians have come to perceive or at least sense in their bones that such a cosmic outcome is inconsistent with the term "Gospel" (Good News) as well as God's nature as Scripture presents it and Jesus as the incarnate Word revealed it. With, I believe, the Spirit's help, I have set out how a truly beneficent providence may faithfully be *adduced from Scripture* without undermining the vital utility of gospel grace or the role of the Church. Like the apostle Paul I have come to know God to be a Philanthropist (Titus3:4 cf. Greek), a depiction utilized by some of the earliest Church fathers as the necessarily small-scale patristic study I have incorporated affirms. Unfortunately for many, such broader benign providence cannot be delineated without critically re-examining the biblical hermeneutics of one of Rome's most revered doctors – Augustine, Bishop of Hippo. His synopsis, whilst not wholly endorsed was substantially utilized by the Early Catholic Church and built upon a thousand years later by the Protestant Reformers who corroborated his emphasis on human moral ineptitude and one-dimensional grace. Such a schema does not lend itself to amelioration; it must either be taken as read or virtually redrawn from scratch. Of necessity I have undertaken the latter, providing, I trust, a thoroughly coherent biblical synopsis, incorporated for the moment here and in my e-book, the latter being an especially timely technological development for the propagation of such a disclosure, providing readers with online access to the Greek and Hebrew linear translations of the Bible as well as to the writings of those earliest (apostolic) Fathers who had not been entirely dependent on biblical exegesis having *heard* the Good

News and its essential soteriology directly from the apostles or their immediate appointees.

I am no academic and this book is hardly the result of a life-long study, for my understanding of certain biblical passages was transformed during the ten or so days I was conscious of the Holy Spirit's immediate presence, a time of weeping, rejoicing and virtual nervous breakdown – an experience that from my conservative Christian background I was not expecting or barely open to receiving. However, the new understanding I have come to has been confirmed at the personal level by its ability to resolve many tensions and inconsistencies within Scripture, in the process demonstrating the existence of evil and its associated suffering to be a necessary part of the transformative process by which all redeemable humanity is being prepared for future participation in God's Kingdom.

INTRODUCTION - REFERENCES:

A. Saint Augustine – *"The City of God"* Book XXI chapter 12

Chapter One

The Hidden Dispensation

*"And **this gospel of the Kingdom** will be preached in all the world as a witness to all the nations and then the end will come"* (Mt24:14 New King James Version)

The book's title is taken from a passage of Paul which we will examine shortly but it was puzzling over the above statement of Jesus *within its textual context* that was the catalyst to transforming what I had intended to be a small-scale retirement writing project for incorporation into a personal website into something so expansive; so a consideration of the prophecy in which it is embedded is where I have opted to start. The verse which will form the focal point for this opening chapter is taken from what most Bible scholars acknowledge to be a distinctly problematical end-time prophecy referred to as the Olivet Discourse. It was musing upon it that set the ball rolling along a personal voyage of discovery which reshaped my understanding of how biblical prophecy in both the Old Testament and the gospels should be approached. The term "gospel of the Kingdom" occurs only four times in the New Testament and is used exclusively when referring to the preaching of Jesus - twice by Matthew (4:23; 9:35) and once by Mark (1:14). The only other occasion this description of God's glad tidings is used is by Jesus Himself, the verse quoted in the chapter sub-heading. The verse is assumed to be referring to the preaching of the current gospel age, but why is it somewhat incongruously located in the middle of Jesus's discourse on the tribulations, referring to the natural disasters and political traumas that would herald His second coming? Or was the Lord referring here to the destruction of the Temple and the events leading up to it? The

8

disciples had asked Him about both in the Matthew account (v3), but the response doesn't clearly distinguish between these two cataclysmic events, as is also the case in Mark and Luke's accounts. It is as if they were expected to occur almost simultaneously, in which case it must be said these passages would have made a lot more sense. In Mark's account, the flight from Jerusalem to the mountains is directly linked to the tribulations which are to affect the whole of humanity (Mk13:18-20) preceding the coming of the Son of Man (vv24-26). It is clearer still in one of two references to these events in Luke's account (chapter 17), where the escape passage (vv30,31) is indisputably linked to the return of the Son of Man, who "must first be rejected by this generation" (v26). Frankly, neither preterist nor futurist can provide a satisfactory solution to this passage, but once one grasps the implications of the "fellowship pertaining to the administration/dispensation of the secret (plan) that had been hidden in God" (*"fellowship of the secret"* for short), such terms become largely redundant outside the allusive book of Revelation.

A large part of the 24th chapter of Matthew is indisputably referring to the end of the age and the universal significance of the second coming. The passage concerning the escape to the mountains (vv15-20) as is clearer from the account in Luke (21:20) indicates a siege of Jerusalem; yet heading for the hills would hardly have been advisable in the context of the first Jewish-Roman war (66-73AD) as events transpired unless there was to be some divine deliverance waiting when one arrived there. That historical conflict did indeed result in a siege of the city and the destruction of the Temple by members of the Roman army in AD70, but Jesus's advice would align better to the prophecy in Zechariah chapter 14 in which a siege of the holy city by Gentile armies coincides with the coming of JHWE as King of the World. The purpose of escaping to the mountains would indeed have been divine deliverance by passing through the supernaturally created mountain valley to safety in "Azal" (Zech14:5), at which point the Lord would sally out and fight the nations who had oppressed His people (v3) in accordance with other Old Testament end-age prophecy. If Jesus had this in mind, it would explain why the passage in Matthew concerning

9

the escape to the mountains directly leads into verses 21 and 22 relating an unprecedented global trauma that if it were not to be shortened would destroy humanity, heralding the return of the Son of Man.

Jesus went on to warn of false messiahs, wars, famines, pestilence, earthquakes, persecution of the faithful, many of whom will betray and hate one another, many being ensnared by false prophets; and because of the increase in lawlessness, the love of many of the faithful will grow cold (vv10-12). Comfort should be drawn from the description of the forecast global trauma as birth-pangs (v8), anticipating what Jesus and Matthew refer to as the renaissance or regeneration (Greek: *paliggenesia*) that is to follow. And so we arrive at the featured verse in which Jesus declares that *"this gospel of the Kingdom"* will be proclaimed in every place and nation as a witness before the end of the age comes. For reasons already implied I believe that what was being envisaged here was a global evangelistic mission (cf. Mt10:23b) rather than what we regard as the gospel dispensation, now entering its third millennium. But even if it were referring to the gospel age, for such a universal witness to be accomplished if Christ were to return imminently, three issues would surely need to be addressed: firstly, there should be an agreed understanding of the Good News message to be announced to the world; secondly and inextricably linked to the first, it would be delivered from a unified or at worst affiliated body of churches; and thirdly, the outreach would be driven and given urgency by a common recognition that to use Jesus's analogy, the fig tree was in bloom (v32), i.e. world events were indicating that the end of the current arrangements on Earth really was nigh. But as some readers will appreciate, for our Lord alludes to it in this prophecy in the context of the Temple as later does Paul in the context of the Church, His return will have been preceded by a cataclysmic ecclesiological event, as a result of which the gospel has a markedly different content depending on which Christian grouping is presenting it, thus making a coherent universal witness quite impossible. If you disagree with that assessment it is probably because you think the other lot, for example Catholic and Orthodox churches if you happen to be an Evangelical, do not know the true gospel

10

anyway; which rather demonstrates my point. Before delving further into that maelstrom some surprising particulars need to be kept in mind with regard to the prophecy under consideration. Starting with one that is explicitly stated in Scripture, the incarnated Son of God was not at that time aware of the precise timetable of events (Mk13:32), for that was known only to His Father. In view of the resurrected Jesus's unwillingness later to answer His apostles' inquiry concerning the restoration of the Kingdom to the Jews (Acts1:6-7), they were not given any indication of timescales when writing the epistles, and most would agree that is evident from the tone of their content. For example, although Paul on one occasion refers to himself as being absent from the body and present with the Lord, i.e. going to Heaven when he dies, he always encourages or warns his readers in the churches in terms of being prepared for the "Day of the Lord" (1Cor1:8; 5:5 2Cor1:14, Phil1:6,10;2:16, 1Thes5:2; 2Thes2:2; 2Pet3:10,12); or "patiently to await the Son from Heaven" (1Thes1:10), rather than speaking in terms of an individual's death and the judgement to follow it. It suggests that he along with the apostles had themselves interpreted the Lord's teaching as indicating such a day might well arrive within a generation, albeit that St Peter suitably reminded his readers that one day with the Lord can be as a thousand years (2Pet3:8).

Restoration of the Kingdom to Israel

But the more salient issue to consider at this point is what exactly the apostles were asking Jesus in Acts1:6-7 and what He said in response, and what is equally interesting what He did not say. *"Lord, will you at this time restore the Kingdom to Israel?"* The enquiry pertained to the re-instatement of the Kingdom role to its intended heirs the Jewish nation, and by implication the related prophesies concerning the physical nation itself. The question obviously cannot relate to Jewish people "getting saved by coming into the Church", for the Church's membership at that point was almost exclusively Jewish and continued to be so up to Peter's revelation concerning the admittance of the Gentiles (Acts10). Jesus in response does not dismiss the apostles' inquiry as irrelevant on a basis that the Kingdom was

11

to be established universally through the Church, but rather He replies that it was not their business *"to know the times and seasons which the Father has put under His own authority"*. Given the timing (post-Commission) and the persons being denied enlightenment on the subject Jesus did not intend it to be the Church's immediate business either. The response also implied that such a re-instatement might indeed be anticipated otherwise He surely would have replied along the lines: "You have not understood my teaching; the question is irrelevant". In terms of Old Testament prophecies relating to what we know as the gospel age, as most readers will recognize, there simply aren't any that come close to envisaging the form it has taken. Without exception they roll together the coming of the Messiah as heralded by John the Baptist with final judgement and messianic rule, as indeed did the Baptist in his understanding and preaching as I will demonstrate shortly. Jesus's reference to *this* gospel of the Kingdom (*touto* to *euaggelion* Mt24:14) that He envisaged would be preached before His return must equate to the Good News message about the coming Kingdom and how to prepare for it that Jesus and His disciples had been preaching to the Jewish people, for it was *this* gospel not another (I said I was pedantic), and a major component of the outreach was physical healing, raising the dead and casting out evil spirits. That was the context of His commission: *"Freely you have received, freely give"* (Mt10:8). For all twelve including Judas Iscariot had been given the power to heal sickness and disease (v1). Yet what Jesus's disciples were preaching and performing (albeit exclusively amongst the Jews v5) as a result of their Matthew 10 commission could have contained no reference to Jesus's death and resurrection and the soteriology focussed around it, for the disciples had no conception of it (Lk9:45, 18:31-34); yet it would be "this gospel of the Kingdom" that the Lord envisaged would be a witness to the rest of the world at the end of the age (Mt24:14).

Already, two seminal points may be gleaned: firstly and more generally, scriptural references to "the gospel", for example Paul's introductory statement in his letter to the Romans (1:1-7) are referring to a proclamation concerning the Lordship or Kingship of Jesus; the gospel *per se* is not a list of instructions

12

about how one gets saved; rather that is the result for those who obey the Good News proclamation. Secondly and more controversially, Jesus's understanding of the "gospel of the Kingdom" as a final witness to the world re-affirms that at the time of the Olivet discourse He was not anticipating (or if you prefer not disclosing) the gospel age of the Church as it has panned out. That is why the Church has never preached the "gospel of the Kingdom" that Jesus's disciples were preaching and enacting, in which physical healing and satanic deliverance were central and the soteriology concerning Christ's Passion quite absent. The gospel the Church *has* been preaching has rightly been focussed on Christ's death and resurrection as the means by which the soul can be healed, the elect of God sanctified, and the world enlightened and salted. Of course, Jesus hadn't died and been resurrected at the time of the Olivet Discourse, but the point that I am typically labouring is that no reference could have been made about His death and its implications for none of the disciples were expecting it let alone would understand it (Lk9:45; 18:31-34).

"Behold the Servant of God who is to eradicate sin from the world"

At least two of John Baptist's former disciples were amongst the twelve so they could not have been aware of it either in spite of the prophet's references to the *"talya d'alaha"*, which John translates in his gospel as "Lamb of God" for that is what the apostle had come to know Christ to be: the Paschal Lamb. But *"talya"* can equally mean "servant" (or "son") in the Aramaic language, and one of those is bound to have been the Baptist's understanding otherwise his disciples that became the Christ's disciples would surely have been better informed and prepared for what was to occur (i.e. their Lord's death). It is highly unlikely that Jesus was referred to as the "Lamb of God" by His disciples during His earthly ministry, which is why it is only to be found in the later Johannine account. For the slaying of the lamb was the focal rite of Jewish Passover, and as His most

13

faithful disciple had assured his Master: "No worries, Lord, that is certainly not going to be happening to You!" (cf. Mt16:22).

Acts: a guide to sound evangelism

Once one reaches the Acts of the Apostles, the crucified and risen Jesus is central to the Good News message. Indeed, Acts is vital in that it indicates how people were called to gospel salvation in terms of what is required of them and once again just as importantly what is not. Examine every sermon in Acts meticulously, including Paul's and you will note that "justification" for example is mentioned but once (13:38b/39). In the apostolic evangelistic preaching of Acts, people were not brought to salvation by apprehending "justification by faith alone", or by "renouncing any effort to be righteous and resting in the Saviour's merits" or "looking to the finished work of Christ and appropriating it to myself" or "believing that Jesus had died *for me* as an individual" or "praying the prayer of faith, asking Jesus to come into my heart" but simply by acknowledging and believing that Jesus Christ is Lord, turning from their sinful ways and being baptized for cleansing of past sin: nothing more, nothing less (cf. Acts8:36,37 & 17:30). The teaching on how the Christian goes on to grow in the faith and in holiness and participate fully in the life of the Church is provided by the epistles. Of course, none of the apostles' writings are specifically evangelistic, being pastoral letters written to the churches, but even allowing for this change of genre (evangelistic preaching to pastoral letter) it cannot be the case that what is essential to saving faith could be excluded from *all* the evangelistic sermons in the Bible and can only be deduced from the Pauline epistles! Of course, the Lord's ethical teaching in the gospels along with the pastoral epistles must be drawn upon to fill out the picture of what it means to commit one's life to Christ; but in terms of what one is required to believe or emotionally experience to become a Christian, and who within the broader Church are to be regarded as such, nothing can supplement the requirements of initiation as preached in Acts. Likewise, if the gospel as one currently perceives it does not match the heralding angel's description of

14

"Good News of great joy that shall be to all people (Lk2:10), be assured one has not yet fully grasped the implications of the birth, life, death, resurrection, ascension and coming again of the Lord Jesus Christ. Angelic messages of Good News and great universal joy lead to joyous outcomes for humanity, albeit not necessarily for each individual; any eschatological depiction that does not reflect that Good News requires revisiting, however revered its formulator may have been.

Saul of Tarsus - The thirteenth faithful apostle

Jesus had called twelve men to the apostolate for good reason, and a richly symbolic one:

*And Jesus said to them, "Truly I say to you who have followed Me, in the Regeneration when the Son of Man will sit down on His glorious throne, you also shall **sit upon twelve thrones judging the twelve tribes** of Israel (Mt19:28 New American Standard Bible)*

It symbolized the reconstitution of God's chosen people: the twelve tribes, only two of which had survived at this point. Judas lost his spot and was replaced by Matthias who it tends to be forgotten was added to the eleven faithful apostles (Acts1:26), surely to complete the symbolism for there was no obvious practical reason for him be recruited at that point. Peter had insisted that one from amongst the larger group of men and women who had been accompanying Jesus throughout His ministry be appointed to make up the twelve who were to witness to Jesus's life, death and resurrection as apostles (Acts1:21,22). Saul of Tarsus on the other hand was appointed "out of due time" (1Cor15:8), personally commissioned by the risen and ascended Christ as the thirteenth faithful apostle[1] now that gospel salvation was to be made available to the Gentile nations. In his own words, Saul of Tarsus was *"chosen to know God's will; to see the Righteous One and hear His voice so as to be a witness to all men"* (Acts22:14,15). Yet surely if Jesus had initially envisaged commissioning a universal body to take over the role of Israel in establishing God's Kingdom on Earth, He would not have ruined the symbolism by appointing a thirteenth

15

apostle at a later stage specifically to target the Gentiles (Rom11:13). That is hardly a strong argument in itself to justify the title of this opening chapter, just one piece of the evidence. For it should become obvious as one carefully reads through Acts that in spite of the Great Commission to baptize and make disciples of all nations, it is not until events recorded in the eleventh chapter that any of the disciples fully grasped that anyone who was not a Jew, Samaritan or proselyte could be granted the same gift of salvation [Greek: *ten isen dorian*] as that intended for the Jews:

*I (Peter) realized **then** that God was giving them (the Gentiles) the **identical gift** He gave to us when we believed in the Lord Jesus Christ; and who was I to stand in God's way? This account satisfied them (circumcised believers in Jerusalem) and they gave glory to God, saying "God has clearly granted to the Gentiles also the repentance that **leads to life** (Acts11:17,18 New Jerusalem Bible).*

One will constantly need to keep in mind that references to "eternal life" or "life" in the New Testament relate to being united to God in Christ now, not "going to Heaven when you die":

*And **this** is eternal life, that they might know You the only true God and Jesus Christ whom You have sent (Jn17:3).*

And: *"Whoever eats My flesh and drinks My blood **has** (present tense) eternal life, and I will raise him up at the last day" (Jn6:54)*

And: *"No murderer has eternal life **abiding in him"** (1Jn3:15)*

St John is referring to something to be experienced now; a higher form and quality of life than that which we can naturally know as fallen human beings; likewise, Peter in Acts. Even the sinless Saviour asserted that He *"**lived by the Father"** (Jn6:57)* in the same way *"those who eat Me shall **live by Me*** (same verse), affirming again that "life" as Jesus, Paul and others speak of it does not relate to "avoiding perdition" or going to Heaven but a present empowering relationship with the divine; "death" being the deprivation of such. This is not to deny that eternal life

16

in the more literal sense is promised for the future; i.e. living in a body that never ages or dies rather than this body which is heading for the grave. Those who have eternal life abiding in them also hope to inherit such everlasting life (e.g. Tit3:7).

The chief apostle will have been aware he had received a universal commission to make disciples for Jesus of all nations. But Acts11:17 confirms categorically he had not up to that point understood that Gentiles were to receive a gift of salvation of the nature that he and his fellow Jews had received; i.e. that which pertained to "eternal life" as we have just defined it. Peter and the other apostles would therefore not have envisaged that those who were to carry the work of the Kingdom forward after them could be Gentile since they had not grasped that non-Jews were to benefit in the same way as they had from the "Good News" of Jesus. This should appear all the more surprising considering that the disciples had spent further time with Jesus after His resurrection receiving instruction from Scripture concerning Himself (Lk24:45,46); surprising that is until one apprehends the "fellowship of the secret/mystery". Peter's realization concerning the Gentiles' inheritance came through his vision of the sheet of unclean animals that he was told to kill and eat (Acts11:1-18) prior to his involvement in the first recorded conversion of a Gentile named Cornelius. Again, does not this surprise you? This man who had spent three years at the Saviour's side and been subsequently filled with the Spirit yet did not realize the Gentiles were to be incorporated into the Church – they were barely to be associated with (Acts10:28); unless of course Jesus had not taught otherwise and this would be Paul's Good News (cf. Rom16:25). In Peter's case he did not grasp the matter until he had received a prophetic vision; in view of the nature and timing of Paul's commission he was in no doubt he had been called to evangelize the (uncircumcised) Gentile nations and regarded Peter as leading the evangelisation of the "circumcision" (Gal2:7,8). Some would make the case that particularly in view of his contribution to the Scriptures, Paul was the supreme apostle rather than Peter and I am inclined to agree with them. Yet paradoxically it re-affirms Peter to be the rock (Greek: *Petros*) upon which Jesus would build His assembly, for as we have just been considering the Lord had

17

originally called twelve apostles, not thirteen. Paul affirmed Peter to be the leader of those apostles evangelising the Jews, yet Jesus had given no indication whatsoever that such would be the arrangement when He commissioned Peter and (at that point) ten other disciples. Paul also had to rebuke fallible Peter for his reluctance to fellowship with Gentile Christians (Gal2:11-14). Not so surprising really since the one apostle had been instructed by the incarnate Word of God as Jewish Reformer (cf. Mt23:1-3), the other by that same divinity as Overseer of His international Church; the one apostle being ignorant of the fellowship of the mystery that had been hidden in the Father (Eph3:9), the other being its discloser having been personally instructed by the Son (cf. Gal1:16, 17). Do not give up on me, all shall be explained within the chapter: my frequent prayerful and not intentionally irreverent refrain throughout my encounter with the Spirit was "You've got to be kidding me".

Prophetic passages in the Old Testament that appear to be anticipating the Church age need to be examined in context. Probably the one that comes closest is Joel chapter 2, and the section we relate to the Church is:

*You shall know that I am in the midst of Israel; I am the Lord your God and there is no other. My people shall never be put to shame. And it shall come to pass that **afterwards** I will pour out my Spirit on all flesh. Your sons and your daughters shall prophesy, your old men will dream dreams, your young men shall see visions, and also on my menservants and on my maidservants I shall pour out my Spirit in those days. And I will show wonders in the Heavens and in the Earth, blood and fire and pillars of smoke. The sun shall turn sun into darkness and the moon into blood before the coming of the great and awesome day of the Lord and it shall come to pass that **whoever shall call on the name of the Lord shall be saved**, for in Mt Zion and Jerusalem there shall be deliverance as the Lord has said among the remnant whom the Lord calls (Jl2:27-32 New King James Version – listed as 3:1-5 some versions)*

Joel's prophecy appears to be depicting a period that will immediately *follow* the restoration of Israel and the vindication of His people in the presence of JHWE, which is the case in all

18

such prophecy. Order or sequence is a quandary for the Old Testament spiritualizing hyper-allegorist; i.e. much of Christendom at present. I am aware that Christians of my former ilk will not be comfortable with that term, but I simply mean it in the dictionary sense of "all Christians everywhere"; likewise with "Jewry", I am referring to all Jewish people, their culture and beliefs. Whilst there are of course frequent allegorical references to Christ and the gospel throughout the Old Testament, there is also a historical context and narrative to be considered, such as the fact that Torah was both practiced and delighted in by the godly (Ps119). Similarly with prophecy, Joel and those who interpreted him understood the promised restoration of Israel in a more literal sense, ending His nation's humiliation, the oppressing "Northerners" being sent packing (Jl2:20); God's people and even the animal Kingdom liberated (Jl2:22) within a restored religious, political and ecological environment (Jl2:23). This would be followed by an outpouring of the Spirit on all flesh in turn followed by the tribulation (Jl2:30,31) and the Day of JHWE. The gospel of the Kingdom would be preached, echoing Jesus's words: *"Repentance for the forgiveness of sins will be preached in His name to all nations, beginning at Jerusalem* (Lk24:47)" Those calling on the name of the Lord and fleeing to the Mountains would "escape" whilst the "remnant" would be safe in Jerusalem (Jl2:32). For sure, Peter draws upon the above passage from Joel in the context of the Spirit's outpouring on the Day celebrating the Feast of the first-fruits (Pentecost) (Acts2:17:21), so the first part of the prophecy had been fulfilled in the context of the apostolic gospel age. Prophets in the apostolic era were relatively commonplace (Acts13:1; 15:32; 21:10), but although Paul confirms their ecclesiological office as secondary only to the apostles (1Cor12:28) they have played no universally accepted office in the Apostolic Church beyond the first century; similarly, miracle workers and healers. Yet Jesus had said *"If I cast out devils by the finger of God then the Kingdom of God has come upon you"* and implied in Jn14:12 that His followers would likewise be given authority to raise the dead, physically heal and cast out demons, indeed do greater works than He had performed; yet again, that is only really the case during the apostolic era. I have

19

concluded that these miraculous events along with the prophetic office were a continuation of the witness of Jesus and His disciples during His time on Earth and were for the same purpose: as a witness *to God's chosen race* that the Kingdom of God had come upon them; and since all the miraculous activity was carried out in Jesus's name, evidence that the One that their leaders had conspired to crucify was indeed the promised Messiah.

The Jews' two-stage rejection of Jesus and His Kingdom

Here is one of several points where confusion has arisen with regard to the implications of the rejection of Jesus as Messiah by His people in terms of the apparent subversion of Old Testament prophecy. The first rejection/subversion is recognized by Christendom but not Jewry whilst the second has been understood by neither, being the fellowship of the secret; initial incredulity for Christendom, potential Good News for Jewry and great news for the world. I will endeavour to unpack what I mean by that statement during the remainder of this chapter.

The key reference to the first rejection or failure to recognize Israel's "day of visitation" together with its implications is outlined by Luke. Jesus approaches the holy city on a donkey and weeps over her:

*"If you had known, even you, especially in this your day the things that **make for your peace**! But now they are hidden from your eyes. For the days will come upon you when your enemies will build an embankment around you, surround you and close you in on every side, and level you and your children with you, to the ground, and they will not leave in you one stone upon another, **because you did not know the time of your visitation"** (Lk19:42-44 New King James Version)*

It must be remembered that many ordinary Jews welcomed Jesus to their city with their palm leaves but their leaders were indignant and already plotting His downfall. This was the first rejection culminating in the crucifixion and as Jesus stated (v42) it put paid to the prophecies indicating that the coming of the

20

Messiah would bring an end to Israel's political and military problems; the promise of peace and security for Jerusalem, evident in much prophecy including the recent angelic annunciations concerning John and Jesus, would not be secured by Jesus in His earthly lifetime, quite the contrary in fact; worse was to come for Israel in about a generation's time. Jesus warned as much in the Olivet discourse we have been considering. But this *per se* is not what resulted in the rejection of the Jewish nation as sole inheritors of the Kingdom that Paul refers to in Romans 11 and Ephesians 3. Such is affirmed in Acts where the apostle indicates that even after Pentecost it was *still* the Jewish people's "day of visitation" and they were still not appreciating it. Paul gave this warning to certain Jews at Antioch:

So be careful! – or what the prophets say will happen to you: "Cast your eyes around you mockers; be amazed and perish! For I am doing something in your own days that you would never believe if you were told of it" (Acts13:40,41 New Jerusalem Bible)

Note the warning is about what will or might happen to the Jewish nation, not what already had happened. Their day of visitation did not end when they crucified Christ: that event that Jesus referred to as His other baptism had been both divinely planned and prophesied (Acts2:23; Is53:5); what was shortly to occur was undoubtedly planned or foreknown (by God) but never prophesied; it concerns the secret fellowship (or community partnership) "hidden in God" even from earlier prophets; it concerned a universal Church. For the Jewish leaders refused to acknowledge that the resurrection and the miraculous signs were the vindication of Jesus's earlier claims. They still rejected His Messiah-ship even now that He had been raised to the highest Heavens and empowered His disciples to work miracles in His name. That, in modern parlance is where they finally blew it. They had already blown the prospect of political peace and security through their rejection of Jesus in His lifetime, now something even more radical was at stake: Kingdom inheritance. The very next Sabbath, these same leaders "filled with jealousy" towards the apostles, just as they had been

21

toward Jesus used blasphemies to contradict everything Paul said (v45), which prompted the apostle to add this:

*We had to proclaim the word of God to you (Jews) first, but since you have rejected **it**, (i.e. the apostle's message) since you do not think yourselves **worthy of eternal life**, here and now we turn to the Gentiles. For this is what the Lord commanded us to do when He said "I have made you (Israel) a light to the nations, so that my salvation may reach the remotest parts of the world" (Acts13:46,47).*

The prophecy from which Paul quotes (Is49) declares Israel to be God's servant, through whom He would manifest His glory (v3) and by whom He would bring saving enlightenment to the whole world (v6). They as His chosen people and future heirs of the world (cf. Rom4:13,14) would have come to know "eternal life", i.e. an intimate relationship with God and life of an eternal quality (Jn17:3) through sanctification in Christ blood (Zech13:1); but as the same prophet foretold this had been prophetically linked with the restoration and liberation of their nation and holy city through the direct intervention of a returning messiah, who as well as residing with his people would act as judge and arbitrator with opposing nations (Is2:4; Mic4:3.) Now, says Paul, as a result of their rejection, the universal enlightenment would go ahead without them by means of a newly formed universal assembly founded by their Messiah and His apostles, none of whom had been drawn from the ranks of the Jewish sacral hierarchy. Although it is only briefly alluded to in Scripture, the longed-for national liberation and the re-instatement of Israel to "the Kingdom" would now have to wait (Acts1:6). After issuing this warning, Paul and Barnabas symbolically shook the dust from off their feet as they left Antioch (13:51), just as the disciples had done to towns and homes that rejected the "gospel of the Kingdom" preached during Christ's earthly ministry. Shortly afterwards at Corinth, preaching as usual in the synagogue, certain Jews "turned against (Paul) and started to insult him". Paul took his cloak and shook it out in front of them, saying:

*"Your blood be on your own heads; from now on I will go to the Gentiles **with a clear conscience**" (Acts18:6 New Jerusalem Bible).*

One is bound to ask why Paul's conscience would not have been clear (literally: clean) if he had brought this gospel to the Gentiles and the Jews hadn't rejected his message: wasn't his message of salvation intended for all? Well, yes and no: *"for as a result of the Jews' rejection, salvation has come to the Gentiles to provoke them to jealousy"* (cf. Rom11:11). I had previously understood this to be merely a question of order, but there would no logical reason for such if the privileges of Kingdom service and the eternal life pertaining to it were from the time of Pentecost being offered to the world; apart from which the apostles would have been quite clear in their minds about the matter, which they certainly were not, with the obvious exception of the lately-commissioned Saul of Tarsus. Apart from which, Paul writing to the Romans is adamant: salvation came to the Gentiles as a result of the Jews' rejection; it was not a question of protocol or order. For as we will see there is salvation and there is SALVATION. The latter was earmarked for the Jews alone in Old Testament prophecy but was to be made available to the nations through Paul's revelation of what in short-hand I refer to as "the fellowship of the secret". "Salvation" as foretold for the Gentile nations meant one would be enlightened, pardoned in the name of Jesus if one acknowledged Him as Lord, leading to acceptance as a subject in God's Kingdom, for all who call on the name of the Lord would be spared (i.e. saved from perdition). SALVATION on the other hand was to be born again by water and Spirit, delivered from corruption by means of sanctification in the blood appointed for sprinkling[2] provided through Calvary (Heb12:24 cf. Greek) resulting in interior communion with Christ, eternal life, participation in God's royal priesthood and a joint-inheritance with the Son of God, no-less.

In the early chapters of Acts, everything appeared to be following prophetic expectations: the Messiah had come, been rejected, executed, raised and ascended. For sure, few if any Jews, even the twelve, had understood His death from Scripture

23

but it could be seen and understood in retrospect, for all references to the gospel being "demonstrated from Scripture", for example to the Ethiopian eunuch in his chariot exclusively utilized the Old Testament at that point. The Spirit had been poured out upon Jews and proselytes on Pentecost, the dead were being raised; demons expelled, numerous miracles being performed, not just by apostles but deacons as well (Acts6:8). Even items of the apostles' clothing or handkerchiefs were taken to people and they were healed. Multitudes came to the apostles for healing, and again, all were healed (Acts5:16). The Good News about Jesus was being preached as a result of which Jews, Samaritans and proselytes were receiving the gift of the Spirit leading to "eternal life", such that at that point Peter could say:

All the prophets that have ever spoken from Samuel onwards have predicted these days (Acts3:24).

But they did not predict what was about to follow, and that had been heralded by the appointment of the thirteenth faithful apostle – O blessed number, for it signified that Gentiles, against all prophetic predictions were to be granted "eternal life" and have equal status with elect Jews as joint-heirs with Christ in His Kingdom. Paul had been appointed *"as a priest in the Good News of God that the offering up of the Gentiles might become acceptable, sanctified by the Holy Spirit"* (Rom15:16 Young's Literal). Having quoted from Joel concerning the pouring out of the Spirit, the apostle Peter goes on to tell his Jewish hearers that the Jesus they had crucified was resurrected and temporarily being retained by Heaven until coming again to establish a universal restoration (Acts3:21). In the meantime, they should repent, be baptized for the forgiveness of sins and thus receive the Holy Spirit (Acts2:38).

So in terms of the Joel's prophecy, the outpouring of the Spirit had been fulfilled, but the part that the prophet thought would precede it concerning the Jewish nation and people had not. The fact that Peter nevertheless draws upon this prophecy in the context of the dawning of the gospel age actually reinforces what is being asserted here – that the terrestrial promises pertaining to the Jews and Jerusalem are not fulfilled or "re-envisaged" through the establishment of the Church, and so the

24

apostle utilizes virtually the only passage that appears to resemble a gospel age rather than apply the imagery of Jerusalem and the nation of Israel being replaced by the Church, albeit that Paul does on one occasion refer to the "Jerusalem that is above", our Mother (Gal4:26), referring to those who dwell in Heaven and form a part of the communion of saints with the Church on Earth (see also Heb12:22). Wherever Old Testament prophecy is quoted in the New Testament, it is not re-envisaged to fit the idea of the Church; rather selective portions pertaining to the particulars that have been fulfilled are quoted, and the rest, such as the restoration of Israel, destruction of the wicked and arbitration with the nations is omitted. Such scriptural dark matter incorporating some of the more cryptic or ambiguous narratives which occur in this analysis are an aspect of what is considered in more detail in chapter five under "progressive revelation". This has undoubtedly been God's stratagem for the Church, just as it has been for the world in terms of the human race's pursuit of scientific knowledge and their advances in medicine, transport and communicative media. For it would hardly have been fitting for television, mobile phones and the internet to have been available for the events surrounding the first coming of Jesus Christ; nor for that matter the printing press, given that Jesus would be founding a Church, not writing a book. In the religious sphere an on-going learning curve has been guaranteed through the intentionally cryptic profundity of Holy Scripture that was never intended to be unravelled until the end of the age, for it contains at least one significant mystery (or secret) that was not to be disclosed until such a time (cf. Dan12:1-4&7; Rev10:4,7). But now let us focus more carefully on that other "*musterion*", usually translated "mystery" which in its context pertains rather to a divine secret requiring initiation.

The fellowship of the secret

The New Testament "elephant in the room": the biblically unexplained and largely undebated non-fulfilment (or subversion) of scriptural prophecy regarding the terrestrial and political aspects of the Jewish apocalypse pertains to a secret disclosure, revealed to and through Paul of which I was

25

previously unaware but now realize is the key to understanding Old Testament prophecy. Still more importantly from a Christian perspective, it reveals the true significance and *context* of "gospel salvation". It also sheds light on the nature of the processes that will be initiated by Jesus at His coming. Addressing Gentile converts in the Ephesus Church, the apostle wrote as follows:

*Surely you have heard about the administration of God's grace that was given to me for you (Gentiles), that is the MYSTERY made known to me by revelation, as I have already written briefly. In reading this then you will be able to understand my insight into the MYSTERY of Christ, which was **not made known to people in other generations** as it has **now been revealed** by the Spirit to His holy apostles and prophets*. This MYSTERY is that through the gospel the Gentiles are **heirs together with Israel**, members together of one body, and sharers together in the promise in Christ Jesus (Eph3:2-6 New International Version). [* i.e. the prophets contemporary with the apostles – NOT the prophets of the Old Testament]*

So the Church was not to be exclusively Jewish: what's the big deal some might ask? Three times in this short passage the apostle refers to a mystery (or secret): who is likely to pay much attention to such a seemingly verbose passage? Who indeed; that is why its implications have been missed for nearly two millennia. I have come to appreciate during this process that neither Paul nor any other contributor to Holy Scripture ever "waffles" or is slipshod with his use of words. Every phrase and grammatical construction in the original Greek or Hebrew has been incorporated and preserved for a purpose; the Holy Spirit as Supreme Editor has seen to it, though translators have not always respected it. The point about this passage is not the mystery itself relating to the Gentiles inheriting the Kingdom, but the fact that it **was** a mystery; in fact, a secret [same word in Greek], into which the apostle to the Gentiles had been initiated through personal revelation. It was "*not made known to people in other generations*", even by the prophets, otherwise it would not be a secret but a fulfilment; nor indeed was it revealed by or possibly to the divine Prophet in the gospels (cf. Mk13:32), at

26

least not at the time He was outlining His expectations regarding His second coming and/or temple destruction that we looked at earlier. For this was a secret to be revealed by Paul that had been previously "hushed up" (*sesigemenou* - Rom16:25 Greek interlinear), the significance of which has scarcely been grasped in the gospel age either. This was *Paul's gospel* (*to euaggelion* __*mou*__ - Rom16:25); the revelation of the mystery kept secret through the ages.

It pertains to a mystery which from Paul and his contemporaries' perspective related to the fact that people outside the race of Israel were not only to be enlightened and offered forgiveness through repentance in the name of the Lord as indicated in Old Testament prophecy but come to "*share an inheritance with the sanctified*" (Acts26:18). In Paul's words they were to be "*joint-heirs with Israel*" (v6). They too could receive the Holy Spirit and have their hearts purified by adherence to the faith (Acts15:9 cf. Greek). Be assured that was *not* the teaching of the Old Testament prophets. Such a blessing would be achieved by coming into a mystical communion with Christ:

The mystery which has been hidden from ages and generations, but ***now has been revealed to His saints****, to whom God willed to make known what are the riches of the glory of this mystery among the Gentiles, which is* ***Christ in you, the hope of glory*** *(Col1:26,27 New King James Version)*

The mystery being outlined in *this* book is that the Gentiles' access to this supreme gift of grace was indeed initially a mystery, even to the other twelve apostles. All this has implications to the interpretation of earlier prophecy: logically one would expect the promises of the Old Testament to be fulfilled in the New Testament age, albeit perhaps in a more spiritualized sense. But such a fulfilment isn't going to happen; it is not intended to happen – at least not all within the current age for earlier prophesies did not envisage the current age as such. From any human perspective, the published plan for the salvation of the world has been changed; not the Man or His supreme act of love at the centre of it of course but the supporting cast. Yet according to Paul, it was not really a change of plan: the Old Testament prophecies set out what would

27

happen if the Jews recognized their "day of visitation" when it arrived in the Person of Jesus. The Father knew the outcome but did not relay it through His prophets; it was kept a closely guarded divine secret, to be revealed (appropriately) by the thirteenth faithful apostle, appointed out of time for an unexpected task. This may appear bizarre, even playful, but then this is our God: *"O the depth of the riches both of the wisdom and knowledge of God! How unsearchable are His judgements, and His ways past finding out. For who has known the mind of the Lord or who has been His counsellor?"* Thus exclaimed Paul, also in the context of the Gentiles' unexpected inheritance of "eternal life", as he outlines it again in Romans chapter eleven. Yet even this more explicit reference hasn't been grasped either; subconsciously readers suspect the poor old chap's throwing another wobbly, or at least he cannot possibly mean what he appears to be writing (especially Rom11 vv11,12,15 &30). On the contrary, the apostle meant exactly what he had written: Gentiles would not have been "saved" in the present age if the Jews had kept Covenant. They could have been enlightened and finally accepted into God's eternal Kingdom, but they would not have been saved in gospel terms, i.e. their souls whilst still embodied could not have been healed, restored and divinely aided so as to experience eternal life by *recovering the divine communion* that was lost as a result of the Fall. This mystery hasn't been grasped because something else hasn't been grasped along with it, without an understanding of which the apostle's comments about the Gentile inheritance taken as read would indeed appear ludicrous, for the Old Testament makes it quite clear that God had intended to reconcile the world not just the Jews to Himself. That "other" pertains to what has already been hinted at and is to be considered in detail in the chapter concerning justification through the faithfulness of Christ; how the benefits of the Atonement avail at two levels. All then will make better sense: "But is it scriptural?" I hear you cry; I intend to demonstrate so shortly.

Non-retractable assurances to the Jewish nation

Blessed is the nation whose God is the Lord; and the people whom He has chosen for His own inheritance (Ps33:12)

The psalmist was referring to the nation of Israel, the first-fruits of God's increase (Jer2:3) and the intended "sons of the Kingdom" who later were rejected or rather, placed on hold (Mt8:12). For what may humanly speaking appear to be a change of plan is not a change of mind with respect to the promises JHWE has made to His covenant people, or else our faith might be in jeopardy. The apostle writes in the same chapter of Romans (11): *"there is no change of mind on God's part about the gifts He has made, or of His choice* (v29). That refers to His choice of the nation of Israel as His special people and that her King would one day become King of the world. That plan has not so much been re-envisaged, spiritualized or even "fulfilled in the person of Jesus"; rather it has been re-ordered, sub-divided and augmented; for God has concluded Gentile and Jew in unbelief that He might have mercy on both (Rom11:32) and give eternal life to both (Acts11:17) through joint incorporation within the Fellowship of His Son. The outcome is now going to be even better; for Jewish disobedience has brought about the opportunity for an alien like myself to be fully reconciled to God now, even whilst in sin-prone flesh. But His first-choice people have not been forgotten either:

For if the casting away of (the Jews) be reconciliation for the World, what shall the reception of them be but life from the dead? (Rom11:15)

This affirms what I was indicating earlier; it was not a question of protocol or order, i.e. preach the gospel to the Jews first then move on to the Gentiles – it was the Jew's "casting away" that led to the Gentiles salvific inheritance as co-equals with His chosen race. It had rather been a case of "offer the privileges of the Kingdom to the sole heirs-apparent first; if they as a nation reject it (i.e. they still reject its King Jesus) then let it be offered to the whole world to rouse the holy nation to jealousy" (cp. Rom11:11). This is surely reaffirmed just a few verses later when Paul refers to his Gentile Christian readers as wild and

29

unnatural appendages that had been grafted into the good olive tree that was the Jewish nation (Rom11:24). That is hardly the language of prophetic fulfilment; the Gentile nations were never perceived in prophecy to be joint-heirs-apparent to the Kingdom. It subverted all expectation; it was *new revelation*; it was the fellowship of the secret hidden in God, the immediate text surrounding which we shall come to in a moment. And it is wonderful news, for grasping this mystery opens up a new perspective on the context of gospel salvation within a vastly broader salvific landscape, as hinted at a few paragraphs ago. But where does this leave us within the re-staged procession of salvation history; at what point are we within such a metanarrative? According to the Old Testament the age in which we are living was to be the time when the Gentile nations were being enlightened by God's Holy priesthood the Jewish nation under their Messiah King of Israel and the World; but instead, elect members from all nations are currently joining that royal priesthood through incorporation into the Church to enlighten the whole world and prepare it for realization of the Kingdom of God at Christ's appearing.

The Jewish Nation: light to the Gentiles

As far as the Old Testament age was concerned, the race of Israel was intended to have been a light to the Gentile nations, living as a holy nation faithful to JHWE, whose Name and Law would become honoured amongst other nations:

*Look, as JHWE my God commanded me (Moses), I have taught you laws and customs for you to observe in the country in which you are to take possession. Keep them and put them into practice and **other peoples will admire your wisdom and prudence**. **Once they know what all these laws are**, they will exclaim "No other people is as wise and prudent as this great nation Israel (Deut4:5,6).*

Some readers will be aghast at Moses' statement - the Law (Torah) actually to be practiced so that the world would come to admire Israel *and her Law?* Yes indeed, that was the divine intention – so that the Jewish race might fulfil its role of light to

30

the Gentiles; a thoroughly positive role for the Law which clearly Moses understood but the likes of Augustine, Luther and Calvin did not. The witness of Israel *being faithful to the Law* was meant to have been the rest of the world's "preparation for the Gospel" i.e. their future submission to the Lordship of King Jesus when He eventually came to do what John Baptist expected Him to do: destroy the enemies and oppressors of God's people and judge the whole world, i.e. put it to rights. Then, supported by the Jewish Nation (the sons of the Kingdom - Mt8:12), He would establish God's Kingdom on Earth; reconciling other nations to God and each other by inculcating a way of peace along the lines of Isaiah chapter two that we will look at in a few pages time.

Such was the consistent expectation of all Old Testament prophecy but instead of that, on the minus side the current age remains under the grip of evil (cf. Gal1:4) for Satan's fate has been sealed but he has not been cast out and continues to deceive the world, whilst very much on the plus side Gentiles are being invited to join with Jews in the Messiah's Fellowship so that together under the direction of the Holy Spirit they may enlighten the unchurched world in preparation for the Lord of the Church's return, "*whom Heaven must keep until the time of the universal restoration*" (Acts3:21 cf. Greek). Then at His coming, supported by a vastly enlarged and racially inclusive sanctified assembly (the sons of God), including those who currently sleep in Christ, He will establish His Kingdom of peace and enlightenment throughout the world. Then what?

Then comes the end when He shall have delivered up the Kingdom to God, even the Father; when He (the Son) shall have suppressed all rule, authority and power. For He must reign until He has put all enemies under His feet...Then when all things have been subdued unto Him, then shall the Son Himself be subject unto Him who put all things under Him, that God may be all in all (1Cor15:24-28 Young's Literal).

The Old Testament prophecies had outlined how that would have been accomplished by Jesus with the faithful from His chosen nation; the difference in the "age" (or "Day" or whatever) to come will be the racial make-up of the Jesus people

31

and the folk still needing enlightenment. But the key point is this: the enemies to be defeated or suppressed will be the same, for they will *not* have been eradicated by the Church: Satan, his structures, his seed (Gen3:15), his sicknesses (Lk13:16) and his death (cf. Heb2:14). The victory over these things has been made possible through the cross but will not be accomplished before the restoration in Christ's presence. The victory over Satan and what he controls on Earth along with the Jewish terrestrial/political expectations of Old Testament prophecy are not being fulfilled or "re-envisaged" in any form within this current dispensation; it has been deferred, effectively to allow for the mystery of the Gentile inheritance to be fulfilled (cf. Rom11:25). The Jewish nation has been provoked to envy; her house has been left to her desolate; yet once the nature and purpose of the current dispensation and the sacred fellowship pertaining to it has been grasped, will she not also say *"Blessed is he who comes in the name of the Lord"?* (cf. Lk13:35).

The fellowship of the secret – unknown to the heavenly sovereignties

It's about time I focussed on the verse of Scripture which gave rise to the title of this book. Paul refers to the revelation of the Gentiles' unexpected inheritance being provided to the "apostles and prophets" (Eph3:2-6). These refer to prophets of the apostolic age (cf. Acts13:1; 1Cor12:28) for the mystery had only been revealed "now" (v5). Even the heavenly authorities were kept in the dark concerning this mystery, as is confirmed by the often mistranslated and barely comprehended verses 8-11:

*Unto me, who is the most inferior of all the saints, was this grace granted that I should preach among the (Gentile) nations, the unsearchable riches of Christ to enlighten all regarding the fellowship of the secret hidden in God through the ages, who created all things through Jesus Christ, that **through** the Church should **now** be made known **to** the sovereignties and authorities in the heavens, the multi-faceted nature of God's wisdom according to the **purpose of the ages** made in Christ Jesus our Lord (Eph3:8-11)*

32

In other words, it was not until the establishment of the Church, indeed *by* its establishment, that this mystery concerning the Gentiles' portion, salvific inheritance and the nature of the dispensation pertaining to it was revealed by God even to the principalities and powers of Heaven, having been "hidden in God" from the earlier age. That is why none of the Old Testament prophesies depict the gospel age or Church in the form it has taken, for it was never envisaged (or disclosed) that the Gentiles would be included amongst Christ's consecrated band of enlighteners, rather that they would become enlightened through association with the Jews, God's elect people. But now according to Paul's Good News, the Gentiles could themselves be made holy and incorporated within that consecrated fellowship and inherit all its privileges (Acts26:18). As explained in the introduction, having completed this writing I was subsequently led to examine again the writings of the early Fathers and was surprised to discover that St John Chrysostom (AD347-407) had come in part to an understanding of this matter, namely that the dispensation of grace to the Gentiles (resulting in eternal life and a glorious inheritance) was unknown to the Old Testament prophets as well as the celestial principalities and powers before it was revealed through St Paul. Chrysostom utilized the Alexandrian NU-textual variant "dispensation" for this verse rather than "fellowship", and the former equally makes sense in the context. This mysterious or secret dispensation Chrysostom recognized had not "come to pass" but had now been "manifested" through the establishment of the Church[3a]. He goes on to write in his commentary:

*"For this is the gospel: 'It is He that shall save His people' – but (note) not a word about the Gentiles. That which concerns the Gentiles the Spirit reveals; that they were called indeed the angels knew, but that it was the **same privileges as Israel**, yea, even **to sit upon the throne of God**, who would ever have expected this? Who would ever have believed it? – (for it had) been **hid in God**"[3b]*

He also affirms my translation from the Greek, i.e. that that the mystery was revealed now (not in the Old Testament), through or on account of (not "to") the Church, to (not "by") the celestial authorities. The fourth century saint and scholar does not work through its implications but at least he had grasped the gist of what Paul was intimating, which is more than most interpreters had done, including myself until revealed by the Spirit. I acknowledge that many early Fathers, unless they had clearly understood Paul's reference to this mystery, would regard the fellowship of the secret as a "strange doctrine" for I find it somewhat peculiar myself. Yet it must be presented for not only was it directed to my mind during what I know to have been a spiritual encounter, it reconciles a great deal concerning the context of the Church and gospel within a yet more glorious plan of loving goodness in which the majority of human tongues will one day willingly confess that Jesus is Lord to the glory of God the Father (cf. Phi2:11).

Returning to Ephesians, in the previous chapter Paul had explained to His Gentile readers how it had become possible for them to benefit from what was not originally intended for them. The reason they had previously been excluded from the promises of Christ was simply because they were not Jewish:

*Remember you were at that time separate from Christ, excluded from citizenship in Israel, **foreigners to the Covenants of the Promise**, without hope and without God in the world (Eph2:12).*

As well as breaking down the horizontal barrier between God and man, a vertical barrier was also broken down through Christ's death and resurrection and that is the one Paul is referring to in this frequently misinterpreted passage (Eph2:11-16). Its focus is not on how the sinner is reconciled to God but how Jew has been reconciled to Gentile and *both* reconciled to God. For Christ is the end of the Law (Torah) for righteousness for everyone who believes (Rom10:4). He had set aside in His flesh the corpus of Jewish Law with its commands and regulations to create in Himself *"one new humanity out of the two"* (v15) as a means of reconciling both to God through the cross by which He put to death the enmity between Jew and Gentile (v16). Thus the Gentile nations could become fellow citizens with God's people (the Jews), both becoming members of God's Household which is the Church (v19). This effectively is the fellowship of the secret, or the revelation of the

34

"mysterious administration/fellowship" and the age pertaining to it that had been "hidden in God from earlier (pre-Apostolic) generations". The exegetical implication is that Old Testament prophecy, instead of being tortuously allegorized to prefigure the Church or the gospel age, should now be understood as relating in part to the period immediately *following* the second coming of Christ, which of course matches the sequence envisaged in all Old Testament prophecy. References to the "Gentiles" or "nations" can now be read as "the un-churched" or "non-Christian". It heightens the importance of the Revelation to John together with the limited prophetic statements contained in the epistles (mainly Paul and Peter), for unlike earlier material these were experienced and set down after the mystery had been revealed concerning the role of the Gentiles in the Kingdom. And what a transmutation! In the Old Testament, Isaiah consistent with his fellow prophets envisaged God's people, the race of Israel under their messianic Leader becoming:

"A kingdom of priests and kings" who would "feed on the wealth of nations and supplant them in their glory" (Is61:6).

Having shared in the fellowship of the secret, John understands God's elect people as:

"the people redeemed for God by Christ's blood, taken from every race, language, people and nation to be a line of priests and kings to rule the Earth" (cf. Rev5:9,10).

St John is of course referring to elect Jews and Gentiles who could be consecrated for sacred priesthood and (eventually) kingship. We have shown that even Peter had not appreciated that the Gentiles could receive an equivalent blessing to God's chosen race (Acts11:17). We have also shown that in Old Testament prophecy the outpouring of the Spirit on all flesh, on the few occasions it is referred to, always *follows* the restoration of Israel through divine intervention and the judgement of oppressing nations; a pattern that is echoed in Jesus's own prophesies, and in John the Baptist's expectation and preaching. Such prophecy foretold that Israel would frequently fail and offend JHWE, receive punishment from His hand yet later be pardoned (Is40:2) and receive her promised inheritance whereas

35

Paul indicated that the Gentile nations were now to be reconciled to God directly rather than through the Jewish nation, and themselves would become a royal priesthood (Ex19:5, 6 cf. 1Pet2:9), thus stirring Jewry to envy (Romans11:11,15). There are plenty of examples in Scripture of God appearing to change His mind or plan in response to events or regretting decisions He had made. At least, that is the way it is presented in Scripture (e.g. Gen6:7, Gen18:21,26; Ex32:14, 1Sam15:11,35; Mt2:19-22) even if from the theological standpoint God foreknew everything in detail. But since He never goes back on His unconditional promises of blessing, His assurances regarding places and people, even if re-ordered will be fulfilled. What for practical purposes I will refer to as Plan A (i.e. what the prophets foretold in the Old Testament) regarding the restoration of the world based on the Jews inheriting the Kingdom was set out most clearly in Isaiah:

*It will happen in the final days that the mountain of JHWE's house will rise higher than the mountains and tower above the heights. Then all the nations will stream to it, many peoples will come to it and say, "Come let us go up to the mountain of JHWE, to the house of the God of Jacob that He may teach us his ways so that we might walk in his paths". For the Law will issue from Zion and the word of JHWE from Jerusalem. THEN He will judge between the nations and arbitrate between many peoples. They will hammer their swords into ploughshares and their spears into sickles. Nation will not lift sword against nation, **no longer will they learn how to make war**. (Is2:1-4 New Jerusalem Bible)*

Such was God's Israel Project: to establish a holy nation of kings and priests amongst whom He would personally reside, initially through His spiritual presence in the Ark, later through the physical presence of His Son Emmanuel (God with us). The nations who had oppressed His people were to be judged, but as outlined in Joel, the Spirit would be poured out and the Good News of the Kingdom proclaimed as a witness to all nations before the final judgement came (our thematic verse). Many Gentiles would come to Israel's light and kings to the brightness of her rising (Is60:3).

Salvation is *from* the Jews

But in God's plan as revealed in the Old Testament, the holistic package we know of as "gospel salvation" was not intended for Gentile nations in the current age. As confirmed in the eleventh chapter of Paul's letter to the Roman Church it is only through the disobedience of the Jews that Gentiles have any immediate part in it, for as Jesus told a Samaritan woman "salvation is from the Jews" (Jn4:22). But in Paul's words the Jews had stumbled, yet, he assured the Roman churches, God had not forsaken His chosen race. But what else did he go on to say?

*"What I am saying is this: Was this stumbling to lead to (the Jews') final downfall? Out of the question! On the contrary, **their failure has brought salvation for the Gentiles**, in order to stir (the Jews) to envy. And if their fall has proved a great gain to the world, and their loss has proved a great gain to the Gentiles – how much greater a gain will come when all is restored to (the Jews)" (Rom11:11-13 New Jerusalem Bible).*

And later in the same chapter:

*"For as you (Gentiles) were once disobedient to God, yet have now obtained mercy **through (the Jew's) disobedience"** (Rom11:30)*

Are you beginning to grasp the implications of what Paul is saying here? Are you ready to take him at his word? – I didn't, not until the "spiritual encounter"; indeed, not until well into the writing of this book, at which point I changed its title. These verses surely make it clearer still that it was not simply protocol that the gospel first be preached to the Jews it was a change to the published plan that the Good News was to be extended to the Gentiles: "a great gain to the world" and "mercy for the Gentiles". The Gentiles were to have been enlightened by the Jews but not "saved" in the sense the gospel means by *soterian*, a word which has as broad a semantic range in Greek as it does

37

in English. But this is not as extraordinary as it may sound for internal sanctifying communion with Christ was not possible even to God's chosen people before the Saviour was incarnated, shed His blood, was resurrected and made way for the Holy Spirit. Yes, sin could be forgiven but not yet taken away (Greek: "*aphairein*" Heb10:4) for the fountain had not yet been opened for sin and uncleanness (Zech13:1). *Soterian* in the gospel sense is healing of the soul (cf. 1Pet1:9) resulting in life of an eternal quality (Jn17:3) even whilst our souls still reside within the "body of this death" (*somatos tou thanatou toutou* Rom7:24) as the apostle aptly describes the intellectual vessel we inherit from our father's loins corrupted through "original sin". For what purpose this *soterian*? – so to become the Jesus people; "*holiness to the Lord and the first-fruits of His increase*" (Jer2:3): the people the Jewish nation were prophesied to become for the enlightenment and healing of the world. Then, in the age to come, having shared in His suffering, such would share in His glory (Rom8:17; 1Pet5:10, 2Thes2:14), having been conformed to His image and likeness through the spiritual gifts, cruciform service and personal discipleship.

In Paul's preaching as recorded in Acts, he had told his Jewish hearers:

We had to proclaim the Word of God to you first, but since you have rejected it, since you do not think yourselves worthy of eternal life, here and now we turn to the Gentiles (Acts13:46 New Jerusalem Bible).

Note that critical little word "it". It affirms that the Jewish disqualification (or deferment) of their role as the "sons of the Kingdom" (Mt8:12) was not a direct result of their involvement with the crucifixion but their rejection of the apostolic proclamation *about* the One they had crucified, as a result of which the apostles "turned to the Gentiles". The Jew's intended role as God's original choice to establish His Kingdom on Earth should be equally clear concerning how Jesus regarded His own ministry:

And suddenly out came a Canaanite woman from the district and started shouting, "Lord, Son of David take pity on me. My

38

daughter is tormented by a devil". But He said not a word in answer to her. And His disciples went and pleaded with Him, saying "Give her what she wants, because she keeps shouting after us. He said in reply. "I was sent only to the lost sheep of Israel." But the woman had come up and was bowing low before Him. "Lord", she said, "Help me." He replied, "It is not fair to take the children's food and throw it to little dogs" (Mt15:22-26).

There is a happy outcome for the Gentile woman as you will probably know. But Jesus makes it quite clear; He had been sent to the Jews (the lost sheep of Israel) so that they might be fitted for the Kingdom role promised for them in Scripture; that is why He initially refused to heal this Gentile woman's daughter. Jesus did not "test the woman's faith" by lying. What He had spoken He had spoken: "*I was sent only to the lost sheep of Israel*". Because of His great compassion He was prepared to help such Gentile folk who came to Him for help. But it is obvious if one reads carefully through the gospel narratives that John the Baptist, Jesus and initially His disciples ministered and preached almost exclusively to the Jews (cf. Mt10:5-6). Through their avoidable failure, the privilege they were to inherit has passed to (or rather is to be shared with) elect individuals drawn from every nation through elective grace, who by nature and birth are just as unworthy to be a nation of priests and kings to our God (Rev5:10) as those who happened to be the seed of Isaac. As we will later demonstrate from the writings of Paul as much as the teaching of Jesus, such is the context of "grace alone" – it pertains to an individual's *selection* for gospel salvation, not the manner of its completion which is dependent on the individual's cooperation, faithfulness and perseverance, albeit *aided* by grace.

The Jewish religious elite had expected to be leading the work of God's coming Kingdom under their Messiah, but instead it was handed to people "*who would produce its fruit*" (Mt21:43). The work would be handed over to His personally trained squad of twelve intimate followers. But these were still exclusively Jewish; it was the Jews who were the "natural branches" whereas elect Gentiles were later grafted in "against nature"

39

(Rom11:24). Jesus had come "*as a minister of the circumcision for the truth to confirm the promises of the fathers **and also** that the Gentiles might glorify God for His mercy*" (Rom15:8,9). The Gentiles were prophesied to be the "and-also's" (as Chrysostom had appreciated): they would be shown mercy under Christ's rule with His people and glorify God for it, but now they could be the equals with those same people and share the glorious inheritance reserved for those who were to be sanctified (Acts26:18). He came to His own (i.e. the Jewish people) to save His people from their sinfulness but His own received Him not, yet as many as did receive Him were given the authority to become the children of God (Jn1:11,12). If one can grasp what Paul was saying in the eleventh chapter of Romans, particularly vv11, 15 and 30, it also explains the opaque nature of our Lord's eschatological narratives considered earlier and the apparent linking of the destruction of the temple within a generation (AD70) with His second coming. For the expectation was that having carried out retribution to Israel's enemies and destroyed the wicked, the Good News of Jesus Christ's kingship referred to as "this gospel of the Kingdom" (Mt24:14), and very much with signs following would be announced as a witness to the Gentile nations so that if they acknowledged Him, at His coming they could be shown mercy "through His name" and become citizens in His Kingdom. But that is not what we have come to understand as "gospel salvation". It is not a restoration of the soul for immediate (i.e. embodied) intimate divine communion (cf. Col1:27). It is not the same gift of eternal life (cf. Acts11:17,18). In view of the above it was no wonder that even after Pentecost, some of the early Christian converts were by no means clear in their minds that the gospel salvation offered to Jews and proselytes was intended for the Gentile nations at all (Acts11:1-3 & 18).

Recapitulation

In summary, what I have been proposing so far is this: if one regards all pre-apostolic prophecy as "Plan A", then the current age is not the fulfilment of that plan in a spiritualized form; rather it is the outworking of a revised, augmented plan of

40

salvation history that God had kept secret (Plan B) which now incorporates elect Gentiles within the supporting cast of Jesus's priestly, kingly enlighteners; whilst the restoration of the nation originally predestined for that role has been placed on hold (Acts1:6; Rom11:31). God's ultimate purpose, which is the reconciliation of all God's redeemable creation to Himself by uniting it under Christ (Eph1:9,10), together with the soteriological focal point (the cross of Christ) remains unchanged. What has deviated from the original published plan (the Old Testament) is the staging and the personnel, largely because the original support cast (Israel) had become part of the problem rather than the solution. Some readers will have difficulty swallowing the idea that our Lord was not fully "in" on these plans at the time of the Olivet discourse: frankly so did I at the time, which is why I would never have thought of it, *and I didn't* – this entire concept was never in my head when I started this writing. But Scripture is quite explicit that the incarnated Jesus did not know "the end from the beginning"; the Father was aware of things that the Son would not have been (Mk13:32); even now seated at right hand of God, Scripture (indeed the Son Himself) affirms that the "times and seasons" are placed under the Father's authority (Acts1:7), Jesus Christ's own authority having been received from the Father (Mt28:18) as was the later Revelation concerning the end times (*apokalupsis iesou christou hen edoken autou ho theos* – cf. Rev1:1). The inner life of God, i.e. the economy of the Godhead is a profound mystery and the Olivet discourse is further complicated by "incarnational Christology", i.e. what our Lord and Saviour as Prophet knew and when He knew it, especially given that we are informed that His wisdom evolved and developed (cf. Lk2:52) and that He was perfected (for office) through suffering (Heb2:10). Earlier Christological controversies should not make us fear to take Scripture and Paul at their word concerning the unexpected manifestation of the Gentile inheritance. We may not be certain what Jesus knew; we can be more certain about what He taught.

Scriptural cohesion – the vital test

Everything presented in this writing can, when taken as a whole, be validated by re-examining and comparing Scripture with Scripture through the lens of a completely open mind to see that it achieves coherence. Yet that is more easily said than done, for the Bible so easily lends itself to interpreters becoming locked into error as I was for many years of my early Christian life. We misinterpret a particular doctrine (e.g. justification) and then interpret another (e.g. the teaching of Jesus) in the light of it: it is an effective error-clamping mechanism and one that has truly stood the test of time. As far as this writing is concerned there is no point in taking one aspect, annexing it your current understanding and expecting it to make sense or reconcile Scripture. The package needs to be examined in its entirety (and we've hardly started yet) and it will be discerned by the prudent that everything gels. The theology of the Protestant Reformers for all the substantial brainpower behind it, clearly fails such an examination in terms of comparing the teaching of Jesus with the apostles, one apostle with another, and the Old Testament with the New (although we've all had the last problem). As a Calvinist for twenty-eight years I am accustomed to living with such biblical tensions, but my attention has also been drawn within this process to the biblical hermeneutics of Bishop Augustine of Hippo, usually in the context of his defence of the catholic faith against various heresies. His approach had not been aided by his reliance on the Latin Vulgate rather than the Greek of the original text in which language he acknowledged himself to be less adept. The way certain scriptural passages were pressed into service to support his polemics against Manichaeism, chiliasm and especially within his anti-Pelagian writings will be shown to be dubious at best. In the latter case it was largely because he had misconceived the nature of St Paul's polemic against Christian infiltrators in the Roman and particularly the Galatian churches who were insisting on Torah observance. He also had rejected principles of natural law which I will shortly demonstrate underpinned many of the earliest Christian writers' understanding of the gospel that they had received from the Apostles or their second or third generation appointees. These issues came into still sharper focus during the

42

Reformation dispute a thousand years later, with the Reformers appealing to this commonly respected Latin Father's emphasis on the ruin of human nature and strictly one-dimensional grace. However, a good number of academics in the Protestant world have developed a "New Perspective on Paul" in terms of what the apostle had in mind in his various references to justification, faith, works and law. This will be considered in more detail in chapter three. Paul certainly did not "invent Christianity" as a few have argued; what will be more of a problem for some is that neither did he in any way subvert the moral teaching of Jesus. What he *did* subvert at the risen Saviour's command was the divine Prophet's initial understanding (or if you prefer "presentation") of the future constitution of God's elect people. Jesus had been entirely faithful to the Law and the Prophets; Paul must also be faithful to a later revelation he had received of which even the celestial authorities had been ignorant: *"koinonia tou musteriou."*

The mystery of Augustine

This Father's manner was especially forthright and uncompromising in his defence of the catholic faith against potential heresies, leading at times I have concluded to some overcompensation. Pelagius had wrongly implied that man's nature at the Fall was not damaged to the extent that he was dependent upon gospel grace (spiritual renewal) if he were to be reconciled to God and experience eternal life (as earlier defined); Augustine, still more perversely came to affirm that fallen man could not so much as do, think or even desire any good at all apart from the grace of the gospel. The heretic Manes propounded a dualistic view of the cosmos impacting upon human anthropology, leading Augustine to insist that Paul could not possibly have been saying that human nature comprised opposing moral influences from flesh and spirit; the millenarians (chiliasts) of his day were carnally minded so the whole system should be repudiated, and man's future destiny be understood as fulfilled within the spiritual sphere. My assertions here are admittedly over-simplifications and relate to Augustine's personal view but such was his extraordinary influence that I

43

have been left in no doubt that they are the root of various distortions of truth within the Western Church. As a late convert to the catholic faith I would sooner not be challenging anything directly related to the Church's teaching, but this is not entirely my work and incorporating what I believe the Spirit has shown me results in a hermeneutical framework, soteriological strategy and eschatological fulfilment that are significantly different from the Church's current understanding. Augustine's insistence that God intended to damn the bulk of humanity had already been undermined fifty years ago by the Vatican Council's pronouncements on God's broader providence in His dealings with those outside the Church, but the foundational biblical theology underpinning earlier narrower conceptions has remained unchallenged. One has only to contrast Augustine's grim eschatological montage as depicted in *"De Civitate Dei"* (City of God) with the sublime richness and inclusivity of Vatican II's *"Lumen Gentium"* to see quite how far the Spirit has enlightened the Catholic Church through the centuries. But to attain coherence one cannot avoid revisiting many of the theological assumptions that led to Augustine's treatise, culminating as it does in a cosmic horror story of breath-taking proportions (Book XXI), albeit one which many Evangelical Christians have come to take for granted.

Augustine placed fidelity to Scripture as he interpreted it above regard for the more philanthropic and open-minded reflections of earlier Fathers who had perceived more than a vestige of God's image being retained in fallen man's nature and perceived a role for natural law within a multifaceted economy of grace. *"Let us reflect how free from wrath God is toward all His creation... He **does good to all** but most abundantly to us who have fled for refuge to His compassions through Jesus Christ"*. Thus wrote Clement[4], fellow worker with St Paul; whilst his namesake Clement of Alexandria (2nd century) enquired *"What is loveable that is not loved by God; and man has been proved to be loveable consequently man is loved by God"*[5]; Justin Martyr (2nd century) spoke of God's benevolence towards those who walk uprightly and in accordance with right reason (*meta logon*)[6]; a God who accepts those who imitate His own qualities of temperance, fairness and philanthropy and who exercise their

44

free will in choosing what is pleasing to Him[7]; blessed Irenaeus (also 2nd century), recognized that God in His providence is present with all "who attend to moral discipline"[8] paying heed to the natural precepts of the law by which man can be justified[9]; or as I have come to discern the matter from Scripture, respond positively to the light of Christ in their conscience and thus be justified by "faith" through the merits of Christ's faithfulness (Greek: *ek pisteos christou*); for we will show that such is the admittedly esoteric undercurrent to the teaching of St Paul. Numerous other examples could be drawn from the writings of the earlier Fathers along the same vein.

But what light did JHWE Himself throw on the matter of His own nature? *"(I) act with faithful love, justice and uprightness on the Earth, and **these (qualities) are the things that please Me***" (Jer9:23,24 New Jerusalem Bible). Our God is wonderfully kind; He is a philanthropist (Titus 3:4 Greek) who loves fellow philanthropists as we have noted Justin Martyr observe. He delights in those who strive to lead a good life utilizing the light of Christ provided to everyman, especially through the faculty of conscience. The Bishop of Hippo on the other hand vehemently ruled out such a benevolent view of the Creator or the idea that He had any positive regard for human integrity, perceiving all humanity to be a "*massa damnata*" (condemned crowd). Man in his natural state was, he believed, instinctively opposed to what is good and never disposed to do what he knew to be right except for selfish reasons. Man, said he, was neither capable of genuine compassionate love toward his fellow man[10] nor was he in possession of any good unless he had or would be saved by "apprehending the grace of Christ". He understood that God's love (*agape*) in contrast to love as it is defined in Scripture (cf. 1Cor13:5b) would not extend to making allowance for ignorance or human weakness and by implication that such intolerance would be reflected in the Son of Man's final judgements. He asserted that God's vengeance and hatred for Adam's offspring was such that He held each child personally accountable at birth for the disobedience of their first parents such that infants dying without baptism must endure an eternity of mild sensual pain (Latin: *paena sensus*) to pay for Adam's sin[11]. Given humanity's total dependency on celestial grace, God's reconciling purposes

45

were confined to those predestined to be saved through the sacraments of the Catholic Church. Yet such fortunate, undeserving folk would very much be in the minority: *"Many more are left under punishment than are delivered from it, in order that it may thus be shown what was due to all"*[12].

Such was God's benevolence according to this man; such was the outworking of the Angel's glad tidings of great joy to all people imparted to the shepherds, and such was his understanding of divine providence. Truly, this was not the Faith passed on to the successors of the Apostles as we will continue to demonstrate; it was based on his own flawed Pauline exegesis. It was neither the Ancient Church's understanding nor that of his Church today:

"Divine providence (shall not) deny the assistance necessary for salvation to those who without any fault of theirs have not yet arrived at an explicit knowledge of God and who, not without grace, strive to lead a good life" (Vatican II – Lumen Gentium 16)

This flatly contradicts the teaching of their famous Doctor and I am glad of it, but such an affirmation will cut no mustard with Evangelicals; they require proof from Scripture and they shall have it. A "Doctor" indeed for the aptly named *Augustine* was highly esteemed having skilfully articulated plenty that was thoroughly orthodox and seemingly supremely spiritual, especially regarding the Christian's inner life of devotion to God; he had also tirelessly defended the Catholic Church from fatal heresy. An enigma indeed, for he concluded from Scripture that Satan's Eden offensive had been such a triumph as to result in God punishing the beings He had wished to unite to Himself by leaving them devoid of any effectual spiritual faculties to know Him, seek Him or please Him. Likewise, the eschatology that resulted from it was the very antithesis of *"euaggelion"* (Good News) apart from for the proportionately few favoured souls who were to be shown undeserved mercy and spared eternal misery. To ascribe such incomprehensible barbarity and unintelligible justice to the One whose kindness, philanthropy and compassionate nature Christian people are called to imitate (Eph5:1) should appal all who grasp that Jesus Christ perfectly reflected that divine nature in His earthly ministry (Jn14:9). The problem is that the black and white, strictly binary theological system Augustine constructed from his understanding of Scripture and his rejection of natural law does not lend itself to amelioration or watering down; it must either be taken as read or busted wide open. It shall be the latter, for even from a Catholic perspective it no longer supports the understanding that Vatican II affirmed fifty years ago concerning God's broader providence, shared by many in other churches who have also been enlightened by the Spirit; apart from which I intend to show in the next chapter that it was flawed at its anthropological foundation. Nor can that Father's assertions concerning humanity's hatefulness and God's harshness towards the creatures created in His image be swept under the carpet and dismissed as the "rhetoric of an earlier age", for as already indicated Augustine's predecessors did not speak in such a way. They had by no means affirmed that man by nature could do *"absolutely no good thing, whether in thought or will, affection or in action"*[13] except they *"had fled to the grace of Christ"*. Whilst In terms of God's justice, Origen for one had perceived the Creator so very differently; *"a just and good God in that He confers benefits justly and punishes with kindness; since neither goodness without justice nor justice without goodness can display the real dignity of the divine nature"*[14]. Phrase by phrase this depiction of a genuinely adorable divinity opposes the later Father's assertions concerning the Creator's nature and its outworking. Origen's theology may have been speculative at times, but he had a personal knowledge of his Subject; he was one to whom had been imparted the love of God, recognizing along with most of his peers that **God is good** even from a reasoned human perspective.

Through a hyper-allegorized reading of the Old Testament Augustine had misread the role of the Law of Moses. He understood in the light of St Paul's teaching that when JHWE had frequently pleaded with His people of the Old Covenant to *"learn to do good, seek justice, plead for widows"* and the like (e.g. Is1:17; Zech8:16, 17), He was not primarily exhorting them to obedience but wished them to acknowledge their moral impotence and "flee to His grace" for aid[15]. That had not been

47

the teaching of the prophets: Isaiah made it particularly clear in one passage that JHWE was not at all impressed when His people demeaned their souls in His presence, hung their heads in shame and put on sackcloth to acknowledge their sins and moral impotence; He wished rather that they would do what was perfectly within their power to do: free the oppressed, share their food with the hungry, shelter the homeless: *"Then your light will blaze out like the dawn and your wound be quickly healed; righteousness will go before you and JHWE's glory come behind you"* (cf. Is58:5-12). Personal righteousness and the establishment of social justice were what JHWE wished His people to pursue so that as His royal priesthood *they could be a light to the Gentiles*. Augustine was also palpably in error when he asserted that the righteous of the Old Testament were saved by *"believing in the incarnation, passion and resurrection of Christ as a future event"*[16]. Whilst Jesus had confirmed that "many prophets and righteous men" had eagerly anticipated His coming (Mt13:17) and that will have included His disciples, even they had not anticipated His death and were equally dumfounded by His resurrection (Lk24:41); how much less of a chance had the people of the Old Testament if they were to be saved by focussing on such events. In the same passage of his writing he insisted that Moses and Abraham were Christians in all but name and had received equivalent gifts of grace; a concept refuted most clearly by St Peter (1Pet1:10-12) and the teaching of Hebrews. He condemned those Jews who had been obedient to God's Law if their obedience were so that they might receive the earthly blessings that had been promised to them, rather than perceiving they related to the promise of going to Heaven when they died; moreover that people through the ages who had discerned the principles of God's law through creed or conscience and endeavoured to put it into practice were exercising worldly pride; asserting their own righteousness rather than submitting to the "righteousness of God" and trusting in His mercy[17]. But JHWE had made it very clear to the people of the Old Testament how His chosen people were to be judged and it could hardly be further removed from such paradoxical notions (Ezekiel 18). A thousand years later an Augustinian monk drew much inspiration from his patriarch's distorted concept of piety and his followers for the last five hundred years have come to regard these sentiments as being at the heart of the gospel. At the same time many within academia have come to discern aspects of the misreading of St Paul within their various traditions but now it will be systematically exposed so that all reasonably adept believers may review and verify the matter for themselves, both from Scripture and the witness of the Ancient Church. Such popular scrutiny would have been quite impracticable before the advent of the internet. Just as the Reformation was facilitated by the printing press so may a re-formation be ventured utilizing the technology of the current age. Intransigent traditionalists have nowhere to hide these days, and if some unknown layman should come along and write unsubstantiated baloney that will make no headway either. Regrettably, such a process cannot but be deeply perturbing for some whilst merely awkward and humbling for others as certain chickens come home to roost. For what has been said in the dark will be heard in the daylight; what has been whispered in hidden places will be proclaimed from the housetops; for whilst the outworking of Augustine's exclusive and fatalistic soteriology may have become abhorrent to many post-Conciliar Catholic ears, the scriptural interpretations that lay behind it are still evident in the Bible translations utilized by Catholics and in various references within their Catechism, and of course the man himself is still highly revered. The role of natural law, the scope of providence and the more positive aspects of human endeavour and culture have been obscured largely through this Catholic Doctor's influence, yet ironically his spectre hangs more heavily these days over those Christian denominations whose forebears chose to depart from the Church he had laboured so hard to protect from schism. Without controversy, it was Augustine's distinctive teaching on grace and law that formed the catalyst for full-blown *sola fide* and *sola gratia,* whilst the gist of his reasoning regarding man's inability to think or do anything pleasing to God apart from gospel grace continues to hold sway for the more traditional Evangelicals who, having turned a deaf ear to many within their own academia, keep faith with the medieval Reformers' reading of Paul.

It has all gone according to Plan

I get exasperated as you see; then I remember that it will have been in accordance with God's inscrutable plan that Augustine's intellect, matchless rhetoric, boundless energy and commitment to the Catholic cause combined to make him such a dominant figure in unifying the formation and systemizing the theology of the Western Church during such a formative period of her history. I keep in mind also that twenty years ago I would have endorsed his analysis of the human condition and happily glossed over the seemingly paradoxical nature of divine love, for this was the inescapable logic of the "all of grace" theology that my former hero John Calvin systematically developed in his "Institutes of Religion" as a guide to the movement that had broken away from Rome. Both those spiritual colossi had been content to bless the Creator whilst regarding as loveless and hateful those made in His likeness: my brethren and sisters, these things ought not to be so (cf. Jam3:9, 10). Such erudition as theirs can be persuasive indeed but sound theology being in the literal sense "a study of God" requires first and foremost a contemplative and experiential knowledge of the Subject whose very nature and name is Love, as those within Eastern Orthodoxy have arguably better discerned. Here in the UK that may also apply to many mainstream Anglicans and associated denominations who tend to be regarded as liberals by those from my earlier background; such believers may not be quite as familiar or literal with their Bibles, but they know their God and their fellow man well enough to spurn the harsh and desolate depictions still accepted by many "Bible-believing Christians" and ultra-traditional Catholics. More liberal folk may come to love their Bibles more once the joyful reality of God's loving-kindness and an admirable justice that is intelligible to sound reason has been clearly expounded. A Bible-based articulation of the long-awaited truth concerning God's loving providence should taste as sweet as honey in the mouth of every child of God, whilst in the gut there will be a bitterness and an urge to bid good riddance to what had historically been understood concerning God's nature and providential intentions (cf. Acts10:34,35; Rev10:10). Yet as we will show, the scope of God's Plan of Loving Goodness will redound even more to His

50

glory, for it has been achieved through the atoning death of the Son He adores, the length, breadth and height of whose love passes all knowledge.

Yet none of this will be entirely new revelation; it is an explication of what has been hinted at within scriptural prophecy and implicit though barely comprehended within the epistles. The true elixir had always exuded from the pens of the apostles and gospel writers if only they had been understood, and the gist of their teaching on God's loving providential purposes was discerned to a greater degree by most of the earliest Fathers of the Church. Why only the gist and not in any systematized form is well described by the blessed Origen (AD185-254). He discerned that the apostles, whilst ensuring that the essentials of faith and practice were carefully explained to the churches in both word and script, less essential matters were, in accordance with the divine will, not always explicated but left for the Church to grasp their significance over the course of time. I have more feebly outlined this principle in chapter five (progressive revelation). Yet as the Church grew and heresies abounded it became essential for doctrine to be systematized, a task in which Augustine contributed heavily, partly in view of his effective prosecution of the key heresies of the period. That is where certain principles especially relating to natural law became obscured as errors were imbedded; none directly affecting the Catholic Church's ability to fulfil its evangelical mission, "merely" its understanding of the fate of those she was unable to embrace. For whilst a measure of moral corruption and doctrinal error that is not fatal to the gospel has been permitted to creep into the Church as it tried to do at Corinth even in Paul's day, the gates of Hell cannot wholly prevail against that which has been built upon the Rock (cf. Mt16:18). Given the Doctor of Grace's extraordinary impact and esteem throughout Western Christendom it is no wonder that only recently has God's wider plan of reconciliation embracing those outside the Church been sufficiently grasped by the Roman Church to the point of being formalized at the Conciliar level a mere fifty years ago. Of course, various Catholic thinkers, perhaps most notably Blessed John Henry Newman were considering and actively debating these issues a hundred or more years earlier and no doubt many before that whose views the Vatican would not have been permitted to see the light of day. It is essential that the enlightened post-Conciliar teaching of the Church be demonstrably underpinned from Scripture if those to whom fidelity to the Book is paramount are to give the matter due consideration.

No apology

It should be evident by now that I am not primarily a Catholic apologist, or I would keep many of these observations to myself. Rather, what I write results from the conviction that *all traditions* will need to review their doctrines and heritage if they are to come together to form the "perfect man" that Paul longed for (Eph4:13). Particularly as the gospel age draws towards a close, the Spirit would wish the "Temple", being all the faithful in Christ to be numerically completed, purified and brought into perfect union for her Spouse. Such a union cannot possibly be established within the current configuration, for Christ, mystically speaking is only to have one bride who must be at one with herself and capable of being sanctified for her Spouse. For such to be brought about *all parties* may have to acknowledge a measure of doctrinal error, which the wise will discern is a more propitious precondition for reunification than if one side or the other had to eat all the humble pie, which is why a conventional apologist with the support of his church could never 'cut it'. For it is not a case of determining who is the best church with the best Christians, for the Holy Spirit has been at work in many of them, rather the question is who is the Mother Church in whom the fullness of Christianity resides and with whom all are being summoned to affiliate or re-assemble? Then and only then shall that longed-for universality be realized, and the bride be made ready. It must start with a broken spirit and a contrite heart as the various parties discern their own historical misconceptions which, resulting from spiritual wickedness in high places in the past, has resulted in a multiple severing of Christ's Body. By such means might the whole Church be renewed. Repentance is particularly relevant to Church leaders, for most Christians have simply been serving Christ in the way they were brought up to believe is right. Pastors and priests who would seek to dissemble the facts or deceive their flock regarding current obstacles to unity must recognize they face the wrath of Christ. His self-declared wish and prayer is that His Mystical Body on Earth be made whole at last (Jn17:22,23), *not* that Christians determinedly defend the tradition in which they happened to have come into the faith. Such partisan apologists frustrate Christ's will and do the devil's work, for Satan's dread is a re-united Church and the powerful witness and enlightenment it would provide for the world.

The apostasy

At the outset I had no intention of revisiting this subject; I prayed that this cup might pass from me, but it was not granted. For Catholics have no desire to revisit this cataclysmic event for their Church bears substantial culpability; but then this project is not my initiative, still less theirs. Here in the book is where it should be considered for it is in the context of the Olivet discourse (Mt24) around which this necessarily expansive first chapter is focussed. Jesus as a Prophet in his own right drew upon the prophecies of Daniel regarding a sacral atrocity which God had revealed to Him would take place at some point before His return. This event is expressed in terms of the Temple, but how would this prophecy apply to the Church applying what I will term the dual perspective principle ("DPP") which I will utilize in some biblical cross referencing. By this I mean that as a result of the restructured timeline to enable people of all nations to be brought into the messianic fellowship, certain prophetic promises have been deferred, such as the removal of the wicked from the Earth, global peace, security for the Holy Land and universal acknowledgement of Christ's Kingship; these will instead be fulfilled after the Parousia. What was thwarted or not completed at the first coming would be repeated at the second, such as reconciling certain "parents and children" (cf. Mal4:5-6) in time for the Lord to come to realize His Kingdom *"to order it and establish it with judgement and justice"* (Is9:7). That is what Prophet John believed he was preparing for with respect to Israel (cf. Mal3:1-5). At the Mount

53

of Olives, Jesus had drawn His hearer's attention to a prophecy in Daniel (Mt24:15), which foretold that a man and his supporters would come to "*profane the sanctuary, abolish the perpetual sacrifice and appoint the appalling abomination*" (Dan11:31). This was directly alluding to the diabolical activities of Antiochus Epiphanes, outlined in more detail in Macabees1. That deuterocanonical account sets out how some renegade Jews eagerly collaborated with this evil prince, leading many others to abandon the Holy Covenant and live without the Law as Gentiles, effectively bringing about an apostasy. Antiochus and his men desecrated the Temple, removing the altar with its ornamental trimmings and libation vessels, and installed an idle (a statue of Zeus) in its place. But Jesus clearly had something else in mind, for Antiochus's activities were some two hundred years *before* Jesus's re-iteration of the prophecy concerning the abomination (or idol) that He said would in the future cause desolation by being appointed a place that was not intended for it (he who has ears let him hear, or rather - let the *reader* understand – Mt24:15; Mk13:14): such would supplant the daily sacrifice (cf. Dan12:11). Jesus anticipated it relating to some events preceding the destruction of the temple (under "Plan A") but applying the dual perspective principle, it would refer to an event in the Church for it is contextually linked with the global distress and the second coming, which we now know pertains to the time of the Church, not the Temple. Jesus's prophecy came very close to being realized in terms of the Temple in the early 40's when self-styled deity Emperor Caligula planned to place statues of himself in the sanctuary and dispatched an army under Governor Petronius to carry it out, but miraculously the Jewish people managed to persuade the governor to countermand his Emperor who was assassinated shortly afterwards. Daniel's depiction does not align with any sacral issues leading up to the Temple's destruction in the 70AD siege of Jerusalem; apart from which, dreadful though the Jewish-Roman war may have been, it was eclipsed as recently as the last century by the Great War and Jewish Holocaust, and certainly did not threaten the continued existence of mankind (cf. Dan12:1; Mt24:21-22). Consequently, many commentators recognize that the Daniel 12 prophecy was not fulfilled in AD70. It is said to be a "sealed prophecy", the meaning of which would be hidden until the "time of the end" (v4). What we are also told in Daniel is this: *"From the time of the turning aside of the perpetual sacrifice[18] and appointing the desolating abomination "* (12:11) up to the time when the *"fragmentation of the authority of the holy people is over"* (12:7 cf. Hebrew text) will be a period of 1290 days (=3.5 years or "times"). *Blessed will be those who persevere and attain a further 45 "days" (12:12) up to the resurrection* (cf. 12:2).

Daniel chapter twelve was intended to be mysterious and so it is (verse 4). Even now I am not entirely certain of the matter, but my interpretation will become evident to those who comprehend this chapter and follow through the links provided. What I can say more definitely is that Daniel's reference to the apostasy which Jesus alluded to is prophetically linked to the historical event Paul writes about in his second letter to the Thessalonians[19]. Jesus's references to God's people being ensnared and deceived by false prophets, resulting in mutual betrayal and hatred (Mt24:10,11) clearly refers to a religious hiatus (an apostasy) as distinct from the earthquakes and famines that are immediately to proceed the Parousia. In terms of the timing of the big event, Jesus did provide a general guideline in form of a parable:

Take the fig tree as a parable: as soon as its twigs grow supple and its leaves come out you know that summer is near. So with you when you see all these things, know that He is near right at the gates. In truth I tell you before this generation has passed away, all these things will have taken place (Mt24:32-34).

By "these things", Jesus must be referring to the tribulation events He had outlined. By "this generation", He is referring to the ones observing and experiencing these events, which I believe He will have understood to be the generation being addressed, particularly in view of His statement in Luke9:27 that some in the crowd would not taste death before they see the kingdom of God established. This is also indicated by His expectation that His followers in the last days *"will be handed over to the synagogues"*(Lk21:12) and that His own disciples *"would not have finished going through the towns of Israel"* before the Son of Man returned in glory (Mt10:23); also that

55

some of the people who will be rejected for Kingdom would be able to plead *"but we ate and drank in your presence and You taught in our streets"* (Lk13:26). The Jewish Teacher of Righteousness also intended to despatch "prophets and scribes" to the synagogues (Mt23:34) before His return. He had earlier instructed His listeners to "keep Torah" (Mt5:18) until Heaven and Earth disappear, and those who failed to teach it in full would be least in the Kingdom of the Heavens (v19 cf. Greek). Likewise, He had instructed his followers *to continue to obey the Scribes and Pharisees* that taught the Torah because they *"occupied the seat of Moses"* (Mt23:1-3). *Caveat: Jesus effectively confirmed them to be leaders of the true "Church" but He was by no means enamoured with them (or their institution); He would go on to replace it and them.*

Nevertheless, Jesus clearly did not regard Himself at this point as founding a new religion; rather He was encouraging a renewed and spiritual approach to being Jewish in preparation for the coming Kingdom. It should also be noted, Jesus was not saying the Jewish leaders were teaching a distorted works-orientated religion; for He said they were to be obeyed. His complaint against these leaders was their legalism regarding the externals of the Law, parts of which were mere human traditions (cf. Mk7:8); whilst they neglected the heart of the Law which was devotion to God and love for neighbour leading to social justice and to act as a light to the Gentiles (Mt7:12). Jesus also knew them to be hypocrites, hence: do what they say, not what they do (cf. Mt23:3). Finally, He said that those in Judaea should be ready to flee to the mountains to be delivered from the indignation to come (Mt24:16-19). All this, together with the various verdicts to be awarded to the cities that had not responded to His call to repentance (Mt11:20,21) must have been in the expectation of a reasonably imminent Judgement, for these verdicts on cities can scarcely have relevance after two thousand years, but they were in accordance with Scriptural end-time prophesies as envisaged in the Old Testament. It did not pan out in that way or at least in that sequence for the reason provided most clearly in Romans11:11 concerning those from the Gentile nations being elected to the royal priesthood "to stir God's chosen race to envy" and re-affirmed by the same apostle in the third chapter of Ephesians through the fellowship pertaining to God's secret plan. Preaching the gospel of the Kingdom to all nations as a witness to the coming Christ could have been undertaken within a generation; then the rest of the world would be sorted out (judged) at His coming in accordance with all Old Testament prophecy. The revised plan that had been "hidden in God" could potentially take very much longer, for now chosen members from every nation and each future generation would be drawn into God's Household to be fitted for Kingdom service now and in the ages to come (cf. Gen15:5). Of course, the current age does not exist merely to recruit Gentiles to the Kingdom, it was to be the age of discovery for the whole human race (hence its longevity); the period when she would really start to engage in the pursuit of knowledge, gain an understanding of science and the universe, discover new medicines and develop ever more sophisticated means of transport and communication; knowledge and innovation that has progressed exponentially in the last century. This has all been working towards an end, which is not to prepare for global annihilation and a spiritualized eternity but for renaissance and resurrection (cp. next paragraph). In the meantime, the Initiator of that regeneration has become the "long expected Jesus": currently physically located where He needs to be to make intercession at the right hand of God for a people who are not only located in the holy city but throughout the world; for -

He is able to save to the uttermost those who come to God through Him, because He always lives to make intercession for them. For such a High Priest was fitting for us, who is holy, harmless, undefiled, separate from sinners, and has become higher than the heavens (Heb7:25,26 New King James Version)).

Just as a universal gospel mission was prophesied to prepare those outside the Holy Land who were living at the time of the expected Jewish Messianic Kingdom, so will such a *unified witness* be needed for the likely billions outside the Church in the generation that lives to experience Christ's second coming; for which reason something radical needs to happen within Christendom.

"Second coming" nomenclature

Jesus describes His future return to Earth as the renaissance or re-birth (Mt19:28 cf. Greek), Luke as the universal restoration (Acts3:21) and "the liberation" (Lk21;28), John as the Millennium of Christ's rule with His saints (Rev20:4,5), and Paul as the restoration of the physical creation (Rom8:21). Many Christians on the other hand still understand it to be the time when those who have received Jesus as their personal Saviour are taken up to Heaven whilst everyone else is despatched elsewhere. But confining ourselves to the biblical depictions, whilst they may appear on the surface to be entirely positive, taken with related passages it is clear that will by no means be the case for all; for divine displeasure will be exercised against "the wicked and godless" who will be despatched from the Earth when Jesus comes to be glorified in His saints and admired by those with "faith" (2Thes1:7-10); the latter being as the early Fathers understood *"that faith through which from the beginning, Almighty God has justified all men"[20]*. Such prophecy as exists within the New Testament apart from the Lord's in the synoptic gospels was received within the apostolic era at the time when the mystery of the Gentiles' shared participation in the Kingdom had already been revealed. Paul indicates that the age to follow this one will still be based on Earth (Rom8:21) and last as long as necessary to subordinate all earthly authorities to Christ (1Cor15:25). This is surely reaffirmed by his warning to the Thessalonian Church not to believe early reports of Christ's second coming *"for that cannot happen unless there will first have been the apostasy"* (2Thes2:3). Clearly, he cannot have been teaching the churches that the Parousia would mean an end of to the time-space universe or else why refer to a letter from the apostles or an apostasy in that context? Wouldn't "the end of the world" have been more significant?

Whilst Christ has already been raised far above all earthly and celestial authority (Eph1:21), at His coming the world will be shown whose authority they are really under. Christ has defeated the devil and, we are told, will one day subdue all earthly authority. But that cannot occur until He comes with His angels and saints; in the meantime, the tares grow alongside the wheat, whilst the earthly authorities will never take their orders from the Church in the current age: historical religious and cultural formation has seen to that (though after Roman Emperor Constantine's conversion, the mid-first-millennium Church might understandably have cherished such expectations). It is not till after all authority has been placed under His feet that Christ submits Himself and His Kingdom to the Father (cf. 1Cor15:24-25). Scripture is also unequivocal that there is to be a new or thoroughly renewed Heaven *and* Earth at some point, which those who have fallen asleep in Christ do not currently experience. Their ultimate destiny is not to be sleepers, "resting in peace" or inanimate contemplation; rather it is to be in communion and active service with the One who is vitality personified (cf. Jn14:6). The dualistic concept that the Christian's eternal future will be confined within the spiritual sphere may be traditional, but it has little scriptural basis; it has more to do with Plato than Paul or Peter, which is not to say that Plato, Aristotle and other great philosophers did not teach much that was good, not least concerning natural law; but it was incomplete – as has been said, merely a preparation for the gospel. But end-time prophecy is not expressed in terms of "going to Heaven" (I refer of course to end-time not end-life). But given that the Heavens are where the Lord of Hosts is enthroned with Christ, His angels and the spirits of the human deceased, it might appropriately be regarded as headquarters, from which a Christian receives his citizenship (Phi3:20), where his name is listed as a "firstborn" (Heb12;23) and his treasure and reward are reserved (1Pet1:4), which the Lord will be *bringing with Him* at His return (Rev22:12).

Just as the universal flooding of the Earth is presented in Scripture as an adjustment to the divine plan in response to events (Gen6:7), the radical re-ordering resulting from the Jewish response to their resurrected Messiah (Rom11:11) was either a result of divine deliberations that we were not privy to between our Lord and His Father late in His earthly ministry, or as Paul appears to indicate was a secret known only to God (by which the apostle always meant the Father). But God does not go back on His favours (Rom11:28). The Jews are to be re-

59

instated in God's Kingdom; also, if the Law and Prophets are to be fulfilled, their land is to be liberated. From a Christian perspective, Jesus Christ has replaced in His Person the Temple and religious institution of the Jews, so even applying the dual perspective principle a re-built temple might appear superfluous, yet it is outlined in meticulous detail (Ezek40-42), so one might wish to keep an open mind.

The World – Love it or hate it?

Regarding the concept of Christ's earthly reign, some would point out that Jesus had intimated to Governor Pilate that His Kingdom was not "of this world". What He actually said (when translated into biblical Greek) was that His Kingdom was not *"ek tou kosmou"* (Jn18:36), that is it was not *derived from* the world and so did not function according to worldly principles *"otherwise my servants would have fought for Me so I would not be delivered to you, but at the present time My Kingdom is not from here"*. One also should keep in mind that references to the "world" (Greek: *kosmos*) rarely refer to planet Earth as such, rather to the world order or the people within it. So when we are told not to love the world or the things of the world, it does not mean we should not love and care for God's good Earth. It is the Lord's in all its fullness (1Cor10:26) and will be inherited by the gentle (Mt5:5); the world system/order (*kosmos*) on the other hand has been the princedom of the devil. Confusion arises for *kosmos* can also refer to the people of the world as in John 3:16: God so loved the *kosmos* that He gave His only Son. Yet John also wrote "Do not love the *kosmos* or the things of the *kosmos*; if anyone loves the *kosmos*, the love of the Father is not in him" (1Jn2:15). John in his gospel is referring to the people of the world; in his epistle he is referring to the world system along with the sensual and materialistic principles that drive it. Similarly end-time references such as "the world is passing away" (1Jn2:17) are not referring to the planet but the world order, though nearly always references *translated* "end of the world" refer to the end of the current age (*sunteleia tou aionos*). Likewise, the Christian's citizenship is said to be in the Heavens, but just as Paul's Roman citizenship was his birth-right and gave him legal privileges wherever he was residing and the ability to appeal to Caesar himself, so does the Christian's heavenly citizenship provide spiritual privileges on Earth and direct access to the Lord of Heaven. It did not mean Paul must reside in Rome or that the Christian's ultimate and permanent destination is Heaven although it is the immediate one for those who die before His return; for God is to renew the present Earth and later prepare a new one - and who knows what else? The exact nature of God's plans for those who love Him is not disclosed in Scripture nor has entered the mind of man (1Cor2:9). The eschatology provided in the Bible may just be the opening gambit concerning God's plans for His eternal Kingdom and especially for those whom the Head of Principalities and Powers regards as His own kith and kin (Col2:10). As for the many Christians who currently fail to perceive from Scripture the future glorious, divine and regal status of the elect, they inadvertently demean the majesty of Christ Himself, for *"He who sanctifies and those being sanctified are one for which reason He is not ashamed to call them brothers"* (Heb2:11) for *"we know that when Christ is revealed we shall be like Him"* (1Jn3:2).

In terms of Jesus's prophecy that we have been considering, it is covered in two separate passages in Luke which provide more detail on natural events and their impact on the world, affirming that such natural phenomena herald a global apocalypse, not merely the siege of a city: (2Cor12:4)

There will be signs in the sun and moon and stars; on Earth nations in agony, bewildered by the turmoil of the ocean and its waves; men fainting away with terror and fear at what menaces the world, for the powers of Heaven will be shaken. And then they will see the Son of Man coming in a cloud with power and great glory. When these things begin to take place, stand erect, hold your heads high, because the liberation is near at hand (Lk21:25-28 New King James Version).

Luke also incorporates the parable of the fig tree. Clearly, Jesus wants His people to be looking out for these things, and not be disheartened by them, because for the faithful it will be a time of divine favour:

61

So brace up your minds, be sober set your hope wholly and unchangeably on the divine favour that is coming to you when Jesus Christ is revealed (1Pet1:13)

"Liberation at hand"; *"when Jesus Christ is revealed"* – this is the eschatological language of the Bible. For as with Paul, Peter's emphasis was for believers to look for the Lord's return, aware that the Christian's destiny is resurrection and "marriage" to the Man Christ Jesus. If the Bridegroom currently enjoys perfect union and joy in beholding the Father's presence (which He surely must), then so shall the Bride, for the Son is not pure spirit, neither shall the resurrected Christian ever be as far as Scripture permits us to foresee. Whatever and wherever our future activity, the principle joy of eternity will be to get to know the Godhead, for that is what eternal life is (Jn17:3) and it can be experienced in measure now for those who dwell in Christ and He in them (Jn6:56).

It is for the reader to discern whether the above Lukan Tribulation events have been set in motion. At the time of writing, would-be eschatologists will no doubt be surveying the situation in the Middle East, though let's face it there has never been a time in history when there was a total absence of wars or rumours of wars whereas extreme natural events could arguably be more significant (cf. Lk21:25). But this writing is not directly concerned with the timing of the second coming or indeed the details of the activity that follows it (for I do not know them), merely its general nature and location. Even the latter is not consistently outlined in Scripture nor was there a total consensus amongst the very early Fathers of the Church concerning St John's "millennial age"; but in terms of those whose opinions we know about, more were for than against. Indeed, Irenaeus who made a point of emphasising the unity of teaching within the churches of his day[21a] (2nd century) believed that the viewpoint of those within the Church *who denied* a future literal millennial rule of Christ on Earth with His saints "was derived from heretical discourses"[21b].

Prophecy – encouraged in Scripture

"*My brothers and sisters; be eager to prophesy*" urged St Paul (1Cor14:39). As acknowledged at the outset, this particularly elongated "word from the Lord" cannot be affirmed by any particular church, for it is neither from nor for any particular church. It is concerned very little with future detail but is a plea for all churches to reflect on what has happened in the past and be willing to review their traditions, even their very foundations. But in terms of the Parousia it has become clear to me from Scripture that creation itself is to be restored and that the current Earth, having been purged and renewed will continue for a period after the wicked and godless are removed from it; also, that the elect will somehow be involved in the "*operation by which (Christ) will subject all things to Himself*" (Phi3:21). In terms of the here and now, the Lord of the Church has never ceased to petition for its unity "*that they might be one just as We are One*" (Jn17:22); especially so in anticipation of this final drama of the gospel age. It was also Paul's wish that we all come to the unity of the faith as one visible Body "*joined and held together by every supporting ligament, growing and building itself up in love as each part does its work*" (Eph4:16). In the historical context it becomes still more essential when the world comes to experience "unparalleled distress" (Mt24:21) and is "put to the test" (Rev3:10) that the Church proclaims a clearly defined message clarifying what exactly is required to be "in Christ" and delivered from the "wrath to come", being the more distressful dimension to the purging and renewal process on Earth, not least as Paul depicts it in his epistle (2Thes1:7-9).

A united witness to the world

"*And this gospel of the Kingdom shall be proclaimed in all the world for a witness to all nations and then the end shall come*" (Mt24:14)

The focus of such a proclamation would be the Kingdom to be realized at Christ's coming and how to be prepared for it. I have made the point that whenever the disciples were sent out by Jesus to preach the gospel during His earthly lifetime they will not have made reference to their Lord's impending death, not least because they were not expecting it nor had they any understanding of its purpose. Of course, that is hardly the case for the Church, yet it is interesting to note that in terms of Jesus's own preaching, the only passage of substance in which He refers to His Passion and its purpose is in John chapter six. Here the Lord bemuses His Jewish hearers by speaking of Himself as the "bread that came down from Heaven", telling them that His flesh is in some sense food that is to be given for the life of the world (v51) and that only those who eat His flesh and drink His blood can experience spiritual Life (v53), know His interior presence (v56) or attain to the resurrection (v54). In other words, the entire focus of Christ's teaching concerning His death, as was the case at the last supper with His disciples, was *in the context of the Eucharist.* So must a unified Gospel witness to the world affirm the Eucharist to be central to the life of the Church and (literally) vital to the lives of Christ's would-be disciples if they are *"to be made worthy of that age"* (Luke 20:35 cf. Greek), being the realization of the Kingdom of Christ within a re-united Heaven and Earth.

The limitations of Ecumenism

Until a few years ago I had regarded myself as a Catholic Ecumenist; content with the progress I observed towards churches coming to a collective understanding of the essentials of the gospel, enabling many denominations to cooperate, at least with certain socio-political aspects of the Church's mission. As Jesus Christ is my Witness and Judge I had no personal desire whatsoever to tear open historical wounds that had begun to heal or re-kindle bad memories that had begun to fade. I had understood that appeasement and accommodation were to be the way forward: "Peace! Peace!" but there is no peace. Examine any multi-denomination Christian forum on the internet and perceive exactly where we are within that process. In the spiritual experience to which I am attesting it was impressed upon me that "forgive, forget and move on" will not do. Yes, such a constructive approach *is* appropriate in many situations, for example the progress that has been made in the last century regarding historical bigotry, racism, sexism and its associated injustices, towards a more inclusive, tolerant and mutually self-respecting society. Let those who are able forgive, may be not forget in terms of erasing from history, but move on for sure. Regrettably such an approach is not always possible in the ecclesiological sphere, for a religious tradition that has been built on a faulty foundation cannot be sustained once that foundation is identified as spurious; it is liable to come crashing down. That is not to say that the edifice, being the faithful people together with their traditions and cults, may not be a precious asset within a reconstituted assembly, for as ecumenists recognize the Spirit has been working, guiding and building in all the assemblies who have faithfully served the Lord in accordance with their own traditions if they have been open to His promptings. Such ecumenical progress that has been made by mutual good-willed endeavour would not be wasted. For the willingness of many to acknowledge past errors (something which delights the Lord's heart and is the key to the solution) gives men and women of faith reason to hope that a corporate re-unification can be brought about, even if there remains a small, vociferous rump that refuses to acquiesce.

What becomes a practical necessity in anticipation of an imminent return of Christ has certainly been aided but cannot be consummated through a gentle process of ecumenism, it requires a *Mirabilia Dei*. Uniformity on the other hand would be neither feasible nor desirable but there can be unity within a wide-ranging legitimate diversity, as is currently the case within denominations and was more universally the case in the first Christian millennium before the Great East/West Schism (1054). There are significant differences in understanding and practice between the Roman Catholic and Eastern Orthodox Churches, but the essential elements of sacral provision and instruction have historically been preserved in both, the one complementing the other as recent Popes have remarked, John Paul II referring to the Eastern Orthodox Church as "the other lung" of Christ's Body. Whilst all Christian traditions proclaim Jesus as Lord and Saviour which is indeed the core message of the gospel, the

65

soteriology surrounding it and what is required for initiation and progression is quite different as I know from personal experience. What I once would have regarded as the "required fiducial disposition for salvation" is missing from the teaching of the Catholic and Orthodox churches, whilst what I now know to be the "indispensable act of salvific participation" is absent from the practice of mainstream Evangelicalism. Be assured my fellow Catholics, you are not "saved" in the eyes of those Evangelicals who have stayed faithful to their heritage except you are relying on Christ's work alone for your salvation and are convinced in your heart that you can contribute nothing towards it. Be assured my former Evangelical friends, the Roman Catholic Church believes the Mass that many of you regard as blasphemous to be the source and summit of the Christian life and you are missing from it; whilst the Eastern (Orthodox) Church concurs that there can be no Church at all apart from that sacred mystery in which the awesome Sacrifice is re-enacted. Such disarrangement within Christendom cannot be sustained indefinitely for applying a newly found principle:

"This Good News of the Kingdom will be preached to all the world as a witness to the unchurched and then the end will come" (cf. Mt24:14).

Hence, not one but two restorations are indicated in the New Testament; the lesser (Mt17:11) to prepare for the greater (Acts3:21 cf. Greek).

Call to the task

In view of the prophetic dimension, this book regrettably must focus a little on myself and cannot be other than polemical. I hope it may be followed by a more concise, less personalised version in due course. As a Catholic Ecumenist I had several occasions during the writing of this book to marvel at the progress I was observing. At the time I first drafted this paragraph I had just returned from a Catholic Mass, the Priest assisted by a Methodist minister, who occasionally provided the sermon. It was held at my then local (St Albans) Anglican Cathedral in which it was announced that the preacher at the

66

next Mass would be a Lutheran Minister speaking on the
Catholic Saint Francis of Assisi. And, some months later as I
returned to edit this paragraph I had attended a Mass at that same
Anglican Cathedral; standing around the altar alongside the
Catholic celebrant were the Reformed Church ecumenical
chaplain, a Greek Orthodox priest and two German Lutheran
ministers, one of whom provided the sermon, and judging from
his emphasis I found him to be a man after my own heart. With
what wistfulness I observed that seemingly united platform –
and yet I knew I still had to go about this business, for it is not
my business. Prior to the revelatory experience that I will
describe shortly, any thoughts I had once harboured following
my transition via Anglicanism from Evangelical Calvinism
(1970-1998) to Roman Catholicism (since January 2000) of
becoming a Catholic apologist had long subsided for I hadn't the
stomach or temperament for it, being a poor communicator
(particularly verbally), timid by nature and easily flustered in
verbal conflict situations. I had also developed a growing
conviction as I continued for a time to meet with Evangelical
friends in Wales before relocating back to England, and
especially having attended some Anglican services at the
aforementioned Cathedral, that the Holy Spirit was carrying out
His enlightening and unifying work in His own gentle way. One
thing I had planned to do after retiring from full time
employment was to set out a Bible-based theological schema
that I had been considering for some years to explain, partly for
my own satisfaction, how those my adopted Church variously
refers to as "people of good-will", non-Christians who "die in
God's mercy" or with a faith "known only to God" as well as
those who respect the one true God in other religions are not
consigned to Hell in the way I had once believed they must be.
These considerations were a spin-off from an earlier more
pressing and personal concern relating to justification, faith and
works; a subject to which I had had to pay meticulous attention
when contemplating whether my spiritual home lay in Calvin's
Geneva or Rome. These considerations were brought to a head
two thirds of the way through a theological degree course at a
Reformed Bible College[22] preparing for full-time ministry which
I briefly embarked upon as a Baptist Student Pastor in South

Wales[23] (1997-8). The course had included a study of New Testament Greek which has proved invaluable for this project; regrettably I did not study Hebrew. Once confirmed as a Catholic at the beginning of the new millennium I soon ruled out any idea of full-time Christian ministry being still unmarried but too old to consider the priesthood; nor did I consider myself literally adept enough to write convincingly about my conversion to Catholicism, although I did start writing a document along such lines which I soon aborted. That was because I recognized the precise understanding of "justification" that I had come to through scriptural interpretation was not strictly Catholic or at least went beyond the Church's teaching concerning how those outside the Church benefit from the atonement (to be considered later). I did however pray earnestly that in some way God would use the unusual breadth of my spiritual journey together with a growing ecumenical heart for the furtherance of His Kingdom. Within weeks of starting work on the planned theological retirement project which I noted retrospectively was begun on Pentecost Sunday, appropriately so in view of what was to follow, unusual things began to happen. Broad though my spiritual journey had been it had completely bi-passed Pentecostalism. Being "filled with the Spirit" was not something I particularly aspired to and about which I had been sceptical having attended several Pentecostal gatherings in the past and having been distinctly uncomfortable with what I had witnessed and sensed in my spirit, yet I am certain that that was what happened to me for a period of around ten days in July 2013. To an outsider it would have appeared to have been an emotional breakdown. I lived alone but was in daily phone contact with a close non-Christian female friend, who I was just about able to convince that I was not going entirely out of my mind. But then she did not personally witness the incessant tears and on one occasion shrieks of horror that emanated from my study during that period (let the *reader* understand). There was abundance of joy too, as certain passages of Scripture became clearer in my mind, particularly concerning the breadth of God's benign providence towards humanity. There were some external (satanic) phenomena, witnessed also by that friend, which were at the same time frightening yet strangely reassuring in view of the task I was about. What also became clear was that the scope of the retirement project was to be far larger, and it wasn't intended for personal edification, but for the whole Church if God would make that possible.

"Confessions"

The emotional turmoil resulted, on a positive front, from a developing sense of God's love for my fellow human beings. At the height of this experience I could look into a person's eyes, even if they were appearing on television and (usually) see Christ there, regardless of whether or not they were Christians (in some cases I knew for a fact they were not), causing me instantly to burst into tears of joy. More negatively, I had a heightened awareness of sins past and present, particularly regarding the relationship with my parents in early adulthood. That hadn't been helped by my teenage conversion to the strict Calvinist brand of Evangelical Christianity through which I came to regard them as cursed by God for not succumbing to my indoctrination. I know from experience that most Evangelical young people do not act towards their non-believing parents as I did, for the relationship had not been good before my conversion. Seeing their photographs on the wall of my room reminded me that they had been better, more humane individuals than I had been during their lifetime. I was also distressed by the hurt I would be causing Christians like those I had once known, loved and still think fondly towards should this writing become better known. Despite a greater awareness of past sin, it is surprising and in context encouraging, that I did not experience any guilt or remorse about my former vehemently anti-Catholic beliefs. Like Saul of Tarsus I had unknowingly opposed the Body of Christ, and like that same man God had mercy on me for I had done it in ignorance (1Tim1:13). Likewise, I have no doubt mercy will be shown to those who heard such a distorted "gospel" from my lips and went on to reject it and Him who came with it. For I now perceive that what I earnestly believed, taught and for a brief period preached was opposed to sound reason; especially concerning the divine nature being in any intelligible sense equitable and compassionate, whilst the perceived providential outcomes were anything but Good News.

Initially, the most disturbing impressions received during the spiritual encounter concerned the sixteenth century Protestant Reformation. Since converting to Catholicism I had naturally come to regard the break-up of the Western Church in a negative light, resulting as it did in ecclesiological fragmentation and doctrinal confusion, yet I was always aware that had the Roman Church not been so intransigent in acknowledging and attending to the malpractice and corruption that had crept in and festered for centuries, the outcome could have been very different. I was therefore content to put the blame on both sides and allow the Holy Spirit to do the healing work that I described earlier. However, during this spiritual and emotional turmoil I became aware of what I had previously suspected but was not entirely clear about – that the cataclysmic ecclesiological and political events of the sixteenth century were foretold in Scripture. On reflection, how could that not be so? Of course, there had been an earlier fundamental schism between the churches in East and West, but that was not what the Bible describes as an *"apostasia"* (Greek for an apostasy, revolt or popular defection 2Thes2:3); the eleventh century event was a disaffiliation resulting from a prolonged and complex process of divergence; neither did it relate to a particular individual and certainly did not result in the "perpetual sacrifice" being usurped by something coming to occupy a place that was not intended for it (Mk13:14). Nor could the apostasy referred to in Daniel and the second letter of Thessalonians be made to fit the development of the papacy (as I once might have hoped) for similar reasons. More fundamentally, the East/West disaffiliation did not result in darkness and spiritual desolation for a third of Christendom (cf. Rev8) since the essentials of the Gospel and its effectual administration were retained by the two disaffiliated parties.

The encounter

Every true Christian has encountered the Holy Spirit; it is just a question of degree. The experience that led to this book was far

70

beyond anything I had ever experienced, although in retrospect I recognized a milder and shorter version of the same on the day I definitively determined to rescind my Calvinist beliefs. It was Christmas Day 1998 and I had been invited to dinner with other single friends; sensing something was happening to me I instead chose to spend the day alone at home with my Bible alongside the Westminster Confession of Faith I had been examining for some weeks, the latter gradually becoming a sea of red ink annotations as the light began to dawn. But this book is not concerned with my conversion to the catholic faith otherwise I would need to explain in more detail how I came to accept and understand practices that were quite new to me and were certainly not clear from Scripture, including aspects of Marian devotion, confession and various sacramentals. In a sentence it pertained to the living tradition of the Church and the principle of authentic development, i.e. how the Holy Spirit progressively has deepened the understanding and devotion of the Church through mystical experience and theological insight expressed through the *sensus fidelium* (sense of the faithful). Some of these issues will be touched upon briefly in the chapter concerning progressive revelation.

The experience of the summer of 2013 was literally ten times the duration, stronger in intensity and physically and emotionally more draining than that earlier denominational conversion experience such that I became an emotional wreck for a month or so. I had been a contented Ecumenist and thought I was to become a Catholic apologist – if only it had remained that simple. For as will already be evident, further revelations involved challenging what I am still clear is the legitimate Mother Church to review her own understanding of several well-established doctrines, which challenge the remit of her infallibility (i.e. its scope and limitations) but not her ecclesiological supremacy or fulfilment of mission. Nevertheless, the Catholic Church will not find what I believe to have been revealed to me easy to accept and there are aspects she will not like at all. Yet this writing will regrettably bring still greater perturbation to others given that I have come to bury Luther not to praise him. I expected the arch-Reformer to come under the microscope within this process, but frankly not so much a fourth century Catholic "saint", and that has been the most unexpected and initially the most troubling aspect of this process - until I came to a better (though incomplete) understanding of my role and indeed his; the greater to sustain a mystery, the lesser to unravel it. So now I may offend the whole Body of Christ, but my over-riding concern is not to offend its Head; apart from which this disclosure is not exclusively about the Christian churches; it also makes a stand for all those who are of God, viz. all *bona fide* members of the human race. For they also receive pardon for their sins through the tender mercies of our God, who is bountiful towards His whole creation, whilst those He has chosen for Christ and prove faithful to their calling are being prepared for a yet more glorious inheritance.

The mystery of lawlessness

But regrettably I must dwell a little longer on the medieval hiatus: this is how the instigator of the Reformation chose to counsel a depressed friend:

"Whenever the devil pesters (you) with these (melancholy) thoughts, at once seek out the company of men, drink more, joke and jest or engage in some other form of merriment. Sometimes it is necessary to drink a little more, play, jest or even commit some sin in defiance and contempt of the devil in order not to give him an opportunity to make us scrupulous about trifles. We shall be overcome if we worry too much about falling into some sin... Would that I could commit some token sin simply for the sake of mocking the devil so that he might understand that I **acknowledge no sin and am conscious of no sin**. *[M Luther letter to Jerome Weller 1530 "Letters of spiritual council" (pp85-87)]*

Most of those who built their theology on this man's prophetic insights would distance themselves from such rank antinomianism – I have bolded the phrase that most concerns me. It provides useful insights into how Dr Luther had recently come to interpret Paul following his own spiritual encounter. It suggests also that he was inclined to confuse a guilty conscience with the pestering of the devil, as did some Evangelical friends

72

in my experience. *"Be assured, if our heart should condemn us, God is greater than our heart knowing all things* (so shall condemn us all the more), *whereas if our heart does **not** condemn us, **then** we may have confidence towards God"* (1Jn3:20,21). (No, I didn't use to interpret it that way either, for I had no conception that the conscience was a spiritual faculty, providing of course it still functions – cf. my chapter six). In terms of Luther's advice, his friend would have done better acknowledging his sins, being ever conscious of them and seeking to avoid them, or else remain guilt-ridden and under the reign of sin (Rom6:12-19).

Even before his ground-breaking conception of salvation through faith alone, the Augustinian monk had been heavily influenced by his monastic patriarch's writings concerning the wholesale ruin of human nature and was especially struck by Augustine's treatise "On the Spirit and the Letter", to which I have had to refer several times in my notes, usually with disparagement. Yet it did not go far enough for Luther for his patriarch had rightly insisted that the principle of God's law needed to be obeyed albeit enabled by grace and that the believer could never be entirely assured about his final salvation. So Luther developed the understanding of a "passive righteousness" in which Christ's perfect justice was imputed to the believer such that he would no longer be judged with regard to his own nature and works but Christ's. I deal with that fallacy elsewhere, but one cannot possibly attempt to do justice to Martin Luther's theology and legacy here. It may be necessary for readers to do as I did to seek a balanced perspective on this momentous period of Church history: read more about the life, work, character and influence of the most significant individual of the last millennium in terms of his impact on the history of the Western Church and the world. Marking the five hundredth anniversary of Luther's birth, Pope John Paul II suggested:

*"A twofold effort is needed, both in regard to Martin Luther and **for the reestablishment of unity**. In the first place it is necessary to continue an historical work. By means of an investigation **without preconceived ideas**, motivated only by the search for truth, one must arrive at a true image of the reformer, of the*

*whole period of the Reformation and of the persons involved in it. Fault where it exists must be recognized, **wherever it may lie"** [Letter to Cardinal Willebrands 31 Oct 1983 - My highlighting]*

In terms of ecclesiological formation, the Christian era may easily be divided into two sub-eras: before and after Luther. In terms of doctrine Augustine may well be our man but he did not lead a revolt which is what I am concerned with for the moment. Whatever you may currently think of the Catholic Church, Pope John was surely right in terms of the need for Christians serious about unity pursuing historical research into Luther and the period of Reformation that is motivated purely by a search for the truth. With that in mind it may be better to avoid Catholic or Evangelical writers and resort or at least refer to secular authors. One I found particularly helpful was the late Richard Marius, once an Evangelical who became agnostic. He was a secular historian but as a former Bible believing Christian had an adequate and a reasonably dispassionate grasp of the theological issues at stake. It provides painful reading for Catholics and Protestants alike and you will need a strong stomach to tolerate some of Luther's quoted obscenities albeit they were not without wit. I am tempted to recall some but will restrain myself. To the surprise of many, he also said this about the Catholic Church:

With the papacy there is a correct Holy Scripture, a correct baptism, a correct sacrament of the altar, a correct key to the forgiveness of sin, a correct preaching office, a correct catechism, Lord's Prayer, Ten Commandments and articles of faith.[24]

Few if any Protestants outside the High Anglican and Lutheran tradition would agree with that statement today, for Luther merely set the ball rolling; a still more marked dissent from Catholic doctrine and teaching followed through the likes of Zwingli and Calvin which distressed the former monk greatly for he was a reluctant schismatic as his statement above affirms; he trusted that once Scripture had been translated into the vernacular and more widely distributed, dissenters from Rome would come to a unified view on the key doctrines such as the Eucharist, baptism and essential church polity, but it was not to be. Through the movement Luther initiated, newly translated

74

into the vernacular, the Protestant Bible would soon come to replace the sacrifice of the altar as the focal object of veneration in the majority of the breakaway churches, with desolating consequences from the perspective of those who believe that sacrament to be central to the faith and the means by which one experiences interior sacred communion and sanctifying grace; desolating also in view of the way that Paul's teaching would continue to be misunderstood and Augustine's one-dimensional grace analysis with its horrid providential implications built upon by the Reformers. As for Luther's immediate legacy, the ecclesiological fragmentation and exacerbated national and global conflict challenges his claim to be prophetic. For if a prophet (and anyone who dares challenge the established ecclesiological order in such a way had better be one) can be shown by the outcome of his predictions to have spoken presumptuously, he is no longer to be feared or listened to (cf. the testing of prophets and prophecy - Deut18:18-22). What Luther had believed and expected would happen did not happen; that is that Christians in the West, liberated from the papacy and with Bibles in hand would come to a united understanding, at least of the *essentials* of the gospel. He personally was distraught at the breakaway movement's sub-divisions even in his own day; let alone what he would have thought of the bewildering plethora of denominations that exist today. There is a good reason for such a disastrous miscalculation: the decidedly non-perspicuous nature of Holy Scripture. Within his personal ministry, Luther also became disillusioned about "the fruit of the Spirit" evidenced by those under his pastoral care at Wittenburg now that they had been delivered from papistry:

I do not know if I will preach anymore to you vulgar slobs, who cannot give four pennies a year out of a good heart. Know this you Wittenburgers: you are altogether empty of good works, giving no salary to the ministers of the Church to educate boys or give shelter to the poor, always passing the buck to someone else...You have been freed from tyrants and papists. You ungrateful beasts are not worthy of this treasure of the gospel (Preached 8th Nov 1528)[25]

But then there is an extraordinary verse in the Bible in which one apostle warns about misinterpreting another and thereby being led away from the saving truth:

Our beloved brother Paul, according to the wisdom given to him has written to you, as also in all his epistles speaking in them of these things, in which are some things hard to understand, which untaught and unstable people twist to their own destruction, as they do also the rest of the Scriptures (2Peter3:15b-16 New King James Version)

If it was "hard to understand" in the apostolic era it might be close to impossible centuries later. The apostle Paul utilizes what to any theologian (let alone the casual reader) is technical language, especially pertaining to his Jewish law-court contextualisation of "righteousness" and its cognate "justification". This is compounded by translation difficulties where the ancient Greek text can be frustratingly ambiguous at the most critical junctures: hence the indispensable nature of the aural element of the sacred deposit which had functioned as a lens for gathering up the whole sense of Scripture; hence also the need for a teaching magisterium and the desolating fallacy of *"sola scriptura"*. As early as the beginning of the third century Tertullian had observed that *"the very Scriptures were even arranged by the will of God in such a manner as to furnish materials for heretics"*[26]. He was implying that the thoroughly unsystematic, sometimes allegorical, often cryptic nature of Holy Scripture was designed to flummox and cause schism when utilized in isolation from the teaching magisterium of the Church. Tertullian implied it, and from the perspective of a further sixteen centuries of Church history I know it for a fact. Indeed, even in the hands of the Church, newly formulated doctrine that had relied entirely upon an individuals' scriptural interpretation could be suspect. "Take and read" with care; the cannon of scripture can be lethal in the wrong hands: misinterpretation can result in darkness, desolation and division for whole societies as well as churches.

Holy Scripture – catalyst for error; arbiter for Truth

Yet the fullness of truth does depend upon an understanding of this parlous yet sacred utility we know of as Holy Scripture which, as if to demonstrate the point, is still being unravelled and its meaning widely disputed after nearly two millennia. So when it is discerned by the faithful finally to have been *made to gel*, we shall have arrived at the truth regardless of the route secured. Such a precarious economy has provided the perfect vehicle for progressive revelation, enabling certain mysteries to be sustained, such as the role of evil within God's munificent providence. As for future ages, given the vital role for personal faith and the calibre of recruits to Kingdom in mind, it should not be surprising that the Lord would wish to conceal what from the world's eyes would be perceived to be the more enviable and ennobling aspects of the faithful's eternal privileges; concealed at least until the very brink of the Kingdom's realization by which point the door will be about to close (cf. Rom11:25; Lk13:25). If doctrinal clarity and historical ecclesiological cohesion had been God's chosen path for the Church it would have been more expedient for a majestic angel or Old Testament-style prophet to visit from time to time to keep the churches in order than for them to rely even partially upon biblical exegesis, which though essential, history has proven to be fraught with difficulty. For what may itself be a holy artefact can become profane if it comes to occupy a place or fulfil a function not intended for it. Were some depraved priest to take the holy sacrament to the farmyard and feed it to pigs, then that which had been a most holy ministry would become an abomination in the sight of God and man, yet it would be easily discerned to be so by the faithful. If, however, that which was likewise a sacred utility were similarly displaced and cast before more sophisticated swine capable of corrupting and repackaging it, what desolation might then be incurred through its propagation?

The culpability of the medieval Roman Church

If I had been the fellow monk who had accompanied Brother Martin to represent his monastery at the papal curia at Rome in 1510, I trust I would have been as troubled and disgusted as he was by the irreligion to be found in that city, not least amongst some of its priests. The behaviour of some at the altar if it was accurately portrayed by Luther would have challenged my faith in the Church, indeed my faith, period. This hadn't happened overnight, but worldliness and corrupt practice had been allowed to grow and fester over centuries as my Catholic Encyclopaedia sets out quite frankly. That statement of substantial culpability reinforced an earlier Conciliar Decree in this context which had incorporated a rare apology: *"We humbly beg pardon of God and of our separated brothers and sisters, just as we forgive them that trespass against us"* [*Unitatis Redintegratio* 21st Nov 1964 – para 7]. For the medieval hiatus we have come to label the Reformation was hardly a straightforward matter of good versus evil. The majority who desired reformation of the Church were good; many in the Roman Catholic Church who had resisted it were bad, stupid, incompetent or a combination of all three. Yet it has been made clear to me where lay the true Body. In the words of Ignatius (A.D.30-107) who had trained under the apostle John: *"If any man **follows him who makes a schism in the Church**, he shall not inherit the Kingdom of God... Take heed then to have one Eucharist for there is one flesh of our Lord Jesus Christ and one cup into the unity of His blood, and one altar"*[27]. Likewise, second century Irenaeus: *"No reformation of so great importance can be effected by (those who would be reformers) as will compensate for the mischief arising from their schism"*[28].

By their fruits…

Another key determinant for assessing prophets and prophecies alongside their legacy is personal character (Mt7:15-20). In Luther's case this was aptly reviewed by Desiderius Erasmus, a highly regarded philosopher who came to be considered the "prince of the humanist". That movement and he in particular

78

were influential in providing impetus to the early Protestant Reformers, for Erasmus had been highly critical of the abuses within the Catholic Church; yet he became one of Luther's greatest foes. His critique of Luther's character would have been shared by many other good people who longed for a reformed Church. Erasmus wrote to the Reformer in 1526 as follows:

What torments me and all honest people is that with your character which is so arrogant, impudent and rebellious, you plunge the whole world into fatal discord, that you expose good men and lovers of good letters to the fury of the Pharisees (Catholic hierarchy); you have provided to vile souls desperate for new things arms for sedition, so that in a word you violently handle the cause of the gospel in such a way that you confuse everything, the sacred and profane.[29]

Erasmus also provided impetus and influenced the much-needed Catholic Counter-Reformation (Council of Trent 1545-63).

Eastern Orthodoxy – the eluded dimension to the Reformation debate

What tends to be overlooked when reviewing this critical period of Church history is the situation regarding the Eastern Orthodox Church. Having nearly five hundred years earlier disaffiliated from the Church in the West and rejected the universal immediate jurisdiction of the Bishop of Rome she nevertheless had retained a good deal in common with the Roman Church's practice and doctrine, both wings holding in respect the deposit of faith containing the written and oral Tradition passed on by the apostles. Eastern Orthodoxy was relatively unaffected by the sixteenth century upheaval and continues today with her estimated quarter of a billion adherents to function as a vital part of Christ's mystical body guided and directed by the Holy Spirit. But the key point is that the centrality of the Eucharist as a sacrifice to God and the substantive means of partaking of Christ's body and blood to become united with Him for personal salvation had historically been understood *in both the West and East*. The very real corruption that had particularly infested the Roman Church, especially during the early second millennium

79

does nothing to invalidate that historical reality. Nor of course did the Eastern Church ever teach "salvation by faith alone" particularly as Luther had re-interpreted faith, and they had also rejected Augustine's and some earlier Western Fathers' understanding regarding imputed guilt from original sin (next chapter). The resolution of Orthodox/Catholic tensions, largely focusing on the function of the papacy, the "Filioque" clause (considered later) and some of the distinctive doctrines of Augustine are a relatively small mountain of faith to climb in comparison to what regrettably still divides the Mother Church and the children of the Reformation, more especially those in the independent churches. It is the latter division that makes this offensive necessary, for these two most influential and world-wide wings of the Church have radically different perspectives on gospel salvation. Examine, for example, the ecumenical progress made through the work of the Catholic scholar Richard Neuhaus and Southern Baptist Charles Colson as set out in their document "Evangelicals and Catholics Together", available on the internet. Many consider it to be the most significant initiative in this area, but one has only to examine the reactions particularly on the Evangelical side to recognize that although these efforts are to be applauded it remains a hopeless cause in terms of ever leading to visible unity. Even those Evangelicals who have endorsed the agreement such as Dr J Packer acknowledged that reality. As for more conservative Evangelicals of my former ilk, they would regard it as undermining fundamental essentials of the Reformation heritage.

The Church is the Body of Christ (1Cor12:27) and cannot be made whole again whilst so many of its members refuse to recognize the Eucharist as the way by which the sacrificial benefits of the cross are perpetuated through the most Holy Sacrament to be the means of grace for ongoing individual forgiveness and sanctification as well as to implement the Church's role as priesthood to the world. Replacing soul-healing sacraments with dead ordinances was a desolating fallacy, yet that was a very long time ago; the disparate Christian communities that have grown out of the Reformation do serve the Lord in many positive ways. Much of what is practiced and preached is beneficial in so far as it is based on the ethical teaching of Christ and the apostles (cf. Phi1:18). In their encouraging of individuals to commit their lives to Christ and the Way, the name of Jesus is honoured and communities may be enlightened and healed to a degree, particularly within traditions that maintain a strong social awareness dimension to their outreach, such as the Salvation Army in whose work the Lord surely delights, as no doubt will have been the case throughout history with regard to those monastic religious communities that have devoted their ministry to the destitute. Such all-round benefits I perceived from my time as an Ecumenist; yet in the higher Anglican circles I moved for a time, I observed that the preaching (some of it being the best I had ever encountered) appeared to draw very little on the key foundational doctrines of Protestantism. Clearly the Spirit has been working and enlightening many within the various churches, drawing them ever closer to the truth. Yet there is still the issue of the foundations, apart from which it is a different picture in the independent sector; twenty years earlier, had I heard those (Anglican) sermons I have just been praising I would have judged that the gospel as I then understood it had not been preached at all. Such is the measure of disorder we are up against, which in view of seasonal factors may no longer be sustainable (cf. Mt24:32). So those who can receive such a message should be prepared to review their heritage (as I had to do, losing many friends in the process), in order that Christ's will for the final times is fulfilled.

Historical witness to the "real presence" and sacrificial nature of the Eucharist

Given that an understanding of the Eucharist is at the heart of longstanding divisions yet simply cannot be compromised, here is brief testimony from Church Fathers from *each of the first four centuries* of the Christian era testifying to the nature of the perpetuated sacrifice offered on the altar and the objective reality of Christ's words concerning His flesh and blood given for the life of the world. The next few paragraphs may be standard Catholic apologetics fare but are important nevertheless. Moving backwards from the fourth century, Cyril of Jerusalem

81

understood the Eucharist to be the means by which a Christian may become *"concorporeal and consanguineous with Christ"*[30]; Clement (3rd century) declared: *"Those who partake (of the Eucharist) are sanctified in body and soul; by the will of the Father, man is mystically united to the Spirit and to the Word"*[31]. From the 2nd century, Justin Martyr speaks of the bread and wine offered at the altar as *"that from which our blood and flesh are nourished through its transformation, which is the flesh and blood of that Jesus who was made flesh"*[32]. From the **end of the first century**, St Ignatius having been tutored by the apostle John refers to the heretics of his day: *"they abstain from the Eucharist and from prayer because they do not admit that the Eucharist is the flesh of our Saviour Jesus Christ who suffered for our sins. Those who speak against this gift of God incur death"*[33a] the bread of the altar being *"the medicine of immortality and the antidote to death*[33b]. In terms of the Eucharist as sacrifice, Augustine, thoroughly orthodox in this area regarded the Mass as the *"highest and true sacrifice..., Christ being at the same time Priest and Victim"*[34]. Even in the oldest post-Biblical authentic writing available (the Didache c. xiv approx. AD96), the "breaking of bread" is referred to as a sacrifice and is explicitly related with the prophecy in Malachi (1:11) to the pure offering with incense being offered by the Gentiles. The Malachi prophecy was understood by the early Fathers to be foretelling the universal and perpetuated daily sacrifice[35] to be provided under the New Dispensation. Moving to the present day, the Eastern Orthodox Church whom we have observed was a relatively stable element in the sixteenth century debacle has historically regarded the Divine Liturgy as *"the awesome sacrifice entrusted to the Church to be re-enacted and given to the faithful for the nourishment of their faith and forgiveness of their sins"*[36]. These essential matters were never intended to be delineated from Scripture alone but were part of the sacred Tradition passed on from the apostles to their successors within the Catholic Church, being the sole depository of apostolic doctrine and the pillar and ground of the truth (1Tim3:15).

The witness of Eusebius AD260-340 (approx.)

Known as the Father of Church History, Eusebius documented the succession of the apostolic sees in East and West, commenting on the faithfulness (or otherwise) of some of their bishops, providing in the process an invaluable perspective on the doctrinal understanding of his time. He would certainly have regarded the above witnesses to the Eucharist (up to mid-fourth century) as orthodox. In view of his own perspective on the matter, Eusebius indicates that natural law, essential to the case I am making, was subsumed within the theological/anthropological perspective of the early Church:

*"The Creator of all things **has impressed a natural law upon the soul of every man**, as an assistant and ally in his conduct, pointing out to him the right way by this law; but, by the free liberty with which he is endowed, making the choice of what is best worthy of praise and acceptance, because he has acted rightly, not by force, but **from his own free-will**, when he had it in his power to act otherwise, As, again, making him who chooses what is worst, **deserving of blame and punishment**, as having by his own motion **neglected the natural law**, and becoming the origin and fountain of wickedness, and misusing himself, not from any extraneous necessity, but from free will and judgment. The fault is in him who chooses, not in God. For God has not made nature or the substance of the soul bad; **for he who is good can make nothing but what is good".*** [quotation from "The Christian Examiner", Volume One, published by James Miller, 1824 Edition, p. 66 – my highlighting]

Reading *any* of the Fathers' writings from the first three centuries, one cannot but perceive the sacerdotal nature and episcopal structure of the very early Church. For sure, the papacy in anything like the form we know it today was a more gradual development arising out of necessity as the Church expanded. Likewise, it should be acknowledged that the early Church did not, and the Orthodox Church still do not employ the term "transubstantiation" when describing the inscrutable mystery of the "real presence", perhaps wisely discerning that no human term can do it true justice; nevertheless, all clearly acknowledge the real and sanctifying presence of Christ in the

83

bread and wine, and therefore the central and soteriological nature of the rite. For (once again) there are not two but three that bear witness to the ongoing reality of Christ's saving presence on Earth: the Spirit, the water *and the blood* (1Jn5:8 Greek – note present tense).

Woe, woe and thrice woe cf. Rev8:8-13

So those within the churches who conceive the sacrificial offering of the Divine Liturgy or Mass to be a medieval fabrication are gravely mistaken. The movement that turned aside the daily sacrifice[37] through rejection of a key element of the Church's foundational truth (the oral instruction received from the apostles) effectively tore the heart out of a third of Christ's mystical body. Luther retained an understanding of the "real presence" but had repudiated the sacrificial aspects of the Eucharist, regarding the Church's universally observed rite (the perpetual sacrifice) as idolatrous. We have just celebrated the half-millennial anniversary of that fateful revolt and most within the bewilderingly fragmented movement that resulted from it now innocently believe they are being faithful to Christ by rejecting that means of grace and priestly offering for the world. Whilst that is the case for any individual it must continue for the sake of conscience, apart from which suitable initiation is required, for as a fourth century Father observed, *"Terrible is the altar; terrible and ineffable is the communion of the sacred mysteries"*[38]. Yet it is the means for the Christian to draw on the spiritual life of Christ (cf. Jn6:57). It is the core of this wondrous salvation in which those called and chosen to be become holy and flawless before Him in love may come to share in His divinity now. As we will see later it is also God's means for advancing the salvation of the world through the sacral activity of His royal priesthood in which every practicing member of the faithful participates (1Pet2:9). Who knows to what extent the Lord has been willing to bi-pass the prescribed means of grace in the cases of genuine ignorance for the Spirit moves where He wills (cf. Jn3:8)? All who respect the name of the Lord will ultimately be accepted by Him, but I have been outlining the means by which one may come to partake of the divine nature

84

and be enabled to gain what St Paul refers to as *"the prize of the high calling of God";* therefore let us, as many as are mature have this mind; and if any of you think otherwise, God will reveal it to you (Phil3:14-15).

Preparing the way of the Lord

Various other prophetic passages came to my attention during the ten-day spiritual and emotional turmoil to which I have referred. They included Rev10:1-11, incorporating the undisclosed secret (or mystery) of the little book or scroll, drawing upon Ezekiel chapters 2 and 3, which I have come to understand relates to the resolve and spirit in which this task is to be approached, and the likely initial response. I will say no more than that I believe them to be pointers to the task in hand. I had not previously understood Jesus to be inferring in Matthew 17:11 that another "Elijah" would be coming to set things right "before the awful day of JHWE comes". It was not until relatively late on in this process that that became clear through a grasp of Ephesians3:1-6, and by applying the dual perspective principle (DPP) to prophecy: "Was it not completed? Then let it be repeated". With that in mind, let us revisit the first century John, for through no fault of his own it was *not* completed; he did not fulfil the role prophesied for him by the angel announcing his birth. Arch-angel Gabriel tells Elizabeth concerning the babe in her womb:

And (John) will bring back many of the Israelites to the Lord their God. With the spirit and power of Elijah he will go before (Christ) to reconcile fathers to their children and the disobedient to the good sense of the upright, preparing for the Lord a people fit for Him (Lk1:16-17 New Jerusalem Bible)

The first point to note is that this is a direct quote from Malachi 4:5-6 which is in the context of Christ's return in glory and judgement. Secondly, in what sense did John reconcile the hearts of the children to their fathers and vice versa? It surely cannot refer to improving family relationships as some have suggested; if so his work was about to be thoroughly undermined by Jesus Himself (Mt10:35). Nor was he able to

85

fulfil the angel's prophecy to "prepare for the Lord a people fit for Him"; indeed, this is at the heart of the matter. The people to be prepared were the Israelites (Lk1:16) for these were exclusively the ones to whom John and indeed Jesus had been sent to minister (Mt15:23-25; Acts10:36). As dying Simeon had prophesied in his "*Nunc Dimittis*", the baby Jesus was expected to become a *light of revelation* for the Gentiles but *glory for His people Israel* (Lk2:32). It was only relatively late in His ministry that Jesus hinted that the people He and Prophet John had come to prepare might be rejected, whilst (Gentiles) from the four quarters of the globe would be amongst the ones to sit down in the Kingdom with the patriarchs and prophets (Lk13:28, 29). A banquet had been prepared, the intended guests invited, many excused themselves, and so the master's servants would need to go out to the highways and hedges and compel whoever he could to come to the feast (cf. Lk14:16-23). The Jews were the ones who had been on the invitation list, but many, especially amongst the leadership were unwilling to come to the party (v24).

Regardless of who would inherit the Kingdom, the salvation of the whole world was always in view, it is a question of how it was to be achieved. It was intended (or rather foretold) to be *from* the Jews (Jn4:22), and by means of the Messianic King, installed on David's throne (Lk1:32) who would exercise swift judgement against Israel's oppressors. "*For the Lord shall arise upon (Israel) and His glory shall be seen upon them. And the Gentiles shall come to Israel's light and kings to the brightness of her rising*" (Is60:1-3). Then no more would be heard the sound of footgear clanking over the ground or clothing rolled in blood. As for their messiah, the government would be upon his shoulder, and his name shall be called "Wonderful Counsellor, Prince of Peace" (Is9:4-6). Having disposed of the wicked, he would arbitrate between many peoples (Is2:4; Mic4:3), and, supported by his Kingdom of priests (the holy Jewish nation), go on to enlighten the heathen nations such that they should "study war no more" (Is2:4), learning the ways of peace and righteousness. Instead of being a target of hostility and oppression, the race of Israel would become an ensign for peace and wisdom, sought out by all the nations, for the Holy One of

Israel would be among them in His greatness (Is11:10,12:6): "*In those days ten people from all languages and nations will take firm hold of one Jew by the hem of his robe and say 'Let us go with you for we have heard that God is with you'*" (Zech8:23 New International Version). The prophetic psalms speak along similar lines:

For JHWE the Most High is glorious, the great King over all the Earth. He brings people under (Israel)'s yoke and nations under our feet. He chooses for us our birth-right, the pride of Jacob whom He loves... God reigns over the nations seated on His holy throne. The leaders of the nations rally to the people of the God of Abraham (from Ps 47 New Jerusalem Bible)

And:

May God show kindness and bless (Israel) and make His face shine on us. Then the Earth will acknowledge your ways, and all nations your power to save... May God continue to bless (His people) and be revered by the whole world (from Ps67 New Jerusalem Bible).

These re-echo the prophecies already quoted from Joel and Isaiah. All the Old Testament prophecies are along the same lines and entirely consistent with each other. What so many great and mighty theologians fail to grasp or choose to gloss is that this was not merely the "Jewish Messianic hope" or Zionist wishful thinking or "Jewish literature" it is Holy Scripture: the Holy Spirit speaking through the prophets about JHWE's declared intentions towards His chosen nation and the whole world. That is how Jesus regarded the matter; He did not subvert it but had intended to be literal and faithful concerning "the Law and the Prophets" (LK24:44b). Apart from which, what of the annunciations – were the angels also Zionists? Gabriel had informed Mary that her Son would "rule over the House of Jacob for ever" – surely a curious analogy for the Church. Likewise, the Baptist's father Zechariah prophesying through the Holy Spirit that his people would be "*delivered from our enemies and those that hate us*" (Lk1:71). The angelic messengers of Good News to Mary and Elizabeth had not intended to be allegorical; these events would indeed have occurred had the Jews heeded

87

their "day" of visitation. The Father who knew the outcome clearly orchestrated these annunciations and prophesies and would not have done so unless He intended to keep His promises, but not in the published order or sequence; i.e. not all in the current age (cf. Rom10:19; 11:11). The following prophecies for His holy nation, one of many such examples, is not currently being fulfilled in any shape or form -

The Lord says (to Israel): You will rule the Egyptians, the Ethiopians and the Sabeans. They will come to you with all their merchandise, and it will be yours. They will follow you as prisoners in chains. They will fall to their knees in front of you and say, "God is with you and He is the only God. There is no other (Is45:14 New Living Translation Bible)

This can be no allegory for the conversion of the Gentile nations as the sub-heading in my Catholic (New Jerusalem Bible) Bible tries to imply. It is the chastened surrounding nations submitting, serving and honouring God and His holy nation under "Plan A". Of course, there are certain parallels with the Church for she is indeed carrying out aspects of the Kingdom role intended for Israel in the current age. It is the Church not Israel who is enlightening and seeking to reconcile the World to Christ (Rom11:15). But it doesn't detract from the fact that the Old Testament prophecies and angelic annunciations depict a very different scenario centred round the physical nation of Israel. There are also numerous warnings and predictions of thoroughly bad things that would happen to Israel's people and the holy city as a result of the idolatry and rebellion of God's chosen race which we are less inclined to apply to the Church. The suffering and determined resilience of the Jewish people has been witnessed throughout their extraordinarily turbulent history. I understand this endeavour to relate primarily to the churches, but I have been given a strong sense of JHWE's intense love for His "first choice" and am clear that the promises He made to them have not been forgotten; neither are all of them being fulfilled through the Church. Israel had frequently disappointed JHWE, but they had paid a heavy price for their disobedience and were now to be forgiven:

Speak ye comfortably to Jerusalem and cry out to her that her warfare has ended, her iniquity is pardoned; for she has received from the Lord's hand double for all her sins. (Is40:2 King James Version)

But what is that prophecy anticipating? What immediately follows it?

The voice of one that cryeth in the wilderness, "Prepare ye the way of the Lord. Make straight in the desert a highway for our God. Every valley shall be exalted and every mountain and hill made low; the crooked straight and the rough places plain. And the glory of the Lord shall be revealed, and all flesh shall see it together, for the mouth of the Lord hath spoken it (Is40:3-5 King James Version)

Israel's warfare with the nations was promised to come to an end for her iniquities had been pardoned - that was the context and backdrop to the ministry of John the Baptist; nor was the holy nation expecting to be usurped as sole heir to the Kingdom and replaced by a partnership (*koinonia*) of Jews and Gentiles. Such was never to be the teaching of John or initially Jesus who was faithful to the Law and Prophets; He hinted at it later in His ministry as He became increasingly frustrated by the "faithless generation" that He encountered (cf. Mt11:16-19). Truly, that generation will have a great deal to answer for (cf. Lk11:50-51). A fuller, yet still cryptic disclosure of this mystery was to come through Saul of Tarsus having received instruction from the ascended Jesus; such was the secret fellowship (the Church) hidden even from the thrones and dominions of Heaven, together with the dispensation pertaining to its administration we know of as the gospel age. John on the other hand had understood he was to prepare the way for a Messiah to deliver Israel from her oppressors, banish sin from the world, negotiate with other nations and establish His Kingdom on the throne of David as "the highest of all earthly kings" (Ps89:27). That is the only way it would have been possible for the whole world (all flesh) to see the glory of the Lord together: many had observed His compassion during His earthly ministry; only a few of His disciples had witnessed His glory. Neither could such universal acclaim arise from gospel evangelisation, it would require a

89

Parousia, expected to occur after the way had been prepared and the path for the Lord made straight, Jesus had undergone His second more dreadful "baptism" and had been received into Heaven only to return within a generation. Much as I thank God for the light shone into my own mind in the past and the Protestant world today through the scholarship of N T Wright [A good number of his sermons, lectures and articles are freely available at [http://www.ntwrightpage.com], did he really believe that *"the Jewish hope that Israel's King would be King of the world had now come true in Jesus the Messiah"*[39], especially when reviewing the events of the century just past. That hope was that their messianic king would be physically present amongst them, would have destroyed their enemies, arbitrated with nations, and surely by extension would ensure that satanic tyrants such as those that led Germany in the 1930's and 1940's and annihilated many of their race could never arise and prosper. Given also that the churches were quite powerless to prevent arguably the greatest human atrocity nineteen centuries into the Christian era there is absolutely no cause to hope that the system of wickedness underpinning what Scripture calls the *kosmos* (world system) can be defeated by the Church in the current age. It has been defeated in principle (by the cross) and will be defeated in practice through some awesome divine/angelic action at the end of the age as confirmed by Jesus, John and Paul (parable of wheat & tares; Rev17 &18 and 2Thes1:7-8), at which time Jesus would in some executive sense be King of the World (Mt25:34).

Continuing the glorious messianic theme:

Rejoice greatly O daughter of Zion, shout O daughter of Jerusalem: Behold, thy King cometh unto thee, lowly and riding upon an ass and upon a colt, the foal of an ass. And I will cut off the chariot from Ephraim and the horse from Jerusalem, and the battle bow shall be cut off. And He shall speak peace unto the heathen, and His dominion shall be from sea to sea (Zech9:9-10 King James Version).

The royal entrance into Jerusalem which Matthew points out was to fulfil the Zechariah prophecy (Mt21:4) or at least a part of it, occurred as we know; the securing of Jerusalem is still awaited.

90

Yet note the precision of the part that has been implemented, down to the precise means of transport for the Messiah. For it is observable that whenever a prophecy is declared to be fulfilled in Scripture it is in a literal rather than an allegorical sense: "Thus was such and such a prophecy *fulfilled*"; not re-envisaged. It also challenges the dualistic idea held by some that Old Testament prophecy is a worldly representation of a spiritual truth for the Old and New Testaments have the same Editor-in-Chief. It could be argued that "peace has been spoken to the heathen" through the gospel, but that was not Zechariah's conception which related to post-liberation arbitration with the surviving nations and inculcating the ways of peace, as is clearer from other prophesies such as Isaiah2:4, for they all follow a similar format. If one is to take Jesus at His word, this and all other prophecies concerning Himself must be realized (Lk24:44), but clearly not in the sequence or precise form envisaged for that has now been displaced; the nations have been enlightened by means of a universal Church, and a third world religion is vying with Judaism for the City of the Great King (Mt5:35).

And the Lord shall be King over all the Earth: in that day there shall be one Lord, and His name one (Zec14:9 King James Version)

How one longs for such a day when God in a meaningful sense reigns *on Earth* and the Lord's name (Jesus) is equally revered by all who worship the one true God. But it is not merely a personal longing it is biblical prophecy and must be fulfilled; but that cannot be an immediate result of the Church's current mission. Entrenched cultural and religious formation ensures that such is quite impossible until the Son of Man is spectacularly revealed to all.

The "Elijah" to come

Behold I will send you Elijah the prophet before the coming of the great and dreadful day of the Lord: And he shall turn the heart of the fathers to the children and the heart of the children

91

to the fathers, lest I come and smite the Earth with a curse (Mal4:5-6NKV)

Our considerations also impact upon prophesies concerning the "Elijah" who was to prepare the people of God for final judgement as Malachi affirms above; but hasn't he come and gone? If you are confused, then so were the disciples:

*And the disciples put this question to (Jesus), "Why then do the scribes say that Elijah must come first? He replied: "Elijah is indeed coming and **he will set everything right again**; however I tell you that Elijah has come already and they did not recognize him but treated him as they pleased, and the Son of Man will suffer similarly at their hands. Then the disciples understood He was referring to John the Baptist (Mt17:10-13 New Jerusalem Bible).*

Old Testament prophecy envisaged a prophet coming with the authority of Elijah to restore everything so that Israel might be ready to receive their promised Christ, who would then exercise judgement, eradicate wickedness from the world and initiate the Kingdom of God within it. Through the prophetically unexpected turn of events, various aspects of these prophecies have been deferred. Although Jesus has already done everything necessary to accomplish it, creation is to be restored at the conclusion of *this* age (Acts3:21; Rom8:21,22 cf. Greek). Yet strikingly the same terminology (*apokatastasis panta*) is utilized to describe Jesus's universal mission and Elijah's ecclesiological mission (Acts3:21 cf. Mt17:11 Greek). More precisely, Jesus affirms that "Elijah" will restore all things (*apokatastesai* -future verb) and according to Luke Jesus will appear at the time of the restoration of all things (*apokatastaseos* - genitive noun). Clearly their respective tasks differ vastly in scope and majesty: the one is to prepare a people, the other has provided in Himself the means for the salvation of humanity. But the point being made is that both missions were expected to be fully restorative within their respective spheres of operation. So we know Christ's work on Earth is not complete; through His atonement sin can be pardoned and purged in the case of His people but the Lamb of God has not yet "taken away" sin from the world as you will observe from your window. He is coming to attend to the matter

92

shortly (Acts3:21) and it will be an awesome experience for many. But what shall we say of His legate? One is bound to ask in what sense did John "sort everything out" or "set everything right again" regarding the children of Israel (v11)? Jesus's assurances concerning restoration through Elijah was made *after John had been beheaded.* Yet in responding to the query from His disciples, He had said "*Elijah is indeed coming to restore everything but if you are* **willing to receive***, then (John) is the 'Elijah to come'*" (Mt11:14). But the Jewish nation was *not* "willing to receive" either 'Elijah' or more importantly Jesus; the bride was not ready for her Husband. The friend of the Bridegroom (Jn3:29) was unable to "prepare the way of the Lord and a make a path straight for Him"; the Lord's path proved to be anything but straight, more especially in His dealings with the religious establishment. Through no fault of the prophet who received the greatest commendation from the One he heralded, John had been unable to get very far at all with the comprehensive commission that had been outlined for him in the subsidiary annunciation; for even "the messenger" was intended to be a cause of much joy to many (Lk1:14-17). The Jewish religious authorities, who humanly speaking were the nub of the problem, wouldn't accept John's baptism; the Temple establishment rejected his teaching (cf. Mt21:25); then he was decapitated by order of the king of the Jews. Would anyone seriously believe Jesus's assessment to be that the Jewish race and its state of religion had been "restored" and "put to rights" through the truncated ministry of John the Baptist? If the answer is in the negative, then according to Matthew chapter seventeen and verse eleven, Elijah had yet to come; particularly as world judgement, the restoration of creation and full realization of God's Kingdom has still to be implemented. Was it not completed? Then let it be repeated. The earlier question was anyway rhetorical – we are left in little doubt by Jesus's admonishment of Jerusalem (Lk13:34-35); for that "faithless and perverse generation" that John had been tasked to prepare would go on to reject Jesus as they had His herald. Of course, John had been no re-incarnation:

93

*So then they asked (John): "Then are you Elijah?" He replied,
"I am not." "Are you the prophet?" He answered "No".
(Jn1:21 New Jerusalem Bible)*

But whether he had regarded himself as Elijah or not, John had
come with his authority because Jesus had said so, although he
never got around to invoking Elijah's awesome powers. A part
of John's mission was to prepare God's people for judgement.
But then of course that didn't prove to be necessary, at least not
in a literal or final sense. Yet in Matthew 11:10, Jesus quoted
from Malachi confirming that John was sent with the intention
of clearing the path for the One who was coming to sit as a
refiner's fire and a fuller's soap to purge the sons of Levi, etc.
(Mal3:1-5). Referring back to the testimonies of the very earliest
Fathers, Clement (AD30-100) who had been personally
acquainted with St Paul (Phil4:3) understood the Malachi
prophecy to be relating to Christ's second advent[40], likewise the
Father of common sense Justin Martyr confirmed also that he
envisaged another "Elijah" would herald it[41]. The Baptist
certainly understood his own ministry in apocalyptic terms when
he gave this warning to certain religious leaders:

*Even now the axe is being laid to the root of the trees, so that
any tree failing to produce good fruit will be cut down and
thrown on the fire… Jesus's winnowing fan is in his hand; He
will clear His threshing floor and gather His wheat into His
barn; but the chaff He will burn in a fire that will never go out
(Mt3:10,12 New Jerusalem Bible)*

This was "the wrath to come" that John warned the Pharisees
about (Mt3:7) and it is obvious from the context that he expected
it to be imminent; nor was he talking about their judgement after
death, but universal judgement expected when Jesus shortly
established the "the Kingdom of God" on Earth. Applying the
dual perspective principle: according to "Plan A", the holy city
was going to be liberated from her oppressors, and by means of
her King's sacramental death, which was always there in
prophecy but barely understood, a fountain for sin and
uncleanness would be opened for her inhabitants (Zec13:1). The
other perspective, being the actual outcome resulted in the
postponement of the "Day of Wrath", whilst the fountain for sin

94

and uncleanness derived from the Saviour's wounds at the Place of the Skull was not to be restricted to the holy city but universally and sacramentally provided via the previously undisclosed multi-racial administration to be established. As a result of the Kingdom role being shared with the Gentile nations, the Jewish expectation regarding their land, nation and Kingdom involvement had been placed on hold (cf. Rom11:2). Their King had promised to return to them eventually but in the meantime:

Look, your house is left to you desolate. I tell you, you will not see Me again until you say "Blessed is he who comes in the name of the Lord" (Lk13:35 New International Version).

But as Jesus also insisted concerning Old Testament prophecy:

Everything *must be fulfilled that is written about Me in the Law of Moses, the Prophets and the Psalms (LK24:44b New International Version)*

There is no indication from Jesus Himself that He had any intention of subverting Old Testament prophecy to fulfil His Own and Israel's mission in an entirely unexpected way as N T Wright and others have proposed. At His arrest Jesus had challenged Peter who was trying to defend his Master by force of arms, "*But how then could Scripture be fulfilled that said it must happen **this way**?* (Mt26:54). Jesus's arrest and execution mustn't just happen, it must happen "this way", as prophesied. So, on the political front, if Isaiah and Micah had inferred that Jesus would personally arbitrate with people and nations to bring an end to human warfare (Is2:3-4), then that is what He expected at some point to be doing. Whilst the Church can pray for peace, preach peace and work for peace, there can be no lasting peace on Earth or universal justice until Satan's seed are removed and his structures of unrighteousness are destroyed from the Earth, which is to be the task of angels (Mt13:41). In the meantime, one looks out of the window and observes the world becoming ever more dangerous and ever more secular as the end of the gospel age approaches in spite of the Church, without whose salt and light things would indeed be far worse. Yet according to Oxfam, the richest one percent of the world's population own more than the rest of the world put together: the world is not currently in any executive sense under the government of Christ. Isaiah had foretold that the Son who had been born of Mary would *"establish (His government) with judgement and justice"* (Is9:7). Neither has Our Lord's judgement been received nor His justice practiced by the world's authorities in the current age. What one currently *can* perceive is the Body of Christ, or at least the part of it that recognizes it has any socio-political mandate, doing all within its power to renew humanity along Kingdom principles. But we are two thousand years into that process and the *kosmos* (world system) is as much under the Wicked One's influence as it ever has been (cf. 1Jn5:19); Satan has been granted a continued jurisdiction (cf. Eph2:2) and has a particular hold over "the sons of intransigence" (same verse) which would not be the case in the messianic age, during which time the arch-fiend would be bound and out of harm's way (Rev20:2), as will those who have become his accursed agents (Mt25:41 cf. Greek). The realization of God's Kingdom on Earth has been deferred and a dispensation (no less) that had been hidden in the Father inserted so that the multi-cultural fellowship pertaining to that mystery can be established to be salt and light for the world and a recruiter for Kingdom from amongst the nations. Even within the religious and spiritual sphere, victory over Evil is not to be realized within the current age (Eph6:12). The spiritual authorities themselves will be aware that they were defeated by the cross and their fate is sealed (cf. Col2:15) but the human agencies they control no nothing of the matter, for they don't "believe" whereas their spiritual masters believe and tremble at the fate that awaits them. Just as the Word, begotten of God before all ages once became flesh and submitted to death to provide pardon for many and to save His chosen people from their sinfulness, so shall the King of Glory leave His throne at God's right hand once more to realize His Kingdom on Earth: *"Lift up your heads, Oh ye gates, and be ye lift up ye everlasting doors, and the King of Glory shall come in"* (Ps24:7). Then, after some fearful mayhem that were best avoided (2Thes1:7-10), the wicked and godless seed of Satan (the darnel) will have been despatched and every foe defeated (1Cor15:25) such that every surviving knee (the wheat) will willingly bow to King Jesus. Such befits the reign of Christ as with any effectual monarchy: all authorities under the sovereign acknowledge his rule, or else. In accordance with all scriptural prophecy firstly the wicked (darnel) are destroyed then the wheat is gathered in (Mt13:30). Note carefully: the wicked (seed of Satan) are removed from the Kingdom, not barred from entering it (Mt13:41). They are to be "*taken out from the midst of the righteous*" (Mt13:49), not the righteous "taken up to Heaven from the midst of the wicked" albeit that the living elect are temporarily "raptured", that is gathered to Christ to be shielded from the aforementioned judicial mayhem and climax of tribulation which the rest of the world must patiently endure (cf. Lk17:34-36). The "darnel" is to be removed because it is poisoning the wheat; the wicked are to be destroyed because they are polluting God's Earth and perverting its people, not because "their righteousness would not avail before a Holy God". They had rebelled against the precepts of natural law; divine light with which they had been innately provided, with dire consequences for themselves and humanity; at Judgement such will be perceived to be abhorrent by all true humanity (Is66:24). So shall creation be purged so that the tabernacle of God can be with men, for He will dwell with them and they shall be His people (cf. Rev21:3).

Preparing the world

In preparing the World for such events, the Church calls people to repentance and allegiance to the coming King through incorporation into the assembly that already acknowledges Him as such. But many *in the churches* also need to be brought to the good sense of the upright (Lk1:17), as prescribed in the gospels by the Baptist, the Messiah and JHWE before them: "*Learn to do good, seek justice, defend the fatherless, plead for the widow: 'come now and let us reason together', says JHWE; though your sins be as scarlet they shall become as white as snow*". (Is1:17,18). The typical gloss has been to disassociate verse 18 (forgiveness) from verse 17 (the pursuit of righteousness through repentance). Likewise, the Baptist prophet, believing the Kingdom and final judgement to be at hand, whilst calling people to receive forgiveness through baptism insisted they must then go on to pursue righteousness, the fruit of repentance: share their food and raiment with the needy; be honest in business and be content with their wages (Luke3:10-14). Clearly, Jesus had been content enough with John's preaching (Mt11:11) and was later delighted with tax collector Zacchaeus when he declared he would pay back those he had swindled: *"Today salvation has come to this house"* (Lk19:8-10). If anyone is still in doubt, such is the nature of repentance.

The ingenious heresy

Taking the teaching of Jesus and John the Baptist at face value will appear facile to some who believe the Saviour's teaching was primarily to show His listeners the impossibility of meeting God's standard of righteousness. That is an example of the locking-in mechanism of scriptural error referred to earlier. In the Reformers' case it resulted from a misunderstanding of Pauline polemics that will be outlined later. The supreme ingenuity of such a heresy and the reason it has so long persisted is that any attempt to challenge it appears to be an act of human pride: the elevation of man and the diminishment of God's grace. But that is a misconception, for anything that is good about man is thanks to His Creator's benevolence, whether it be through a response to the Gospel or via natural precepts and the fact that man's soul/spirit is created in God's image - the loving Creator's wish being to enlighten man concerning his moral behaviour, for the benefit of his society, the creative order set under him and the wellbeing of his eternal soul. The Reformers on the other hand believed that Adam's disobedience resulted in such a triumph for Satan at Eden that what was intended to be the pinnacle of God's creation mutated to the point of becoming innately incapable of escaping eternal punishment at their Creator's hands. We will show that it is the former rather than the latter that pertains to man's true moral status and destiny, not to mention an infinitely worthier reflection of God's own nature and providential care. For the Godhead shall ultimately be worshipped and adored even by the majority who are not to form a part of His royal priesthood (Israel and the Church) when the One who obtained their pardon comes to be glorified in those

98

who have remained faithful to their Messianic calling. Moreover, it will demonstrate the equitable way the God of grace exercises His favour and shows kindness to all who are willing to receive it.

Preparing the churches

It can only be the Christian Church who prepares the world for the cataclysmic events to come, what Scripture typically refers to as the "revelation of the glory of Jesus Christ" (e.g. 1Pet4:13); urging as many as will listen to repent, be baptized and believe the Good News. But how exactly should they repent? What does baptism itself achieve and should they bring the kids along? What exactly *is* the 'Good News' and the 'Kingdom of God' and what else must be believed or participated in to be fitted for it? The churches can provide no unified answer to any of the above which surely we can acknowledge is unsustainable. If the Second Advent were to be the end of the space-time universe, the Church's fragmentation might be less of an issue. But the task that the Lord with His Church will face is to bring the whole world into subjection to its Creator. That cannot be achieved with His assemblies in such a divided state, nor according to the Bible will it be initiated without divine and angelic intervention. Such was to have been the task of the Jews with their returning Messiah but in view of their rejecting their "day of visitation" and Paul's revelation concerning what I have styled "the fellowship of the secret", the whole case has been re-ordered.

Review of emphasis

Through the centuries, the Apostolic Church's emphasis has been spiritually to equip people for life and ensure they are prepared for death and the judgement that follows it on order to be assured of the peace and joy of Heaven. But as all who acknowledge the Creeds should recognize, language such as "sleeping in Christ", "resting in peace" and "repose of the soul" pertain to the period before the Parousia and general resurrection, for new spiritual bodies will not be for resting, sleeping or exclusively gazing, but abundant life, action and service when the Kingdom of God comes in its fullness. There are some related mysteries that had previously been inessential for the Church's historical mission but are needed for the benefit of the elect and righteous *"who will be living in the 'day' of tribulation when all the wicked and godless are to be removed"* (Enoch1 ch1 v1). What many believe to be the inspired Book of Enoch that was necessarily excluded from the biblical canon is considered in the next chapter where it is utilized as a subsidiary reference source regarding the Fall and the Flood.

The context of the gospel

This disclosure is, amongst other things, explaining why within the apostolic writings the gospel is hardly ever expressed in terms of being the means to "get to Heaven". For that is not the gospel, Church or her sacraments' purpose, which is to prepare what the Bible makes clear is *a minority*, elected through unmerited grace, to become kith, kin and consort to the Lord of Glory (Heb2:10-11). As explained earlier, Matthew's references to the Kingdom of Heaven is synonymous with the Kingdom of God and is not referring to the place spirits go after death. Of course, human spirits/souls once separated from the body at death do go to Heaven and some elsewhere: but avoiding perdition is not a matter that has ever required special revelation or even religious practice as we shall continue to demonstrate; it pertains to natural law and is intuitive for those having been made in God's own image. For God is concerned for the eternal wellbeing of *all* humanity, not just the men and women He has given over to His Son, for whom the Latter gives Him special thanks (Jn17:6). Christians are not the lucky escapees from Augustine's *Massa Damnata;* they have been called out *from* the world to be a special blessing *to* the world and become fitted for glory in the age(s) to come. The fact that many who remain outside the Church or have no religious faith at all can ultimately be delivered from perdition is something the Catholic Church has only clearly articulated since the mid-twentieth century (Vatican II Lumen Gentium 16), whereas Evangelicals' primarily concern when presenting the gospel is to affirm that *all* human salvation is dependent upon Jesus Christ and His atoning death. This incontrovertible truth shall now be *re*-affirmed, albeit within the context of the broader benign providence being outlined.

The crucicentric nature of all human salvation

Whilst it would be perverse to regard an instrument of torture as a theological end in itself, the cross is a vital means to an end; that end being glory (cf. 1Pet5:10; Heb2:10). It is central to Christian soteriology, not just for the benefit of specific individuals but *"for the life of the world"* (Jn6:51). Yet according to the One who was crucified, it is only those who in some meaningful sense partake of His flesh and blood that experience its full benefits in the present: *"Most assuredly, I say to you, unless you eat the flesh of the Son of Man and drink His blood, you have no life in you. Whoever eats My flesh and drinks My blood has eternal life, and I will raise him up at the last day. For My flesh is food indeed, and My blood is drink indeed. He who eats My flesh and drinks My blood abides in Me, and I in him. As the living Father sent Me, and I live because of the Father, so he who feeds on Me will live because of Me"*. God's plan to restore the world and its inhabitants from the damage of the Fall is entirely dependent upon the Passion of Christ. But as we shall show in chapter seven, those who partake of His body and blood and daily take up *their* cross with Him are not merely to be restored to a state of Adamic innocence but glorified and perfected for future service in a way that could not have occurred had the events that *led* to the cross not come to pass. That was the introduction of evil to the world through the permission granted to Satan to test humankind in her primeval infancy. And having failed that test God's decision to utilize our disobedient first parents as the sin-polluted procreative fountain source for future humanity. As we will explore more fully in the last chapter, the resultant suffering, division and humankind's ongoing struggle with Evil provided the grist needed for Satan's enemies to be prepared for future glory, Heb2:10 perhaps providing the clearest clue to this mystery. Christ as human creation's firstborn (in the sense of its representative/leader

101

Col1:15) epitomized that suffering and He did so on the cross; hence St Paul's emphasis:

God forbid that I should glory except in the cross of our Lord Jesus Christ, by whom the world has been crucified to me and I to the world (Gal6:14 New King James Version).

Paul could have gloried in his own labour and suffering for the gospel – but he knew it was nothing compared to the munificent sacrifice and undeserved suffering on the part of the Word Incarnate, needed to remedy Satan's treachery and our first parents' disobedience. For as Eastern Orthodox Christians are keen to emphasize, the cross defeated the devil and his hold over death. In fact, that is the sacred Victim's most direct reference to the matter (Jn12:31); but in view of our primary subject matter the full fruits of that dimension to God's victory at Calvary have been deferred.

So much for the Christian, but the historical reality is that much of human creation has not had the opportunity to hear the Good News of Jesus Christ and His Kingdom faithfully rendered, particularly as for the last 500 years about a third of the Church has had a substantially different rendering concerning what is required for Christian salvation than the rest. Given that God our Saviour *"will have all men to be saved and come to a knowledge of the truth"* (1Tim2:4), do you for one moment imagine He would permit such a situation if avoiding perdition were dependent on a particular understanding of "justification by faith" or whether one had had the opportunity, understanding (or more likely the cultural background) to receive the sacraments of the Roman or Greek Church? That is not how the perfect justice of our God functions, being impartial yet merciful and generous towards all. Neither need this be anymore wishful thinking or intuition; it pertains to the context of gospel salvation within God's broader salvific plan, all of which we have just emphasized is entirely dependent on the cross of Christ. The next chapter will carefully examine the biblical account of the incident at Eden that demanded such a drastic remedy, its effect upon human nature, and how and to whom the fruits of the Passion are applied.

Notes: CHAPTER ONE

1. Paul listed as 13th apostle (excluding Iscariot replaced by Matthias) in the listing somewhat confusingly entitled by the editors "Hippolytus on the Twelve Apostles" – "Appendix to the works of Hippolytus"

2. The epistle of Barnabas chap. 5 (approx. AD100)

3a. Chrysostom Homily VI and VII on Ephesians covering (Eph3:5-11) and Homily V on Colossians covering Col1:26-28; 3b.) Ibid. Homily VII on Ephesians (Eph3:8-11)

4. Letter to Corinthians of Clement (c. AD30-AD100) chaps. 19 & 20

5. Clement of Alexandria "The Instructor" Book 1 chap. 3

6. The first apology of Justin chaps. 43 & 46

7. ibid. chap. 10

8. Irenaeus against heresies Book III chap. 25 (para 1)

9. ibid: Book IV chap. 13 para 1

10. Augustine interpreted 1Jn4:7 to mean that only a baptized Christian has the capacity to love since love is from God and no one outside the Catholic Church can be "born of God". Augustine's teaching that man is innately incapable of love is also evident in Anti-Pelagian writings; "On grace and free will" chap. 37.

11. New Advent: Catholic Encyclopaedia: Augustine's insistence on the eternal misery of unbaptized infants – under Heading "Teaching of St Augustine"

12. De Civitates Dei XXI chap. 12

13. Augustine's "On Rebuke and Grace" – chap. 3

14. Origen de Principiis Book II chap. 5 para 3

15. Augustine - Anti-Pelagian writings "On the spirit and letter" chaps. 22 & 27

16. Augustine: "Against two letters of the Pelagians" Book III chap. 11

17. Augustine - Anti-Pelagian writings "On the spirit and letter" chaps. 22 & 27

18. Daniel's "perpetual sacrifice" as referring to the Eucharist: Hippolytus Fragments from Commentaries "On Daniel" 2nd fragment (22)

19. 2Thes2:1-12 The key point Paul wished to assert is the sequence: the Parousia will not occur until an "*apostasia*" (apostasy, revolt or popular defection) from the Church has occurred in history.

20. First epistle of Clement chap. 32

21 a). Irenaeus against heresies Book I chap. 10 para 2; b) ibid Book V chap. 32 para 1

22. Bryntirion Reformed Evangelical College; later known as Wales Evangelical School of Theology (WEST)

23. Bethel Baptist Church Bassaleg, Newport South Wales

24. Luthers Werke 26: 147 – Weimar: Hermann Bohlaus Nachfolge

25. ibid. 27:408-411

26. Tertullian: Prescription against heretics chap. XXXIX

27. Epistle of Ignatius to the Philadelphians chaps. 3 & 4 [utilizing "shorter version"]

28. Irenaeus against heresies Book IV chap. 33 para 7

29. Opus Epistolarum Erasmi Roterdami (April 11th 1526)

30. Cyril of Jerusalem: Mystagogical Catechesis IV,3

31. Clement: "The instructor of children" – "Faith of the early Fathers" Vol 1:410 (W Jurgens)

32. St Justin Martyr – Apologies, chap. 66

33a) St Ignatius: Letter to Smyrnaeans chap. 7; b) Epistle of Ignatius to the Ephesians chap. 20 [both utilizing the "shorter version" deemed as more reliable]

34. Augustine: *De Civitate Dei* Book X chap. 20

35. Cyprian (A.D.200-258) Epistle 53 para 3 – affirms daily sacrifice of Eucharist

36. Greek Orthodox Arch-Diocese of America – Fundamental Teachings

37. The epistles of Cyprian (AD200-258) Epistle 53 (3)

38. St Chrysostom (fourth century – Homilies on the gospel of John #46 re Jn6:52 para 4.)

39. N T Wright: "What St Paul really said" [Lion] chap. 3 p53

40. First epistle of Clement chap. 23

41. Justin Martyr dialogue with Trypho chap. 49 (ignore editors' heading – read text)

Chapter Two

The Fall, the Flood & the Eluded Covenant of Life

*As through one transgression there resulted condemnation to **all men**, even so through one act of righteousness, there resulted justification of life to **all men** (Rom5:18)*

This verse from Romans alludes to the eluded universal Covenant of life as does the passage below. I have translated directly from the Greek which clarifies how the basis of justification at the universal and trans-historical level is Jesus's faithfulness (culminating in the Atonement) not an individual's faith in Jesus:

*But now **apart from** the Law, God's righteousness has been revealed witnessed by the Law and the Prophets; even the righteousness of God through the **faithfulness of Jesus Christ** for all who believe. For there is no distinction for all have sinned and come short of the glory of God being justified freely by His grace through the redemption that is in Christ Jesus whom God put forward to be a propitiation through Faithfulness by means of His blood to display God's righteousness, because in His forbearance He had passed over previous sins. It was to demonstrate His righteousness in the present time – that He Himself might be just whilst justifying people **by Jesus's faithfulness** (Rom3:21-26)*

The reference to "God's righteousness" (v21) and the "righteousness of God" (v22) should be understood as a subjective genitive; it pertains to God not to the believer and refers to His saving justice and faithfulness with respect to His covenants. Justification is what concerns the believer and is freely granted through the merits of Christ's faithfulness to all who "believe". Thanks to the gospel it is now being revealed "*apart from the Law*", not "without law" as some translations infer. The Jews needed to understand that faith is and always has been the badge of acceptance before God, not the deeds of the Torah (works of the Law), for Abraham and righteous men before Him predated the Law; they and all Gentiles subsequently had been accepted (justified) through the merits of Christ's faithfulness applied to those who demonstrated an underlying faith, positively responding to the divine enlightenment they had received. When Paul refers to the Jews seeking to establish their own righteousness instead of submitting to the "righteousness of God" (Rom10:3), he is not referring to some misguided moralism, sometimes referred to as "proto-Pelagianism"; on the contrary JHWE had constantly urged His people to learn to do good (cf. Is1:17), be holy in themselves and administer social justice. Mary's son had been disclosed to be the Incarnated Word or *Logos,* the One by Whom human souls are created and provided with a measure of wisdom, reason and divine enlightenment imparted by their Creator. And it is by the Son of Man's death that the racial barrier that had prevented Gentiles from participating in the privileges of the Covenant of Promise had been broken down (Eph2:12), justification in that context was no longer to be on a racial basis signified by circumcision and Torah observance but by submitting to the "righteousness of God". This had now been revealed separately from the Law (Torah) and enacted through Christ's faithfulness to His death on the cross. It meant that the physical seed of Isaac if they wished to form part of God's augmented and now racially inclusive royal priesthood must exercise faith and allegiance to the very One their leaders had crucified so that they could be sanctified through obedience to the Christian Faith.

Christians and the Jewish nation before them are members of an exclusive covenant evidenced at its inauguration when Abraham's own beloved circumcised son Ishmael was excluded together with his offspring (Gen21:8-20). Yet Paul was also aware of an inclusive covenant to which God was being faithful by which the likes of Ishmael and the righteous before him had been accepted on the basis of their "faith" through the merits of Christ's faithfulness. This Universal Covenant of life is more explicitly referred to in the fourth chapter of Genesis which we will look at in a moment and again in more detail in chapter six of this book in the context of those who default from it; for it is a key to understanding the mystery of evil. In terms of "the Fall", a short-lived implicit covenant was in place relating to God's warning to our first parents not to eat fruit from a certain tree and the implied promise that if they were obedient all would go well otherwise they would die on the day they ate of it. Some have called it the "Covenant of Works" but really it is also a Covenant of Faith, for acceptance with God has never been on the basis of "attaining a standard of worked merit" but of the obedience of faith and remaining faithful. Justification consists of demonstrating that one is a valid participating member of a covenantal community such as the Church, or indeed the redeemable human race that benefits from the Atonement in the context of the eluded covenant to be considered. This is closely related to the issues raised in chapter three (justification through the faithfulness of Christ). With this overlap there is bound to be a measure of repetition; tiresome for some but hopefully helpful for others less theologically minded and to whom some of these concepts will be quite new, for they are somewhat new to the author.

Covenantal Membership: grace to get in; faithfulness to stay in

Everyone entering into a covenant with God is there by unmerited grace, i.e. divine favour and generosity not dependant on merit (which as we will see is not always the case when receiving "grace" or finding favour with God). Unmerited grace clearly applied to a Jewish baby born within the Abrahamic Covenant; equally to the Christian baby baptized by the Church and incorporated within the Covenant of Christ's blood; also, to the adult convert given faith to apprehend Christ (Eph2:8) and receive Christian baptism; and the human baby, starting with Cain as the world's first infant, freely incorporated within the universal Covenant of life through the two-way age-enduring merits of Christ's righteous act (Rom5:18). The issue then becomes how one retains the benefits of that covenant as opposed to defaulting. The answer is faith or faithfulness [same word in biblical Greek] evidenced by "fruit". The Jew who turned from JHWE to idolatry defaults his covenantal privileges;

those in Christ who fail to produce fruit may remain in the Church but will be finally rejected by God (cf. Jn15:2); members of the human race who fail to produce any fruit in the form of compassionate love (*agape*) like Cain and the Matthew 25 "goats" remain on Earth (for the time being) but become alienated from God's loving care; they have a new master to look after their interests, and at least as far ahead as Scripture permits us to foresee will not be incorporated within God's eternal Kingdom but will receive post-mortem punishment (Mt25:45-46).

As the apostle James emphasized, justification requires evidence in the form of obedience or works to confirm that the faith is "formed" as opposed to "dead" (Jam2:17, 22). For devils believe in God's existence as did Cain; but they are not thereby justified for they never respond positively to that belief. Eve and Adam defaulted from their implicit covenant because having been led astray they ceased to be faithful and showed it by disobeying God's command concerning the tree of knowledge. We will work through the implication of our first parents' disobedience shortly, but this chapter is equally concerned with an incident concerning their two sons which is just as significant though has certainly not been recognized as such.

Cain, Abel and what God required of them

I suggested that the verse quoted from Romans in the chapter sub-heading alluded to a covenant; the following verse from Genesis is unquestionably covenantal in form, though most theologians for the last two thousand years have chosen not to regard it as such:

If thou (Cain) doest well, shalt thou not be accepted? And if thou doest not well, Sin lieth at the door. And unto thee shall be his desire, and thou shalt rule over him (Gen4:7 King James Version)

The translation of this verse from the Hebrew is admittedly problematical: "Will you not be accepted?" (Hebrew: *seeth*) could equally be "will your countenance not be lifted?" which is utilized by some versions of the Bible. The King James Version quoted above recognizes "sin" to be a person (the Sinful One), which makes sense since it or he is lying or crouching (Hebrew: *rabats*) at the door and "desires" to control Cain. Sin *per se* could hardly be "at the door" in Cain's case, it's already in Cain's heart and about to wreak havoc. Cain is described elsewhere as "of the evil one", confirming that the Sinful One was indeed at the portal of his soul and was able to master Cain and thereby control him; indeed, own him (1Jn3:12). From the human perspective, that would not have been so if Cain had responded differently to the challenge JHWE presented to him in Gen4:7 (however one chooses to translate it), so the verse effectively reflects a Universal Covenant for fallen humanity; for Abel was fallen but he was accepted. The purpose of the Cain and Abel story which is drawn upon in the New Testament is not to show how Abel "got saved" it is about how Cain became reprobate (rejected), indicated by the vital yet typically glossed references to "this day" and "now" regarding the elder brother's fate. The day he killed his brother he was cursed and entirely alienated from God and not before that day. When God told Cain to "do well", He was not seeking perfection but to do what the young man intuitively knew to be right: offer like Abel the first-fruits of his crop and preferably not go on to slaughter his innocent brother in cold blood. For no one is born devoid of at least one "talent" (the light of reason and a sense of justice) but some choose to bury it in the ground and they will be condemned (cf. Mt25:14-29). Cain, an agricultural farmer (4:2) was not expected to steal from his livestock farmer brother Abel to sacrifice an animal in offering for his sin, as some would dissemble (e.g. the Young's Literal translators). Comparing Scripture with Scripture we see that Cain and his sacrifice were not accepted because his works were evil whilst his brother's works were righteous (1Jn3:12). That was because the one exercised faith and the other didn't, for one was a child of God, the other as confirmed in later Scripture was or had become satanic (1Jn3:12 cf. Greek). As second century Irenaeus had expressed the matter precisely in this context: "*It is the conscience of the offeror that sanctifies the sacrifice when (the conscience) is pure and thus moves God to accept the sacrifice as from a friend"[1]*. Abel showed by his works and a good conscience that he had "faith" so was justified by that faith with reference to works (offering the best of his flock), not by achieving a standard of worked merit (justification by works). Why was perfection not required by either of them? – it was in view of the Sacrifice of atonement effectual throughout human history that St Paul was referring to above. Through the faithfulness of Christ (*ek pisteos christou*), which more theologians and the more recent Bible translators are recognizing needs to be distinguished from cognisant faith in Christ (*pisteos en Christo*), expiation has been provided for the faults arising from human weakness for those who themselves seek to be faithful to God (cf. Rom1:17 Greek: Faith applied to faith) i.e. the atoning benefits of Christ applied to all those who in turn are faithful[2]. The understanding of some that Cain and Abel were expected to anticipate a future Sacrifice for sin by killing an animal is unsustainable; cultic sacrifices were not clearly established as a religious system until the Law of Moses. Paul, James and the writer to the Hebrews make it clear why Abraham had been counted as righteous, being a belief in the God he had encountered evidenced by obedience, in his case that he would be rewarded with a great family (cf. Gen15:1). No one in the Old Testament is declared to be justified by offering an animal sacrifice, so Abel cannot be an exception. As will be demonstrated from Scripture, Old Testament folk and all "people of good will" were and still are accepted by God through Christ's faith/faithfulness being applied to those who are deemed to fear God through their positive response to the divine enlightenment they have received. The Faithfulness of Christ[3] (*pisteos christou*) does indeed relate to His atoning Sacrifice at the centre of history, but the beneficiaries do not necessarily have an awareness of it; universally so in Old Testament times (as we have shown, none of the twelve disciples initially had a clue about their Lord's future death, further evidenced by their initial despair after His crucifixion in spite of Jesus's assurances). Abel exercised faith and produced fruit in the form of good works (1Jn3:12). Abel didn't "get saved", he remained accepted (justified) and was acknowledged as righteous within the Universal Covenant; Cain reprobated (became rejected) and

111

was brand-marked for Satan, and to scare the life out of all who would dare cross him, but that was not at the point he failed to offer his first-fruit in sacrifice, for although God was not pleased with his offering, He still held out an olive branch. Rather he was called to account immediately he had killed his brother. The issue was never the brothers' religious observance *per se* for God has always delighted in compassion rather than religious offerings, as is affirmed by Jesus (Mt9:13). Cain's reprobation resulted from a total absence of the fruit that is the evidence of justifying faith: godly fear or that still small voice of God speaking through conscience. These are the criteria that distinguish those who are or will become the children of God from those who become the delegates/envoys/messengers/agents of Satan (*aggelois diabolou* - cf. Mt25:41). Like Adam and Eve, Cain and Abel were uniquely special, being the first siblings to be born of woman. That is why they are representative within the Universal Covenant to demark how fallen man is regarded by God on an individual basis. The criterion of judgement being "faith" resulting in the fruit of *agape* fully aligns with Christ's final judgement of "the nations", that is those (under Plan A) outside the Abrahamic Covenant (Mt25:31-46). This will be dealt with in considerably more detail in the next chapter.

The demise of the Adam-project

Returning to the error of our first parents, why from a human perspective was God's "Adam project" allowed to go so horribly wrong, almost resulting in global annihilation by water within ten generations? Who was at fault; to what degree and what were the respective penalties handed out to the guilty parties at what we know as "the Fall"? Account also needs to be taken of a subsequent cosmic drama cryptically referred to in Genesis 6:1-2 which impacted upon humanity, but as with the elusive Universal Covenant, in accordance with God's stratagem of progressive revelation it has not been taught or generally understood by the churches, even though the earliest Fathers refer to it[4]. Once clarified, our loving God's decision to flood the Earth, obliterate Sodom and Gomorrah and annihilate the men, women *and children* of the Canaanite territories will be

112

better understood, indeed perceived to be necessary. With that in mind and again contrary to my personal intentions I have been led to refer to the extra-biblical Book of Enoch[5], as it throws considerable light on Gen6:1-2 and matters concerning judgement and the age to come. In recent times fragments of copies were found amongst the Dead Sea Scrolls. This is literature that was regarded as inspired and a genuine work of the Patriarch by early Church Fathers such as Clement, Irenaeus, Origen, Augustine and Tertullian, which is hardly surprising since it is directly quoted in the New Testament (Jude14,15). Tertullian specifically regarded Enoch as falling within the remit of 2Tim3:16 concerning "all Scripture" being inspired and useful[6]. He believed the book had been rejected from the Jewish Cannon because it contained this prophecy pertaining to Christ:

And there was great joy amongst them and they blessed and glorified and extolled because the name of that Son of Man had been revealed to them. And He sat on the throne of His glory and the sum of judgement was given to the Son of Man and He caused the sinners to pass away and be destroyed from off the face of the Earth, and those who have led the world astray (En68:26,27).

More likely, Enoch was excluded from the Old Testament Cannon (apart from that formulated by the Coptic Orthodox Church) because of an unacceptable degree of variation in the manuscript copies available to the early Church councils that determined the composition of the Biblical Canon. Apart from being directly quoted in the Bible, this Scripture clarifies some otherwise obscure verses which themselves are quite important and cannot be properly understood by comparing canonical Scripture with Scripture. None more so than the opening of Genesis 6, vital to a rounded understanding of God's nature and *modus operandi*, together with the respective culpability of the human and celestial agencies that contributed to the fall and the flood. The latter was another reason it was more conclusively rejected by the later Fathers who believed it did not place sufficient emphasis on man's culpability for those cosmic disasters, especially having endorsed Augustine's austere take on the matter. This extra-biblical literature also clarifies less

113

important but nevertheless intriguing issues such as "the blood that speaks better things than Abel" (Heb12:24), Enoch's walk with God (in much detail) and the ethnicity of Adam, Eve and their offspring (hinted at in Genesis5:3). It also reveals, albeit cryptically, the ethnicity of Noah's three sons, and for that reason alone, especially in view of Gen9:25, it was providential it was excluded, and until relatively recently not readily accessible. But it also re-affirms the fact that the wicked are to be removed at the Parousia and the Messianic Kingdom established on Earth for a period before the Earth is written down for destruction and the New Heavens and Earth prepared at the general resurrection. With the aforementioned early Christian writers I have no doubt the book is inspired and should be consulted to aid completion of the biblical jigsaw. In the present context it also contains certain prophecies regarding the final mystery of God that would not have remained such a mystery had the book been received within the canon and historically focused upon within the Church.

Enoch's exclusion from the biblical canon will have been in accordance with God's will, for if we do not accept that the early Church councils were infallibly guided in determining which of the alleged "gospels", "epistles" and "revelations" were genuine and divinely inspired then we cannot trust the Holy Scriptures at all. Researchers into the matter will note that an agreed canon was not properly settled until the late fourth century, and for some time thereafter very few Christians would possess a Bible, for before the invention of the printing press the complete manuscripts would have been rare and extortionately expensive. Much later the Protestant Reformers relegated seven books (classified as deuterocanonical having been included in the Septuagint but not the Hebrew Bible) and these have subsequently disappeared from most Protestant Bibles. Yet some of these books are referenced in New Testament Scripture and you will observe that many were utilized as proof-texts in the writings of the early Fathers. Had Luther had his way James, Revelation, Hebrews and Jude would have disappeared along with them for these more than most challenged his concept of salvation through "faith" alone as he redefined it. But there is another reason to believe Enoch was not intended for the Church throughout its history yet is relevant for today as "profitable reading" – that is the very opening verse:

The words of the blessing of Enoch, wherewith he blessed the elect and the righteous **who will be living in the day of tribulation** *when all the wicked and godless are to be removed (Enoch1 ch1 v1)*

And at the end of Enoch there is a prophecy concerning the book itself and other books:

But when they write down truthfully all my words in their languages, and do not change or remove anything from my words but write them all down truthfully – all that I first testified concerning them; then I know **another mystery,** *that books will be given to the righteous and the wise to become a cause of joy and uprightness and much wisdom. And to them shall the books be given, and they shall believe in them and rejoice over them, and then shall all the righteous who have learnt therefrom all the paths of uprightness be recompensed (Enoch104:11-13)*

This is quite remarkable: the idea of books or scrolls being made widely available for distribution is a concept nowhere to be found in the Cannon of Scripture and was beyond human envisaging before the invention of the printing press. If you have ever read through Enoch you are bound to agree that that book of itself could never be the cause of widespread joy or enlightenment, neither can "another mystery" be referring to the propagation of the Protestant Bible in the Middle Ages, for the Reformers like the Catholic Church did not regard Enoch as canonical, apart from which Enoch's prophecy pertains to the generation living at the time *"when the wicked are removed from the Earth"* (En1:1). For there will be something quite unique about that generation (our generation?): unlike all Christians who have gone before them, they will not have visited HQ before the Lord comes to realize His Kingdom. As St Peter indicates in his epistle (1Pet4:6), those who have died will have had the opportunity to be acquainted and fully prepared for the next age whilst in Heaven; not so the Christians alive at His coming. "But surely we have the Church and the gospel to prepare us?" Which Church and gospel did you have in mind?

115

The Jews had the Law and the Prophets, if only their scribes could have interpreted them – JHWE had to make further provision to prepare the way for His Son to come and inaugurate His Kingdom in the form of a messenger prophet (cf. Mal3:1). It is sobering to reflect upon these "scribes" of Jesus's time: how even the true Faith and it Scriptures could be misinterpreted to the point of crucifying the One who was meant to be their fulfilment.

In terms of the Genesis story, the ultra-metaphorical reading employed by the likes of Augustine has resulted in some essential principles and events being glossed. Clearly, he was right even in his time to recognize that the creation story as presented in the Pentateuch was not intended to be a scientific account of the various creative processes; still more so in view of what we know today. So the seven "days" of creation will hardly be referring to 24-hour periods; Scripture elsewhere testifying that "one day with the Lord is as a thousand years and a thousand years as one day" (2Pet3: 8), or as Augustine pointed out, Sirach18:1 (which he regarded as canonical) refers to creation being made at once (*creavit omni simul*). However, when the Lord tells Cain "*Now you are cursed*" and Cain replies "*from this day I will be hidden from thy face*" (Gen4:14), that has a theological significance which has been quite eluded. Most Christians acknowledge that the whole of human history has been tainted by the disobedience committed as an act of free will by Cain and Abel's parents against their Creator; but there has also been a tendency to understate the influence of the third player in this catastrophe, for Satan (the snake) was its instigator, not Eve or Adam and this is fully reflected in the punishments. These are radically different in degree once the prepared remedy is applied, for it benefits the one guilty party at the expense of the other. The eternal Word's incarnation as a Man and His death on the cross would bring about the ultimate destruction of the one guilty party, whilst for the other it would result in forgiveness, salvation and ultimate theosis (union with the Godhead), so that in the words of one of the last Church Fathers to be revered in both the Catholic and Orthodox Church, St Maximus the Theologian, "*we may consort with God and become gods, receiving from God our existence as gods*"[7].

116

Having created what we now know to be a staggeringly immense universe, our sun just one amongst an ever-increasing but scarcely reliable estimate of 100 octillion stars (cf. Gen15:5), the Lord of the universe through His Spirit prepared this pinprick within space we call Earth to receive life (Gen1:2). But not just any life; for He had determined to initiate within this perfectly suited physical environment a relationship with beings created to be both physical and spiritual in makeup; made according to His nature so that they themselves could come to share in His divinity (cf. 2Pet1:4) and support His activity by subduing the Earth (Gen1:28). So from the outset, man was to act as God's vice-regent, overseeing and caring for all that had been created on Earth. Provided with an equal yet complementing helpmate, Adam was placed in the Garden of Eden to tend and care for it (Gen2:15). The garden contained all the trees required for this first couple's eternal sustenance (cf. Gen3:24). It also contained a tree with the ability to give them knowledge of good and evil, intended for their future participation in the divine life (cf. Gen3:22). Meanwhile they were forbidden to touch it; but having been tempted by the devil to do so, these two children of God who were created innocent yet pliant disobeyed their Father and immediately lost their original state of righteousness. At that very moment they "died" just as foretold (Gen2:17). That death pertained to their relationship with God, whilst what had been a perfectly complementing union between man and woman became subject to tensions and marked by lust and domination. In terms of their morality, their demise had the effect of weakening the soul's ability to master the latent tendencies of the procreated body for the latter had become fatally subjugated to the pleasures of the senses, covetousness for material goods and ostentatious pride. This is a triple concupiscence pertaining to "worldliness" as summed up by St John:

All that is in the world: the desire of the flesh, the desire of the eyes, the ostentation of life is not of the Father but of the world (1Jn2:16)

Through Satan's treachery and our first parents' disobedience, man together with the whole visible creation became subject to

117

physical decay and death, and by procreation the human body became a corrupting influence on the soul that would come temporarily to inhabit it; what Paul and Peter refer to as our earthly tent (2Cor5:1; 2Pet1:13, 14) or vessel (1Thes4:4). However, we're only a few chapters into Genesis and already some traditional theological assumptions need to be challenged. Firstly, it is erroneous to intimate that the Fall led to "death of the human soul", for that implies that the whole person including the human's spirit had become entirely alienated from God and no longer had any effectual enlightenment. The historical error of mainstream Christian theology since its systemization in Late Antiquity has been as basic as failing to distinguish between disobedient Adam and his psychopathic eldest son; that was not the case amongst the earliest Fathers such as Irenaeus[8a] and Origen[8b] who classified fallen Adam with Abel not Cain. Adam was the first man to be created; Cain the first to be born of woman; the one was the federal head of humanity and the progenitor of "original sin", the other being the type of the "damned", being those who through an act of free will leave the intuitive path of sound reason and deference to conscience *"to walk in the way of darkness, and rejoice in evil and delight in the waywardness of the wicked, whose ways are perverse and devious"* (Prov2:13-15). I am aware that "sound reason", even conscience itself will not instruct a man how to be a disciple of Christ - His demands go well beyond such faculties and require special revelation, spiritual empowerment and the means of sanctifying grace. However, innate human reason (informed by conscience) is effectual and normative regarding what is to be pursued and what is to be avoided in the cause of *being humane,* and that is the basis upon which everyman is judged, being without excuse if he has opposed and rejected the light that he has received (Mt25:31-46). Cain did just that, killing his innocent brother in cold blood and so was cursed whilst Adam had never received such a curse (Gen3:17); Cain became alienated from such Light, Adam did not; Cain came under Satan's mastery, Adam did not; Cain was a plant of the devil, Adam a lost child of God (cf. Mt13:25; Mt 15:13); Adam was "dead" in trespasses and sins, Cain *twice* dead and pulled up by the roots (Jud1:12); Adam typified those on a long and arduous

118

path to theosis; Cain to those on the road to what the Bible describes as Hell. The understanding has been that Abel was the first man to be "saved"; the reality is his brother was the first man to be damned, the latter also acknowledged by the earliest Christian writers. Nor would my affirmation of man's innate ability to walk uprightly and attend to morals or observe sound reason have appeared heretical to them, for they recognized that such is quite distinguishable from being raised to eternal life through an interior communion with Christ (Col1:27; 1Jn3:2), which is what the Bible means by "being saved".

Why the Universal Covenant has been eluded

Clearly theologians cannot rely on a single passage in Genesis but must compare Scripture with Scripture, and the concept of a Universal Covenant for fallen humanity implicit in the Cain and Abel story (explicit when utilizing the Masoretic text) hardly fits in with much else as it has been historically and universally interpreted ever since Christian doctrine was systematized. Moreover, the Greek Septuagint (LXX) renders the key verse about God's warning to Cain somewhat differently and that is the version to which most of the apostles and the early Church will have referred. The Hebrew (Masoretic Text) is at least as reliable as the LXX but it simply was not utilized by the apostolic Church, the Greek language being *lingua franca* for the Roman Empire and therefore the Greco-Roman Church. It is therefore no surprise that the apostles do not make direct reference to this verse (Gen4:7) whilst the early Fathers always quote from the LXX, which intriguingly refers to Cain's incorrect division of his offering and that he should "be at peace and rule over him"; somewhat meaningless and surely a corruption of the Hebrew, presumably the "him" referring to the devil. I understand such obscurity to be an intentional veiling on God's part regarding an understanding of a Universal Covenant, yet it is not dependant on this verse alone but can be deduced from Cain's punishment and curse in which he became excluded from the nature of the relationship with God that his brother, his fallen parents and Cain himself experienced before the fratricide (Gen4:11-14.). But the principle reason for what might in a dual

119

sense be termed "the Lost Covenant" concerns the nature of the
Bible itself which was never intended to be a comprehensive
account of God's creation, for example we know relatively little
about the angelic realm from which evil had sprung and with
which we will one day participate; rather Scripture's focus is the
salvation history for the world centred on Christ and His peculiar
peoples (the Jewish nation and the Church). Hence Abraham is a
vastly more significant figure than Abel; both had "faith" and
were justified by it, being representatives within covenants, but
Abraham initiated the exclusive covenant by which God would
work from within through an elect people to enlighten and
reconcile the world to Himself. The inclusive covenant in which
Abel was declared to be righteous and Cain defaulted does not
have a direct role in that salvation story, firstly because it
pertains to that which is intuitive, so is not dependant on special
revelation, and secondly because individuals are not "saved"
through it, i.e. they are not cleansed from sin and raised to
eternal life. The Universal Covenant determines a person's post-
mortem fate, but also prior to that his involvement or otherwise
with Satan as an agent within God's mysterious providential role
for evil (chapter six); that is why the "type" of those rejected
from it being Cain was brand-marked and protected rather than
wiped out there and then. These issues are, as it were, the
unilluminated side of the revelation globe, pertaining to the
mystery of God (cf. Rev10:4,7). Consequently, biblical
theologians have for ever been attempting to fit three square
pegs (soteriological categories) into two round holes
(soteriological outcomes); hence the numerous, seemingly
intractable tensions in Scripture typified by the "narrow way"
leading to life that few will attain on the one hand and frequent
intimations (not least by Paul) of God's broader scale intentions
to reconcile all redeemable humanity to Himself on the other. It
is also to be observed that Adam had three sons as did our
postdiluvian Patriarch Noah, and from these have sprung all
humanity: Adam's son Seth and Noah's son Shem represent the
elect line; Adam's son Abel and Noah's son Japheth the
"righteous" within the Universal Covenant whilst Adam's son
Cain and Noah's son Ham were the accursed defaulters albeit
that only one of Ham's sons was cursed (Canaan) as Ham had

already received a blessing (Gen9:1). Once we arrive at the Abrahamic Covenant, Isaac represents the elect line resulting in Israel whilst Abraham's other son Ishmael who (*nota bene*) was blessed by God (Gen17:20) and remained in His favour and care (Gen21:20) had not been elected to the exclusive Covenant of Promise.

The children of Hagar

Paul regarded Ishmael's mother Hagar as an allegory, effectively for a second exclusive covenant: "the Mount Sinai in Arabia that aligns with the Jerusalem that now is" (Gal4:24, 25). The prophet Mohammed was yet to be born but this may in part be a prophetic reference to those children of Abraham (Muslims) that serve the One True God in accordance with their scriptural Law. The one true God worshipped by Muslims, Jews and Christians delights in all who fear Him and submit to a disciplined way of life for the sake of future reward (cf. Heb11:6). He well knows that each must respond to the creed that his conscience directs him to follow in the context of his cultural background and understanding, for to do otherwise would be a sin. The Church however has been commissioned to go into the world and exhort all in every nation to follow Jesus Christ, yet it is God alone who determines who shall come into the community of His Son, being a matter of elective grace, not wisdom nor indeed any other merit (Jn6:44). Those *"chosen in Christ before the world was made to be holy and faultless before God in love"* (Eph1:4) do not achieve that end and the glorious reward that goes with it by following a prescription of regulations and religious duties; they are spiritually empowered to serve God in spirit and in truth, albeit that also requires substantial self-discipline. As such they not only worship God and seek to observe His commandments they come to delight in Him and His law of liberty and relate to Him as a Friend; likewise, they not only seek to do the right thing by their neighbour, they love him as they do themselves. Yet many who are considered Christian do not live such a life as other faith groups would be the first to point out; that is because many are Christian in name only (the West is more secular than Christian) whilst others though sincere

121

have long been in a measure of doctrinal darkness concerning their need to pursue personal righteousness as you may have discerned having read this far.

As for the many who have no part at all within such faith groupings, they nevertheless remain within the inclusive Covenant of life from which Cain defaulted provided they do not follow in his way (Jud1:11). Such multi-dimensional effectual grace (innate and celestial) can only be perceived and systemized *within a sacramental and synergetic soteriological framework* so it is no wonder such a schema has yet to be established, for on the one hand it undermines some early (fourth/fifth century) Catholic biblical theological groundwork whilst on the other is entirely incompatible with the Protestant conviction of total depravity, *sola fide* and one dimensional *sola gratia*. (The Reformed concept of "common grace" is not linked to the atonement and is deemed ineffectual for forgiveness or the avoidance of perdition). Since Vatican II through the Spirit's prompting the Catholic Church *has* effectively acknowledged a "third hole" being all people of good will who do not find their way into the Church but will ultimately be accepted into God's eternal Kingdom. Completing the analogy what has been lacking for the last fifty years from the Catholic side is the third peg, being a workable biblical underpinning for such a hope, for that cannot be provided without substantial doctrinal deconstruction and who within the Catholic Church would be crazy enough to attempt that?

Having acknowledged that the Genesis account is not a scientific description of creation, I have otherwise been content to take references to trees of life and knowledge and a garrulous snake literally. To regard the whole account as fanciful or purely allegorical might be acceptable providing one takes stock of the events and what they are intended to symbolize, given that all the key players in the saga are often referred to in New Testament writing. Augustine in reviewing these events had at least the good grace to acknowledge that their interpretation was difficult and that the Catholic Church should be willing to change its view on the matter if new information became available[9]. But in his analysis of our first parent's disobedience

122

and its consequences, not only did he fail to distinguish between Adam and Cain's transgression and their respective punishment, but he did not take on board the extenuations indicated in the Book of Enoch (expanding on Gen6:1,2) in spite of the fact that along with many of his contemporaries he had regarded it as genuine and inspired writing. I shall do, for otherwise the nature of both fallen man and His Creator is distorted.

The origin of the soul

In examining Genesis I am applying the "creationist" understanding of the soul's origin, affirming that each person's soul/spirit (that which is separated from the body at death) is created directly by God and planted into the embryo procreated by the parents. That has been the prevalent view within Eastern Orthodoxy and is in accordance with the catholic faith although Augustine himself wavered from it. It was accepted by the later "schoolmen" with Thomas Aquinas asserting it to be heretical to say otherwise. Through original sin, the divinely created soul finds itself within a morally sickly environment, or expressed another way is required to operate through an impure medium (the procreated "body of death"). Physiologically the physical and spiritual entities (body and soul/spirit) are in union, yet they have opposing moral impulses. Augustine, arguably the first recognized Christian anthropologist had started well, aptly applying the analogy "your body is your wife": the couple were once in perfect harmony but following the Fall are in combat with one another. St Paul however goes further: these two entities are influenced by separate and distinct laws or engrained principles; the body, being the corrupted medium through which the soul/spirit (or inner man) must function has mysterious impulses of its own:

*For I am gratified by the law of God in my inner man, but I perceive **a different law** in my bodily members warring with the*

123

law in my mind and bringing me into captivity to the sinful law that is in my bodily members (Rom7:23 Greek interlinear).

In fact, the "law in one's members" is not that mysterious; it refers to the senses perceived through the members of the body that are of course processed by the physical brain, the latter being a part of the procreated intellectual vessel through which the divinely planted soul/spirit must operate. Like the rest of the body it ultimately derives from fallen Adam's loins and is heading for the grave or incinerator. The human psyche, emotions and motivations cannot be contained within that vital organ or entirely derived from it, for when the soul leaves the body it is conscious and memory-retaining as Scripture affirms; the rich man wondering why he must experience suffering in Hades was told by Abraham to "*remember that in your lifetime you received good things and likewise Lazarus evil things, so now he is comforted and you are tormented*" (Lk16:25). The members of the body themselves can be a problem (one in particular - cf. Mt19:12) but hacking off arms and legs resolves nothing as Jesus well knew (cf. Mt5:30,31) for worldly concupiscence has been programmed into the brain thanks to Adam and Eve and original sin and must be controlled by the spirit. As for Paul's reference here to the "law of God", he is referring to a moral sense of what is right and just, particularly exercising love and consideration for others, which the apostle confirms was always the law's (and the Torah's) heart and purpose (Rom13:9,10). It is intuitive, being the outworking of the human conscience (Rom2:15) which is clear when we obey that principle, guilty when we do not. You will need to refer to the Greek throughout this examination of Pauline anthropology in the context of "original sin", for its heart has been obscured in many translations through a process of redaction.

The tripartite nature of man

Again, largely through Augustine's influence and partly as a reaction to the Pelagian controversy, the post-Nicene Church defected from the predominantly tripartite understanding of the earlier Fathers who believed man to be comprised of body, soul

124

and spirit[10]; the latter being provided directly from God and means by which we receive right reason and a pure conscience, the Light of Christ by which little children cannot but "believe" in Jesus the Word (cf. Mt18:6). This has exacerbated our difficulties when interpreting Romans chapter seven in particular; the "spirit" not being conceived by most readers to be a separate entity (a component of human nature) distinct from the Holy Spirit. The fact that trichotomy was the orthodox teaching of the early centuries is indicated by the fourth century "Apollinarian Error" being the notion that Christ's spirit was pure *Logos* and therefore He was not fully human, the point being that such a heresy could not have gained traction if the understanding had been that man had consisted only of body and soul. Paul refers more frequently than others to the human spirit because of his substantial handling of the "inner struggle" concept. On one occasion he refers to "body, spirit and soul" together (1Thess5:23) in terms of them being sanctified "as a whole". Likewise, the writer to the Hebrews speaks of the word of God penetrating between soul and spirit as it does between the joints and marrow (Heb4:12). The latter two materials of the body are closely related yet distinct, as are the soul and spirit. Justin Martyr (second century) spoke of the soul housing the spirit just as the body houses the soul[11] the latter being a kind of ethereal interface formed in the outline of the body enclosing the spirit - invisible when it leaves the body at death yet clearly visible in the realm it inhabits prior to resurrection (cf. Lk16:23). Irenaeus largely concurred: the soul possessing the figure of the body in which it dwells[12a] whilst *"the complete man is composed of flesh, soul and spirit. One of these does indeed preserve and fashion the man – this is the spirit; whilst as to another it is united and formed – that is the flesh; then comes that which is between the two – that is the soul which sometimes when it follows the spirit is raised up by it but sometimes it sympathises with the flesh and falls into carnal lust"*[12b]. Later in the passage he fails to distinguish carefully between the Holy Spirit and man's spirit, unlike the apostle Paul who declares that in the Christian the Spirit witnesses with our spirit that we are the children of God (Rom8:16) and that Christ's spirit unites itself with our own (1Cor6:17). In the New Testament the Greek word for soul (*psuche*) is often translated as "life" for it more often relates to the physical: *"Take no thought for your "psuche" what you shall eat or what you shall drink"*, etc. (Mt6:25). Those who seek only to gratify the flesh are described by Jude as "soulish" i.e. having no spirit (*psuchikoi pneuma me echontes* v19).

Non-generic anthropological substance dualism – the nature of "original sin"

Now one cannot avoid getting somewhat technical in considering the Apostle Paul's distinctive anthropology, albeit it is no different from any other apostle's but is considerably more detailed and often misunderstood. But firstly, I need to explain my own terminology for this interpretation is quite new to me also, being a direct result of the spiritual "encounter", at the height of which I would open the Bible and sometimes accompanied with tears or laughter come to understand a passage in quite a new way. In applying the term "anthropological dualism" I am not simply contrasting the actions or out-workings of the body with that of the mind, for as can be easily demonstrated, the negative "works of the flesh" listed in Galatians5:19-21 could be equally carried out by an embodied or disembodied soul, such as the sin of jealousy or pride. Nor am I referring simply or in an unqualified way to "substance dualism", the fact that man comprises a material body (flesh) and an immaterial soul and spirit. The point is that flesh and spirit have opposing moral inclinations as a result of which the human mind becomes a battleground, receiving conflicting advice or motivations from each: the selfish creaturely inclinations derived from the bodily members processed through the brain on the one hand; the more idealistic sometimes altruistic impulses arising from the conscience governing the God-given spirit on the other. But neither am I saying that the immaterial part of man (the soul and spirit) is in any Platonic sense generically superior or purer than the material housing or "vessel" (the body) because the former happens to be immaterial, hence this busman's clumsy "non-generic" prefix. The dualism in the form of moral antagonism arises from the *immediate* source of the components parts; the spiritual

126

components are pure not because they are immaterial but because they are from God; the body is impure not because it is material but because it is procreated from the loins of fallen Adam and carries the contagion of sin. It should hardly need to be said there could be no such contagion from God yet many (fellow creationists) who recognize that the eternal soul or spirit is not contained within human sperm also believe it to be sinful by nature. All readers will surely agree sin must be derived from man (or Satan) not God; Paul once he is understood explains how precisely that affects human morality and how for Christians the matter is partially remedied by gospel salvation, yet not wholly so for anybody until resurrection (cf. Rom8:23). This duality was certainly recognized by some of the very early Christian writers. In the epistle to Diognetus (c. AD130), Mathetes, the anonymous disciple likens the soul's relationship to the body to that of the Church to the world: the latter (equating to the flesh) wars against the former (the soul) and hates it because it is perceived to restrict its worldly enjoyment, whereas the Church (the soul) loves the body (the world) and seeks to preserve and sanctify it[13]. Likewise, Cyprian (A.D.200-258) recognized the body to be of the Earth and the human's spirit to be from Heaven and that through the Fall they have opposing natures. He affirms that Paul's references to the spirit being opposed to the flesh (e.g. Gal5:17) are not referring to the Holy Spirit but the human's spirit; similarly, the fruits of the spirit[14].

There has been such a spiritual and physical dimension to man since his creation: Adam was formed from the dust of the Earth; the Creator breathed into his nostrils and he became a living soul created after God's own nature (Gen2:7). Dust however reconstituted could never relate to God; man as a whole can for he is body and soul/spirit. It cannot be over emphasized, having a body is not the problem; it is an essential aspect of being human. The problem is *this* body and from whom it has been procreated. From that statement it should be evident I am not depicting what some refer to as "extreme anthropological dualism". That is the unbiblical threefold proposition that the soul is special to God but the body isn't; the after-life is of value but this life in the body isn't and that the soul is autonomously immortal. On the contrary, a human being is quite incomplete without both body and soul in union for they are wonderfully and intricately inter-related. The problem is, as Augustine recognized but did not carry through to its practical outworking, they are currently not fully in union in terms of their moral inclinations as a result of original sin.

What principally has failed to be observed is the way Paul (in particular) distinguishes between the different inclinations acting upon the mind in view of the different law or principle acting within the material and immaterial constituents of human nature; particularly in Romans chapter seven which will be examined later. The apostle summarized the matter as follows: the disposition of the flesh is death whilst the disposition of the spirit is life and peace (Rom8:6). Straight away it is assumed Paul is referring to the Holy Spirit – he is not, for it would hardly need to be asserted that what is divine is disposed toward life and peace. The implanted spirit is rather like Adam and Eve at creation: pure and innocent but pliant, i.e. liable to corruption, except that in the soul's case it is certain to experience corruption through the intrinsic unrighteous bias of fallen human nature as a whole. God never creates what is evil or impure of itself, so that must apply to the human soul/spirit but fallen man can and does procreate what is impure, and then they are combined in the human embryo. Yet it is not like pouring wine (the spirit/soul) into a bottle (the body): the body, soul and spirit are so closely inter-related that the material soon compromises the integrity of the immaterial, yet they remain separable identities, being parted at death. That which was derived from the dust of the ground returns to the ground to await a radical transformation (resurrection) whilst that which was given by God returns to God. But the soul will inevitably have been tainted by its association with mortal flesh unless a person has been "saved" (soul-healed) through the gospel. For through original sin the physical component's latent instincts as they are processed within the brain are intrinsically corrupting, tending to concupiscence (disordered desire), and will inevitably gain the upper hand over the divinely planted soul and spirit unless aided by divine grace. Through divine ingenuity, the punishment devised for fallen humanity provides a means by which mankind

128

will ultimately come to benefit more than if Adam and Eve had remained faithful; but that will not become evident unless one comes to grasp the reason for human suffering provided in chapter seven as well as the anthropological model presented here. Once one comprehends the latter then that which was once irreducibly beyond elucidation becomes a seamlessly coherent tapestry of light and truth. Well almost; I refer of course to the Pauline passages, particularly in his epistle to the Romans and especially those concerning the interrelationship between the flesh, spirit and Holy Spirit. The inner conflict arises from the material and immaterial components' disparate immediate origins; the "inner struggle" is not between human nature in its entirety and the Holy Spirit for it applies equally to those who do not possess the Spirit. Rather it is a conflict between the inclination of the bodily members (Paul's temporary "vessel" or "tent") and the influence of the human's spirit; the one governed by concupiscence, the other by conscience; the one having been created after God's own nature, the other created originally from God's good Earth but degenerated through "the Fall" and procreated therefrom. *"O wretched man that I am; who can deliver me from the **body of this death**? I thank God it is through Jesus Christ our Lord"*. For in the Christian that battle is aided and can be turned into victory through the empowering of the Holy Spirit and communion of the human spirit with Christ's spirit (1Cor6:17). It certainly was in the life of the apostle who knew as his death approached (though not necessarily earlier cf. Phil3:12-14) he was to inherit a victorious crown (2Tim4:6-8). Luke gives us a rare insight into a reaction to this profoundly misunderstood apostle's teaching or more specifically his personal evangelism during the discussions he had with Governor Felix whilst under his custody in Caesarea. Paul's emphasis we are told was on future judgement and the need for personal righteousness and self-control, causing Felix to tremble and defer any further discussion (Acts24:25).

Anthropological dualism in the Gospels and non-Pauline epistles

Anthropological dualism is not exclusive to the writings of Paul. Jesus uses the terminology of the "heart" when referring what Paul's describes as the "inner man" or "spirit":

A good man out of the good treasure of his heart brings forth that which is good (Lk6:45a King James Version)

Jesus is obviously referring to the man's heart not God's in which the treasure resides; similarly it is the human spirit not the Holy Spirit that directly produces good fruit, for contrary to the wishful thinking of the devil and the teaching of some who have been deluded by him, those who do not possess the Holy Spirit can still exercise genuine love, kindness and patience which are fruits of the spirit. That is nothing for anyone to boast about for these virtues come from God as the human's soul/spirit comes from Him and it is created in His image regardless of whether it becomes empowered by the Holy Spirit. *But then there is "the flesh".*

In the gospels Jesus utilizes metaphorical language to describe the would-be disciple's inner struggle with the spiritual and physical components of his nature, and it is a good deal starker than Paul's but is teaching the same principle. The self-mutilation passages recorded in Matthew5:28-30 and Mark9:43-48 are referring to the need to control the bodily members so that the soul or "heart" is not polluted. It is clearly allegorical for it is obvious that cutting off an arm does not make someone a better person: they will still find a way to steal if that is their inclination. In this chapter we are focussing on "original sin" but Jesus's teaching here has still more important soteriological implications (next chapter) for it re-affirms the disciple's personal and urgent involvement with regard to Paul's misunderstood references to *"putting to death the deeds of the body by means of the spirit"* with the aid of the Spirit. Jesus is highlighting the need for a disciple (his soul/spirit, not the Holy Spirit) to keep his bodily members under tight control otherwise the whole person will be damaged. But note the reflexive: "If your eye *offends you* pluck it out; if your arm *ensnares you* hack

130

it off" etc. Others may be offended by my stealing and lustful ogling but that is not the point Jesus is making. As with the apostle's teaching, it pertains to the disparate moral dispositions of spirit/heart and body. The "you" that is offended, ensnared or led into sin is your spirit/soul/heart, being that which is from God and survives physical death; the offenders or ensnarers are your bodily members driven by the physical senses processed through the brain pertaining to the temporary "earthly tent" (2Cor5:1). If the latter is not controlled it pollutes the former and the soul may need to be purged or salted in fire (Mk9:49,50). Only Jesus specifically alludes to this post-mortem aspect which we will return to in due course, but otherwise Peter teaches the same principle albeit less dramatically than Jesus and with less proneness to being misunderstood than Paul since he refers more inclusively to the "soul" rather than "spirit", such that there is no lexical ambiguity in translation to confuse spirit with Spirit.

"Abstain from fleshly lusts which war against the soul" (1Pet2:11).

Peter's "fleshly lusts" equate to Paul's "flesh". His "soul" incorporates Paul's "spirit", but in Peter's case it is unambiguous for the Bible translators, much as some might wish, cannot equate "soul" to "Holy Spirit", yet to be consistent with the way Paul is normally understood in this area Peter might have been expected to write "Abstain from fleshly lusts that war against the Holy Spirit" (cf. Gal5:17). The various apostles' teachings are consistent throughout: the spirit (or soul or "heart" or inner man) is constantly at war with the earthly tabernacle (or vessel or body or flesh) into which the spiritual essence is diffused (cf. 2Cor5:1) and the battleground is the mind that determines the will. The internal struggle is not restricted to the Christian; the difference is that the believer is not dependent upon his own resources being aided by the Holy Spirit and the various means of grace as well as having had his mind renewed and re-motivated by divine teaching (Rom12:2).

131

Only sin "disables" the soul

Such an understanding clarifies and reassures concerning the nature of human disability, especially that affecting the brain or mind. Even in cases of severe dementia or brain damage there is no fear that the real person i.e. their eternal soul/spirit is changed or damaged even though they may cease to recognize their own loved ones or no longer be able to articulate their faith. The people they truly are is retained and imprinted within the immaterial spirit that returns to God when the body dies. Sickness, aging and accident may damage the body and brain but only sin can corrupt the soul and so it will to an extent for those who are not "saved" through the gospel unless they die in early infancy. The special grace of the gospel is required to restore and maintain a purity of spirit that enables the soul to experience "eternal life" whilst diffused within the mortal body. Some within the Faith who have discerned such a dualism have used it as an excuse for sin, believing it is not they who are sinning (citing Rom7:20). They fail to realize that in so doing they place themselves in a state of bondage (Rom6:16) and in continually sinning against the light they fatally disrupt their relationship with God – in Paul's language they "die" (Rom6:16). In Peter's language they are also endangering their eternal soul (1Pet2:11). Jesus likewise as we have just seen.

Human nature: inclined to sinfulness

Just as Paul has been misunderstood so has the human condition been misdiagnosed, especially within Western Christianity. Eastern Orthodoxy has somewhat more fittingly presented the matter, being less enamoured with Augustine and careful to adhere to the corpus of Faith as it had been handed down by the apostles. Orthodoxy believes that human nature cannot be intrinsically sinful being created in God's image, but through the Fall has become open to evil intents and actions and so is ever "inclined to sin". More strictly though it is the soul or spirit that cannot be sinful in itself; it becomes "inclined to sin" through infusion with that in which it is associated, so one would have to conclude that *human nature as a whole is sinful in itself*, for the

132

body (flesh) is very much a part (albeit a temporary part) of human nature. That is why man has been deprived of the quality of Life and divine communion that God ultimately intends for him whilst he remains in mortal flesh except he encounter the grace of the gospel. But fallen man is not morally rotten at heart for the core (the spirit/inner man) is directly supplied and enlightened by God. He does not look at the outward appearance of man but observes the core (the heart) and finds it to be quite variable (cf. 1Sam16:7), sometimes even in accordance with His own (1Sam13:14). Yet neither is mankind "morally neutral" but has an unrighteous bias, always tending to err unless aided by divine grace (which Pelagius seemingly failed to recognize). For whilst our Heavenly Father does not create or assign what is rotten and morally degenerate, our human father unavoidably does, and it becomes the spirit's earthly tent or vessel. The human spirit having been enlightened by Christ (Jn1:9 Greek) has clearly discernible impulses of its own that we know of as the conscience, which unless it has been rendered inoperable (cf. my chapter six) genuinely guides and restrains. In taking heed to his conscience, even an otherwise irreligious man exercises a form of godly fear and does or at least tries to do what God would have him do in any situation. By means of this commonly provided divine enabling or *effectual* common grace, a person made in God's image even without the spiritual provision available through obedience to the gospel may live a decent, upright and worthwhile life, leaving the world a better place than he or she found it; even contributing to the building of God's Kingdom on Earth, just as the Gentile Cornelius had done before his conversion (Acts10:31). However, as we saw earlier, these lost children of God though they may be decent, humane and live purposeful lives have yet to fulfil the *purpose of life itself* which is to be united and in a meaningful relationship with one's Creator. Through original sin and the inherited "body of death", they cannot live a victorious, spiritually fulfilled life, or be "free indeed" from the enslavement of sinful concupiscence which requires not merely the common grace of enlightenment and sound reason but *"the exceedingly abundant grace which is in Christ Jesus"* (1Tim1:14). Those receiving such a "supreme gift of grace" (cf. Acts11:17) not only aim for what is right but

133

having been spiritually renewed are provided with the ongoing spiritual resources *to practice it* (cf. 2Pet1:3). For such come to possess the indwelling Christ who unites Himself with their spirit (1Cor6:16,17). Those lacking that vital divine communion in Pauline language are somewhat radically described by him as "dead". Yet those who have been blessed to experience Life with a capital "L" will know why he uses such language and proclaim with the apostle - *"For me to live is Christ; to die is gain"*. Meaningful communion with God *is* life; anything short of it, whilst fine for the animal kingdom, is not worthy of the name for those who specifically have been made in the Creator's image for *an eternal relationship with God*. Those who are not in Christ are currently alienated from the life of God; they are "dead" in that sense. Yet every human life is valued by the One who gave it and each person's experience within the corrupted intellectual vessel inherited through the fault of their first parents provides a test and preparation for the eventual fulfilment of their eternal purpose: to be reconciled to God through an introduction and willing submission to Jesus Christ. In a certain sense they already know Him (Jn1:9) and serve Him (Mt25:40) whenever they show compassion to anyone in need. In the language of Vatican II: *"Whatever good or truth is found amongst (these people) is to be considered a preparation for the Gospel"*[15]. That was clearly the case for Cornelius. Yet such virtue as they do possess is a result of the grace they have received, albeit the universally provided enlightenment provided by conscience with which, unlike Cain, they have co-operated.

Original sin and baptism

Whilst Scripture calls the Christian convert to be baptized to *wash away past sins* (Acts22:16) and be given a clean slate, baptism does not re-orientate what Paul refers to as the "law of the members" operating within the human body (Rom7:23). This body by nature and inclination remains "dead because of sin" even in the Christian (Rom8:10); as the next verse affirms that will not be fully resolved until the resurrection; yet when the soul is spiritually renewed through the grace of the gospel, the mortal body may be presented as a living sacrifice that is holy and acceptable to God (Rom12:1) so that the life of Jesus might be manifested even whilst in mortal flesh (2Cor4:11). Adult baptism is *"the response of a good conscience towards God"* (1Pet3:21); a conscience and spirit that inclines to moral truth and through elective grace understands such to have been perfected in the teaching of Christ. It opens the way to the means of grace by which the spirit of man is united to Christ and empowered to over-ride the instincts of his bodily members so that in Paul's words he may ***"possess his own vessel in*** *sanctification and honour"* (1Thes4:4). Through baptism the Christian convert is cleansed and pardoned from past sins, but the ongoing cleansing is provided by the blood of sprinkling. In the context of infant baptism, the issues of conscience, personal co-operation and pardon for personal sin do not apply; rather it replaces circumcision as the sign and instrument by which newly born infants are united to the Body of Christ and incorporated into the care of the Church. It should be evident from a reading of the gospels that unbaptized or uncircumcised infants were never abhorrent in Jesus's eyes, and He alone determines where they are to spend eternity (cf. Jn5:22). This has always been intuitive to the Orthodox Church, but for those still hankering after scholasticism: unbaptized infants are not to be barred from Christ's loving embrace for it can be adduced from Jesus's teaching that such are not guilty of sin (cf. Jn15:22); they have not themselves broken a law and where there is no law sin is not imputed (Rom4:15 & 5:13); where there is no personal knowledge of evil God does not assign guilt (Jn9:41); sons may be afflicted for the sake of their father's sins but are only held accountable for their own (Deut24:16). Most definitively, Adam's act of disobedience has been universally expiated by Christ's Act of righteousness (Rom5:18) within the Universal Covenant under which all infants fall, being at that stage incapable of defaulting. This is the historically eluded Universal Covenant for fallen humanity represented by the first two male sibling to be born of woman. As for the comparison with circumcision, under the Old Law Abraham was justified in God's sight before he was circumcised (Rom4:10) whereas his son Ishmael was circumcised but not admitted to the Covenant of Promise. But contrary to the teaching of Pelagius (which

135

nevertheless is more orthodox and faithful to the earliest Fathers than many suppose), babies inherit the physical and moral consequences of Adam's sin in the form of corruptible and corrupting bodies, which apart from gospel grace are anything but benign; so entirely irrespective of whether infants are baptized they will demonstrate the concupiscent impulses of the "flesh" as their parents quickly discover. Whilst the Roman Catholic Church had initially gone along with Augustine regarding the forensic aspects of "original sin", the Church now entrust deceased unbaptized infants' eternal welfare to the mercy of God. The Eastern Orthodox Church largely rejected Augustine's theological approach, not a few within her regarding him as a major factor in the East/West schism[16], as well as the "the fount of every distortion and alteration of Christian truth in the West"[17]. Such believe that he subverted aspects of the teaching and tenor of the ante-Nicene Fathers, which I am convinced is the case. His especially narrow and fatalistic cosmology derived largely from his interpretation of the Pauline epistles that he had utilized in his disputations with the likes of Pelagius and Manes.

Manichaeism – misplaced dualism

Manes had developed a sophisticated form of Gnosticism in the third century, the central tenet being a metaphysical dualism resulting in the cosmos and consequently human nature being divided through the influence of two opposing deities; one good the other evil with neither being sovereign. Before his conversion to the catholic faith, Augustine had been a follower of Manes and like him believed mankind's sinful inclinations could be explained and partly excused by an alien nature within him. Like many heretical perversions of the Faith, an element of truth may sometimes be present, and the danger is a polemical over-reaction, resulting in this case in Augustine's unwillingness to discern or acknowledge a form of anthropological substance dualism in the writings of St Paul. Archelaus (Bishop of Caschar) had also erred somewhat in an earlier attempt to protect the Church from the heresy of Manichaeism. His dubious reasoning is evident in the following response to Manes' (valid) insistence that body and soul are in moral tension: "*If the body is the work of the wicked one (as Manes believed) in as much as it is so corruptible and antiquated and worthless, it would follow that it was incapable of sustaining the virtue of the spirit or the movement of the soul, and the most splendid creation of the same*"[18]. But surely the body *is* incapable of sustaining the virtue of the divinely planted soul and spirit (cf. Wisd15:11) apart from the grace of the gospel; it is why one needs a second birth through water and the aid of the Spirit if one is to sustain Life, i.e. communion with the divine. Manes who had difficulty accepting that God could ever have created the being who had become the Prince of Darkness was quite right to affirm that there are two opposing moralising agents within man and that Paul had asserted as such (Rom7) but was in error concerning its origins, nature and the ethical implications. Unlike Manes, the apostle had taught that the components making up human nature derive from the one God, but, the immaterial components (soul and spirit) are directly planted by Him (as indeed Archelaus had rightly affirmed) whilst the material component is transmitted in a degenerative state ultimately from fallen Adam's loins. This is a form of dualism nevertheless being the result of original sin. On reflection is not such a condition preferable to the concept of human nature being defiled in its totality? Actually, what might be preferable is hardly the issue; such moral antagonism is what Paul was teaching and is the observable reality of human nature: often noble in aspiration, less so in practice.

Bodies are for loving

Paul is nevertheless insistent that this disordered human body is to be loved and cherished by its owner, satisfied by its sexual partner if it has one (1Cor7:5), and for the Christian acts as a temple for the Holy Spirit. Even this carnal version is a wonder of science, fearfully and wonderfully made (Ps139:14) and potentially beautiful to behold, whilst what remains of it will eventually be utilized to create a glorious new body. In a real sense the body we currently inhabit will always remain a part of our identity. "Your body is your wife"; physical and spiritual have become one but will be later separated and the physical component redeemed and ennobled before being reunited with its eternal spiritual partner such that body, soul and spirit become a holy and inseparable unity. In the meantime, the Christian must pummel the temporary vessel and bring it under subjection (1Cor9:27) for the disciple of Christ has been set a course to run (Heb12:1); he is like an athlete straining for a prize, which is the high calling of God (Phil3:13-15). It is to be observed from the writings of two very early martyrs Polycarp and Ignatius having been trained by the apostle John that they had begged their churches to do nothing to save them from martyrdom otherwise they might fail to "attain to God" and would have continue to "run the race" of the Christian life, being in their estimation as least as arduous as being thrown to the lions or burnt alive[19]; the point being they certainly did not regard Christian discipleship in any passive sense of simple trust or "coming to an end of one's own efforts to please God" but rather the pursuit of personal holiness so as to be worthy of the age to come (*kataxiothentes tou ainos ekeinou tuchein* - Lk20:35).

St Paul describes this temporary vessel as "the body of this death". Regrettably, "*Somatos tou thanatou **toutou*** (Rom7:24) is often inadequately translated, such as in my Catholic edited New Jerusalem Bible where it is "the body doomed to death". That is not what the Greek relays and entirely misses the point. The apostle is not referring to the human body's fate but its *current condition*, for it is the degenerative procreated intellectual vessel that leads the divinely planted soul into death (i.e. disruption in divine communion). Such deprivation is what the apostle means by "*this* death", i.e. the death the person he was illustrating was currently experiencing: it is not "damnation" or total depravity, which would pertain to the soul or whole person, not the mortal body *per se*. Of course, the body we currently possess is "doomed to die"; an obvious fact but not the point Paul was making; for that issue can and will be resolved at resurrection. The body of this death on the other hand requires a more immediate remedy for those who are to relate to God *whilst still within it* so that the soul may be fashioned for a still greater destiny: that remedy is participation with Christ (Rom7:24,25).

It all stems from the Garden of Eden incident and God's previous warning to Adam:

*You shall not eat of the tree of the knowledge of good and evil; for **in the day you eat of it** you shall surely die (Gen2:17 Word English Bible)*

Again, the New Jerusalem Bible translation misleads employing "doomed to die" whereas the Hebrew is indicating that these children of God would "die" the very day they ate the forbidden fruit, and so they did; their relationship with God was disrupted from that very moment. That is the cessation of the "Life" God has intended for the pinnacle of His creation: intimate communion of the human soul with the Source of its eternal life. This is recoverable only by being "born again" and coming to know the sacred interior presence of Christ who restores life to those who feed on Him (cf. Jn6:57).

O *sin* where is thy sting??

One needs to observe carefully what the apostle is saying here concerning spiritual death (1Cor15:54-56): "*The sting of death is sin and the strength of sin is the law*" (v56). The converse idea, namely that the sting of sin is death is better understood and Paul quotes as much from Hosea in v55. But once again the apostle intends exactly what he writes. He is indicating that something being dead results in sin which then in turn leads to a further form of death. In terms of the latter, being "mortal sin", Luther and his followers are mistaken to imagine that such is no longer an issue for the Christian, but then St James was never the Reformer's favourite apostle: "*When lust has conceived it brings forth sin, and when sin is consummated it brings forth death: do not be deceived, my beloved brethren*" (James1.15,16). It should be noted James was here addressing Christian believers. The point Paul was emphasizing by inverting the more readily intelligible quote from Hosea regarding sinful practice resulting in death was that sin itself *results from* death, i.e. the "body of this death" by which in responding to the body's natural inclinations the soul rebels against the divine light of conscience and so disrupts the relationship with the Source of its spiritual

139

life. So what had been conceived in sin (Ps51:5) has "died" leading in turn to sin that destroys Life once the "law" (a sense of right and wrong) can be perceived and is invariably breached (Rom7:9). Hence the need for heavenly grace by which one can be spiritually purified, receiving ongoing cleansing of the soul so that those predestined to it may serve God whilst still in mortal flesh and be able to be re-fashioned after Christ's image for an eternal partnership with Him. The apostle had further asserted that *"death will be swallowed up in victory"*, yet even celestial grace does not fully resolve the problem of mortal embodiment:

*"For **when** this corruptible has put on incorruption and this mortal has put on immortality, **then** shall be brought to pass the saying that is written: "Death is swallowed up in victory""* *(v54).*

God intends to save our soul and body, but He does not do so simultaneously (also Rom8:10). So even the Christian is still tempted to sin whilst in mortal flesh which is why it is his body that is to be offered as a living sacrifice (Rom12:1) *"so that the righteousness of the law might be fulfilled in us who walk not after the flesh but after the spirit"* (Rom8:4); for it is the latter (spirit) that having been supplied by God loves His law and wishes to serve righteousness. Not until "this corruptible" (body) has been transformed at resurrection will death (physical and spiritual) finally be swallowed up in victory when the body itself is redeemed (cf. Rom8:23). The soul's "vessel" in its current degenerative state is the cause of the human problem being the outworking of original sin; the final solution will not be for the soul to lose a body altogether so as to be eternally at rest in Heaven (which is a spurious dualism), but to be re-clothed in a new body which is *from* Heaven (2Cor5:2) and to be married to the Man who is God and actively participate within His realm (hence the arms and legs); that will be joy unspeakable and full of glory.

But Paul doesn't leave the matter there: *"The sting of death is sin and the strength of sin is the law"*: sin is empowered by a growing awareness of right and wrong (the law) such as when an infant loses his innocence and grows into maturity. *"For I was alive without the law once; but when the commandment came,*

140

sin revived and I died' (Rom7:9). I am aware that the context of the preceding verses is the Law (Torah) rather than an individual sense of right and wrong but if this verse were applied in the covenantal sense it would imply that Gentile pagans remained spiritually alive because they weren't provided with the Law (Torah) whilst God's Covenant people spiritually "died" which cannot have been the apostle's meaning. He is reverting here to an individual application which continues through the focal inward struggle passage a few verses later, to be considered in more detail later.

Corruption of the mind

Thinking back to our first parents it cannot only be the "flesh" that can corrupt the soul: Adam and Eve in their state of original righteousness could not have had a problem with concupiscence for their bodies were created directly by God, not procreated from sinful parents. The pure but pliable souls of these children of God were nevertheless corrupted by a direct assault on their minds through the deception of Satan, as a result of which their perception of the Creator became distorted, leading to their disobedience and punishment. But unlike Adam and Eve in their original state of righteousness, procreated infants starting with Cain and Abel have an innate tendency to be disobedient, greedy, selfish and the like through concupiscence; unlike our first parents they do not need to be persuaded by the devil or anyone else to be naughty and disobedient, it is entirely natural to them because of the law of their members (i.e. the processing of the brain) (Rom7:23 Greek). However, their loss of innocence can be greatly accelerated or exacerbated by the corrupt communication or behaviour of others; or alternatively they can be aided by good parenting and teaching. But how ever sound the latter may be, their mind and will cannot avoid being distracted from a consistent path of goodness; their soul cannot maintain its innocence and so they cannot sustain "eternal life" as Scripture defines it unless they are saved by the gospel and become associated with the life of Christ (cf. Rom5:10).

141

The mystery of holiness

Herein lies the mystery of holiness according to this revelation, for again it draws upon ideas alien to my previous understanding for it is an outworking of the new anthropology: unless by some means the soul can be restored to the purity of that of a little child, it cannot enter the Kingdom of God (cf. Mt18:3). Holiness is purity of soul: child*like*ness without the naughtiness (child*ish*ness); guarded and preserved by wisdom. Purity of spirit/heart/soul is not inviolable perfection which God alone possesses (Mk10:18). He does not expect it or require it as is evident if one carefully analyses Jesus's dealings with His disciples and JHWE's earlier dealings with His intimate servants such as Abraham, David, Job, Moses and the prophets who each related to their God as a child to a father. So what are the distinctive features of a young child which the Lord would have His disciples emulate? It is surely a humble acknowledgement of one's need for guidance, provision and discipline from Father God and Mother Church; a sweet and intuitive simplicity, credulity, a sense of wonder and a keenness to please. What a young child does not possess is a sense of self-loathing or conviction of moral impotency. And nor should he, for looking intently into the eyes of a young child one is observing the windows of a soul newly supplied by God and enlightened by Christ; not one "formed after the mind and will of Satan" as at least one "spiritual master" of the past had concluded (next page). Yet still there is the flesh, so to maintain a childlike purity of spirit one has to be enabled to control the concupiscent inclinations of the body, requiring both self-discipline and heavenly grace. Only then can one hope to become worthy to inherit the promises of Christ. Such is the mystery of holiness; it is not one-sided grace but sanctification of our spirit *"by personal obedience and the sprinkling of the blood of Jesus Christ"* (1Pet1:2 cf. Greek). Such a symbiosis is affirmed in Paul's exhortation to believers to work out their own salvation with fear and trembling (Phi2:12). Thereby may a Christian be united to God whilst still in mortal flesh to be prepared for Kingdom service. That is restricted to those who have been born again by water and the Spirit; not "all people of good will" but children of the Church, walking in her light and receiving the

142

ongoing cleansing from Christ's blood for those venial sins that beset even the most devout (1Jn1:7 cf. 1Jn5:8). No one can be *"saved to the uttermost"* apart from the Apostolic Church where alone are dispensed the mysteries of *heavenly* grace. Yet there is a broader, communal context to holiness also, for those individuals and communities that practice it are as a witness to the world, living and behaving in the present as God would have all humanity to live in the ages to come. That is what the world was meant to see in Old Testament times when they observed the nation of Israel living in accordance with God's Law in righteousness and peace and exclaim *"Surely no other people is as wise and prudent as this great nation"* (Deut4:6); it was not to be. Now wider society is meant to look to the Church (which therefore must be a visible distinct entity) and discern such a model of loving fellowship, sanctity and charity. It is one reason Jesus prayed for her to be -

"...perfected in unity so that the world may believe it was You who sent Me and that You have loved them as You have loved Me" (Jn17:23).

Truly, the world will be the more inclined to believe it when they see the Body of Christ united and at peace with itself.

Dualism misplaced

The carefully nuanced dualism that this layman has to the best of his ability outlined regarding St Paul's anthropology has historically been eluded, although as we have seen it was recognized to an extent by the likes of Cyprian and no doubt other ante-Nicene contemporaries whose writings are not available to us. Such dualism later became diffused into Christian eschatological cosmology where it has no place to be: the notion that the physical realm is correlative with carnality and corruption and is inferior to the spiritual. Corruption is the consequence of disordered desire, not materiality. Jesus has already demonstrated that the resurrected body such as He came to possess will be thoroughly material (spirits do not eat breakfast - Lk24:42). Such misplaced thinking was behind Augustine's influential change of mind regarding the

143

Millennium; he came to regard the concept as overly carnal, partly in reaction to certain Millenarians of his day that he cited who regarded the millennial "Sabbath" as something of a perennial knees-up. These early chiliasts' extraordinary distortion of the concept of Christ's rule with His saints to establish global righteousness whom Augustine refers to in "the City of God" brought the whole system into disrepute; certainly it is the only grounds he provides there for dismissing the earlier broader consensus of the ante-Nicene Fathers and constructing an a-millennial or some would perceive a post-millennial explication for the latter part of Jesus Christ's Revelation to John which the Church has tended subsequently to utilize. His interpretation of the two resurrections as set out in Book XX chapter 7 of his "City of God" will hopefully be discerned by readers to be untenable to the point of not warranting serious analysis; but to be fair we do have the inestimable privilege of historical hindsight. Cosmological dualism (spirit good/material bad) may be refuted from scripture and creed in one word: RESURRECTION. For as we have endeavoured to show, the problem is not having a body but having *this* body disordered by original sin. Returning to Paul's "inner struggle" passage (Rom7:14-25), "s*arks*" refers to the "flesh" not the "human nature" as some translations infer for the mind is a vital part of human nature and is often opposed to the "flesh"; something which Augustine appears to gloss over in his comments on this crucial passage of Scripture. In his "Confessions" he alludes to this teaching from his favourite apostle then immediately appears to contradict him as well as himself:

*"For though a **man be delighted with the law of God according to the inward man**, what shall he do about that other law in his members, "fighting against the law in his mind" and captivating him in the law of sin that is in his members? Thou art just O Lord but we have sinned, we have committed iniquity, we have done wickedly and thy hand has grown heavily upon us and we are justly delivered over to that first sinner, the ruler of death, because he (Satan) **turned our will to the likeness of his will,** whereby he stood not in thy truth [Confessions – F J Sheed Book7/ XXI - my highlights to demonstrate the contradiction]*

144

One is bound to ask how man's will is said to be conformed to
Satan's will since the writer has just quoted the apostle as saying
that the former delights in God's law "in the inward man" and
Augustine affirms it himself in the first sentence. Did he really
believe that Satan also "delights in God's law in his inner
being"? This is a typically convoluted piece of reasoning; Satan
would affirm our species to be accursed and rotten to the core;
not so Holy Scripture (e.g. Jam3:9). Man's will would not be
conformed to that of the Adversary (Hebrew: Satan) for he is
man's adversary as much as God's; he was envious of us and
God's plans for us indicated by the fact that following the
incarnation of the Word of God it is humanity rather than a
prince from the angelic realm that has been incorporated into the
Godhead. Satan's mind and spirit are united in evil whereas
human beings have a divided nature, sensing and often desiring
what is right and just but often failing to achieve it thanks to the
opposing "law within its members" (Rom7:22,23). For sure,
unregenerate man is in captivity to that "law" or carnal principle
whilst imprisoned in mortal flesh as Augustine rightly asserted;
but only when the human spirit and thus the mind and
conscience become entirely defiled (cf. Tit1:15; 2Tim3:8) does
the human heart, mind and will mirror that of Satan's, at which
point a person would have no ability or even the desire to do any
good at all. That will not happen whilst a working conscience is
retained by which the whole person is effectively plugged in to a
measure of divine enlightenment concerning the benefit of the
good and the need to avoid evil for the sake of peace of mind. In
his account of his conversion Augustine appears aware of such a
conflict of wills, especially as he becomes convicted by the
claims of the true catholic faith. For whilst in the inner man he
wished to embrace it, his notoriously lustful character which he
readily acknowledged inclined him to say, "Lord make me
chaste, but not yet." His better part desired the benefits to be
obtained through allegiance with Christ; his fleshly part the
pleasures of the present world. But ever conscious of his former
error within the dualism of Manichaeism, Augustine was
reluctant to work through the implications of the opposing moral
inclinations of the material and immaterial components that
make up human nature. Having applied the perfectly good

analogy of our body being our wife with whom we now bicker, he contradicted the concept of opposing wills again in his "Confessions". In the examples he gives of people either appearing to have more than two "wills" or of both wills being bad or good he fails to make the obvious distinction between opposing wills and opposing minds. The first pertains to the opposing inclinations of the spiritual verses fleshly nature whereas the second simply refers to the weighing up available options. His reasoning here which you can judge for yourself (Book8 - X) is either extraordinarily inept or subtly devious. It is unlikely to be the former for overall his standard of rhetoric appears inimitable and in keeping with a true Doctor of the Church. Readers will readily be able to draw upon Augustinian writings that appear to contradict what I am saying for he was somewhat prone to contradict himself, especially in the context of free will, asserting it at one moment, denying it at the next[20]. Indeed, he has just denied it by asserting (above) that the human will has been "turned to the likeness of Satan's will". The enigma continues, yet the extraordinary path of discovery set for the Church required that this man be revered such that his assertions concerning human nature and grace would be substantially utilized by the Church and reinforced by others who would later depart from her. Thus, the reality of God's *universal and effectual revelation* to man so that even through the application of natural precepts he can preserve his soul from perdition has been obscured until coming more sharply into focus through the writings of John Henry Newman in the early nineteenth century. Being a senior Churchman (eventually a Catholic Cardinal) he was not well placed to work through his enlightened theories to their logical conclusion without undermining some established doctrine. This writer on the other hand, albeit with scarcely a tenth of that man's intellectual prowess, is operating from total obscurity and with the Spirit's help has endeavoured to do just that; in particular to show how this universal revelation and the innate faculties by which it functions is also linked to the Atonement, resulting in the munificent providence I have been outlining whilst not detracting from the superior and immediate Life-giving

146

privileges granted to faithful disciples of Christ, to Whom belongs the glory for His love and faithfulness, even unto death.

Returning to Augustine and the origin of the soul, whilst initially accepting the prevailing Catholic creationist view it didn't sit well with his interpretation of original sin so he put forward the hypothesis that God created only one soul being Adam's, and that all subsequent souls are identical to Adam's fallen soul prior to assuming their own particular lives. Apart from departing from the teaching of most earlier Fathers (with a notable exception being Tertullian), such spiritual traducianism (surely a contradiction in terms) is challenged by Romans chapter nine, in particular verse 21, which indicates that not all human souls (vessels of the spirit) are identical, but some are adapted or "scaled down" to fulfil the Potter's purpose (cp. v22 Greek interlinear). Such souls destined for indignation will appear inscrutable to those Christians who are keen to assert the Potter's equitable nature, but I have come to understand they are a necessary part of God's plan for humanity, which is clarified in the last chapter concerning the purpose of human suffering. Those of us who are creationist in the context of the soul's origins must surely recognize that God does not directly create what is evil, nor the soul of man in a state of ruin, so it has to be explained why humans are so inclined to sinfulness. The failure to recognize the opposing laws or governing principles within the material component and the immaterial components acting upon the mind (Rom7:23) has led to the historical misconception within the Western Church concerning both the nature and forensic consequences of original sin, for I am aware that Augustine's view was endorsed by numerous Councils. In insisting that human nature was fatally degraded in its totality through a staunch resistance to Mane's distorted dualism, Augustine's strictly one-dimensional perspective on grace was in turn derived from an over-reaction to Pelagius' exaggerated conception of man's innate spiritual faculties. From what we are informed of Pelagius' teaching by the Catholic Church (for most of his writing was destroyed), he had mistakenly believed that the Fall did not result in a part of the human nature being fatally damaged, physically and morally. On the contrary, the degraded "flesh" (the visible yet replaceable part) is entirely creaturely;

147

never desiring the spiritual good, always selfish and pleasure-seeking:

*For I know that in me (**that is, in my flesh**), nothing good dwells; for to will is present with me but how to perform what is good I do not find (Rom7:18NKJ)*

This verse is not referring to Paul as a Christian, who, enabled by the Spirit is and must be able to perform what is good, as the apostle assuredly did. For he is required to be righteous in himself, not "be clothed in Christ's righteousness"; being a concept nowhere to be found in Scripture. If 1Cor1:30 springs to mind, one should ask whether His wisdom also forms part of the package. Christ's personal righteousness, wisdom and sanctification are not imputed but progressively infused or imparted in measure through association with their Source. But in Romans 7 Paul is referring to a person in his natural state providing he has retained a conscience, for in those who go in the way of Cain there is no longer an "inner struggle", for the physical and spiritual components are now dead (in the Pauline sense of being alienated from divine light and conformity), so there is nothing left to struggle. Likewise, the distinction between flesh and spirit would scarcely be relevant for those upholding traditional Reformed teaching since they regard fallen humanity as depraved in its totality. Applying Calvin's dulcet phraseology, "all men's thoughts, inclinations and efforts are corrupt and viscous", it scarcely matters if Paul were talking about the spirit or flesh, for there is no genuine goodness in either. The Catholic Church was influenced but thankfully never entirely accepted Augustine's dire prognosis for the human condition and his undermining of effectual free will as earlier Fathers had outlined it[21]; and through the progressive enlightenment of the Holy Spirit certainly takes a less pessimistic view now:

The human person with his openness to truth and beauty, his sense of moral goodness, his freedom and the voice of his conscience, with his longings for the infinite and for happiness, man questions himself about God's existence. [Catechism of the Catholic Church #33]

She recognizes that fallen man is capable of discerning, desiring and often practicing what is right and just in the ordering of society as well as in individual acts of compassion and courage. Yet she cannot deny that her venerable Doctor believed and taught to the contrary, constantly asserting the existence of free will on the one hand yet declaring it to be ineffectual on the other. He believed, as once did I, that such free will as had been notionally provided was to ensure that those (the majority) not chosen to benefit from God's mercy would be justly condemned to eternal torment "to show what had been due to all". Protestants who have kept faith with their heritage focussed on the five *solae* likewise understand something along those lines; I certainly did for the first twenty-eight years as a Christian, whilst being aware that a good number of my fellow Evangelicals either did not have the stomach for such teaching or perceived it to be inconsistent with the nature of God as revealed in His Son as well as with human nature and society as they encountered it. Yet if their watered down "moderated-Calvinism" and Arminian viewpoints prevalent in Evangelicalism today cannot be coherently systematized from Scripture (which they assuredly cannot) then the Good Book so many rely upon is undermined and with it any solid grounds to substantiate one's hopes for eternity. This presentation on the other hand has been determined to keep faith with a literal sense of Scripture which after some substantial Spirit-led unravelling *can* be reconciled with itself, potentially enabling a truly God-honouring and credible providence to be affirmed to the world.

Paul and "original sin"

For sure, the apostle affirms the concept of "original sin". In Romans 5 he states that "*death reigned from Adam to Moses even upon those who did not sin in the manner of our first parents*" (v14). But it is "this death" again, i.e. that which is currently being experienced; not "damnation" but the carnal body disrupting our fellowship with God whilst we inhabit it (except we encounter the Son who can make us free indeed to serve the living God). Adam's degenerative body we inherit, his guilt we do not; for sin is imputed to the degree that the law known to the transgressor has been transgressed and where there is no known law to defy, sin is not imputed (Rom5:13). So up till the time of Moses (Rom5:14) and indeed beyond for those outside the Law (the Gentile nations), the law and standard by which people were judged can only be that known to them innately through the conscience once they are of an age to discern it, by which faculty they became a law for themselves (Rom2:14 New Jerusalem Bible).

Flesh, soul, spirit and Spirit in the language of St Paul

Focussing specifically on Romans 7 and Paul's references to the "flesh" or "spirit", it tends to be assumed that whenever the apostle speaks positively about the spirit, he is referring to the Holy Spirit rather than an immaterial component within man. Firstly, let's be clear about the distinct identity of the human's spirit in the language of Paul; for *pneuma* (spirit) as in English can sometimes refer to a state of emotion, e.g. the spirit of friendship or anger. This clearly is not the case in the "inner-struggle" context: he is referring to the human spirit created by God that is separated from the body at death. In the opening chapter of Romans (v9) he affirms: "*I serve God in my spirit in the gospel*"; he writes that as Christians we experience the witness of the Spirit with our spirit that we are already the children of God (Rom8:16); that ideally women should remain single so that they (i.e. their soul or whole person) can focus on being holy in body and spirit (1Cor7:34), whilst in 1Cor6:20 he exhorted Christians to "*glorify God in your body and in your spirit which is of God*" (not "are of God" – some versions) - *pneumati homon hatina estin tou theou*. This latter reference to the human's spirit and its origins is omitted in some English translations which employ the Egyptian NU-text variant (e.g. New International Version and Catholic NRSV and New Jerusalem Bible). The writer to the Hebrews employs *pneuma* (spirit) to refer to individual purified "souls" in Heaven (the spirits of the righteous having been perfected (12:23)), and likewise Jesus on the cross "gave up His spirit" (e.g. Jn19:30) after which His body was lifeless. In her *Magnificat*, Mary magnified the Lord in her soul whilst her spirit rejoiced in God

150

her Saviour (Lk1:46,47). We have seen that central to Paul's thought is the fact that as a result of original sin, man has become a psychologically disordered union between the flesh (the sensual bodily desires) and spirit or inner man (e.g. 2Cor7:1; Gal5:17); the latter verse referenced from Galatians typically being wrongly understood to be referring to the Holy Spirit, the give-away phrase being –"*that is why you cannot do the things you would wish to do*", which if it were referring to the Spirit could hardly apply. The verse is referring to the point the apostle was making in Romans 7:15 that apart from the grace of God he would not do what his mind and conscience tells him he ought to do but to gratify the flesh the things his spirit and its faculty conscience abhors. The Christian's spirit is aided by divine grace, so it understands and is strongly motivated to do what is right yet is still opposed by the flesh. Aptly the apostle closes his letter with the benediction: "*May the grace of our Lord Jesus Christ be **with your spirit*** (cf. Gal6:18). The Christian is to follow the dictates of his spirit (walk in the spirit) "*for the disposition of the flesh is death but the disposition of the spirit is life and peace*" (Rom8:6). His soul is to deny the impulses of his body, for an opposing law governs it to that which governs the spirit or inner man (Rom7:23) "*so those that are Christ's have crucified the flesh with its affections and lusts*" (Gal5:24,25). When the "flesh" is crucified (denied) one can then follow the dictates of the spirit (inner man) which is guided by the conscience and aided by the Spirit. St Peter writes that only those who "*escape the corruption that is in the world through lust*" may partake of the divine nature (2Pet1:4). Paul likewise exhorts us to "*present our bodies as a living sacrifice holy and acceptable to God*", which he regards as our reasonable service (Rom12:1). That is calling for a sacrificial commitment on the Christian's part to deny himself, or rather the inclinations of his body (cf. 2Cor7:1 "ourselves" = our souls or whole life). Those who continue to live according to the impulses of the flesh rather than the spirit cannot please God. Yet in those like Cain who have given in to evil and the Evil One (1Jn3:12), the flesh like everyone else's is dead (in the Pauline sense) but the spirit is also dead or non-functional (i.e. twice dead –Jude1:12) so material and spiritual are no longer in tension. Dead (flesh)

151

versus dead (spirit) results in a chilling serenity in which the soul is unhindered in its response to the instincts of the flesh; it may satisfy its worldly and carnal appetite by any means. Unlike all who are or will be liberated as the children of God (Rom8:21), these desolate ones have no "inner struggle" for what is dead does not struggle. They therefore may be cool, calm and at peace with themselves as they pursue evil. *This* is death of the spirit; *this* is total depravity of the soul, and *these* are the damned (not a distinct Scriptural word in the Greek but you'll know what I mean: they are going to be punished in Hell). They are the wicked and godless (spiritless) who must be despatched at the renaissance, for they were not planted by God (Mt15:13) but by His enemy (Mt13:25). This pertains to the mystery of providential evil, explored more fully in chapters six and seven. The concepts are alluded to by Jesus in His parable of the wheat and darnel (tares) and explicitly affirmed in His interpretation. In terms of the very early Christian writers, Ignatius (first century) understood those not planted by the Father to be the children of the evil one[22]. The concept of the devil fathering human offspring (in the adoptive sense) is indicated in -

The Proto-Evangelium

As we have seen, Adam and Eve were not cursed by God (cf. Gen3:14,17). That pronouncement was given to the arch-instigator of mankind's downfall represented by the serpent (the devil). Adam and his male descendants were condemned to a life of arduous toil, aging, decay and death, for the soil was cursed for man's sake (Gen3:17-19), whilst woman-kind would additionally endure male domination and great pain in childbirth, for at least in Paul's eyes she bore the weight of guilt (1Tim2:14). Through Satan's victory, he was granted control of the world order (Greek: *archon tou kosmou* Jn12:31), yet as we shall see it was all for the greater good. Amidst the apparent debacle, a ray of hope is already apparent. God tells the snake (representing the Evil One):

I shall put enmity between you and the woman, and between
your offspring and hers; it (or He) will bruise your head and you
will strike its heel (Gen3:15)

It provides a shadowy glimpse of the Good News concerning a
coming Messiah (the woman's offspring), for the omniscient
God had already envisaged His plan of salvation for humankind,
the central event of which would be the sending of His own Son
to be the Saviour of the world. Satan would strike Christ's heal
through his apparent victory at Calvary, but the death and
resurrection of Jesus would prove to be the bruising of the
snake's head, assuring Satan's ultimate defeat. It is not just
Satan but *his offspring* who are to be at enmity with the
woman's offspring; nor is the latter referring exclusively to Jesus
(Rom16:20). Satan's seed pertains both to the outcome of
Gen6:1-2 (no longer an issue) and the human seed adopted by
Satan, who following their own free choice of reprobation is
permitted to gain their mastery (cf. Gen4:7 Masoretic). This also
could only be by divine decree; it is a providential arrangement
with (not an obligation to) Satan who could have no inherent
rights over God's property. It is an ingenious contrivance on the
Creator's part (for He is sovereign), but one will not discern any
positivity to it until one has more deeply penetrated the mystery
of evil considered in the final two chapters.

The cross is the unspoken heart of the proto-evangelium and
central to the gospel for *"as in Adam all die, even so in Christ*
shall all be made alive"; and *"since by man came death, by Man*
came also the resurrection from the dead"! It would seal the
fate of God's true enemy, the seducer and accuser of mankind.
Approaching death, Jesus declared:

Now is the judgement of this world; now shall the prince of this
world be cast out. And if I be lifted up from the Earth, I shall
draw all men unto Me. (Jn12:31,32 King James Version)

This is already achievable, but it is not to be realized before He
comes again. Satan hangs on as god of this world (2Cor4:4); he
still deceives it and is permitted a measure of control (Eph2:2).
Consequently, the majority who have lived and died were never
drawn to Christ, let alone "all men". The deferral is the

downside of the fellowship of the secret but is for the greater good. For it is indeed God's intention to restore what mankind had lost at the Fall and Christ is the beginning, middle and end of it, and will be acknowledged to have been so by all for the glory of the Father (Phi2:11). The universal condemnation for all humanity regarded as being "in Adam" is nullified by the universal justification of life provided by Christ's obedience to an undeserved death. *"The Son of God loved me and gave Himself for me"* (Gal2:20). Many have the right to say that; only the Christian currently knows that. For Jesus is described in Scripture as dying as an offering for sin rather than particular individuals. He *became* sin for us (2Cor5:21); He gave Himself *for our sin* (Gal1:4); He bore our sins in His own body on the tree (1Pet2:24); He suffered once *for sins* (1Pet3:18); the iniquity *of us all* was laid upon Him (Is53:6). Sin throughout the ages has been punished in Jesus; not just the sins of individuals who would come to be His disciples. Through an Eternal Law there can be no forgiveness of sin without the shedding of blood (Heb9:22) and Jesus more than satisfied the penalty owed by human sin. But the once-for-all atonement *per se* neither establishes "eternal life" nor abolishes physical death within this universal exchange because that historical event was never intended to rectify the nature of the vessel transmitted from our first parents that the human soul/spirit is to inhabit. Be assured, God was quite content that the human souls He created would inhabit such a corrupted vessel or he would have destroyed Adam and Eve there and then (for they had been warned); instead he continued to utilize this shamed couple as the procreative fountain-head for humanity (cp. Rom8:20). The fact that He did so was an astounding act of love on His part, not least in view of the consequences for the Godhead, but I suspect few readers will currently see it that way in view of the consequences for the bulk of humanity as many currently perceive them.

Such then is the nature and consequence of original sin: an immaterial soul/spirit created in God's own image (i.e. nature) is planted and diffused within a corrupting procreated vessel. Such is the outworking of Adam's sin for his children. Pardon and ultimate deliverance from such a predicament will demonstrate the glory of God's grace and the depth of Christ's love to provide it. Yet that is only a part of the rationale behind such an extraordinary alignment as we will explain in chapter seven. After the few decades of human life the offending vessel is discarded: "*Then the dust will return to the Earth as it was and the spirit will return to God **who gave it**"* (Eccles12:7). Later our earthly tent will be mysteriously located, decoded and glorified, or in second century language "*our bodies having been nourished by (the body and blood of Christ) and deposited in the Earth... shall rise at their appointed time*"[23] But in terms of mankind's guilt and condemnation arising from their association with the sin of their federal head, it is pardoned regardless of individual cognisance or cooperation:

*As through one transgression there resulted condemnation to all men, even so through one act of righteousness, there resulted justification **of** life to all men (Rom5:18 New American Standard Bible)*

St Paul does not intend to deceive: "all" means "all"; this is a universal exchange and continues to avail as long as one remains within the Covenant of life, which of course includes all who die in infancy for they do not have the wherewithal to default. The next chapter concerns the bulk of humanity who are not the first-fruits of God's harvest (cf.1Cor15:23; Jam1:18) yet demonstrate by *their* fruit that they are destined to be "*delivered from the bondage of corruption into the glorious liberty of the children of God*" once the sons of God are revealed (Rom8:19-21).

Notes: CHAPTER TWO

1. Irenaeus against heresies Book IV chap. 18 (3)

2. So, N T Wright, although I assume he exclusively had Jews and Christians in mind: "What St Paul really said" chap. 6 p109 Lion

3. The theologically crucial distinction between our faith in Christ and Christ's own faith or faithfulness as the ground of justification in St Paul's letters is still not distinguished in earlier English translations

4. e.g. 2nd Apology of Justin Martyr (AD110-165) – chap. 5; Transgression of angels & Irenaeus against heresies Book IV chap 36 (4)

5. Book of Enoch: (Select R H Charles version)

6. Tertullian – On the apparel of women Book 1 chap.3

7. Philokalia Vol 2 p178 (see Wikipedia "Theosis" under heading "Divinisation – citation 6")

8. a) Irenaeus against heresies Book III chap. 23 (5)   b) Origen de Principiis Preface (4)

9. Augustine: De genesi ad litteram 166.27

10. Listing of early Fathers who were Trichotomist and Augustine's objection is referred to in Wikipedia "Tripartite (theology)"

11. Justin on the resurrection chap. 10

12.a) Irenaeus against heresies Book II chap. 19 (6)   b) Irenaeus against heresies Book V chap. 9 para 1

13. Epistle to Diognetus chap. 6

14. The treatises of Cyprian - Treatise 4 para 16

15. Refers to excerpt from Lumen Gentium 16

16. Reception of Augustine in the Orthodox Church – Refer to "Orthodox Wiki"

17. Christos Yannaras: The Freedom of Morality (p151)

18. Archelaus: The Disputation with Manes (18)

19. Epistle of Ignatius to the Romans chap. 2

20. Extract from Augustine's "On Rebuke and Grace" – chap. 2: *"It is to be confessed therefore that we have free choice to do both good and evil; but in doing evil everyone is free from righteousness and a servant of sin, while in doing good no one can be free unless we have been made free by Him who had said 'If the Son shall make you free then you shall be free indeed.'"*. Hence, he is affirming that no one other than the Christian can ever choose a good action or have any kind or good affection; this is clearer still in his next chapter (three): *"For the grace of God through our Lord Jesus Christ must be apprehended – as that by which men alone are delivered from evil and without which **they do absolutely no good thing, whether in thought or will, affection or in action"**.* Likewise his treatise "On Grace and Free Will" [Chap. 7] his opening provides a false hope of his orthodoxy which is soon dashed: *"We have now proved by our former testimonies from Holy Scripture that there is in man a free determination of will for living rightly and acting rightly; so now, let us see what are the divine testimonies concerning the grace of God **without which we are not able to do any good thing.**"* In other words he is affirming as he always does that innately man has no effectual free will whatsoever, merely that is able to determine what he ought to do; thus, like Satan, man can only will, think and practice what is evil except he receive celestial grace (for there is no other grace that he acknowledged, either which is innate or imparted except through the sacraments of the Church). That is consistent with the teaching of the later breakaway Reformers (apart from his insistence on sacraments)

but opposes the available witness of every earlier Father representing the assemblies that had received the catholic faith from the apostles; his teaching on providence and the denial of natural law was (at last) contradicted in spirit and substance within the Dogmatic Constitutions of the Second Vatican Council.

21. Origen systematically challenges the use of certain Scriptures that later Augustine and the Reformers employed in their attempts to limit or deny the free will of individuals to perform what is right in consequence of a "ruined nature"; also their obscuring of the goodness and natural justice of God in the way that He was inclined to favour some whilst willing the destruction of others. These were passages such as "It is not him that wills or runs but of God who shows mercy" and "God has mercy on whom He will have mercy and whom He will He hardens (from Rom 9). Origen explains the context of these passages (as do I but he is Origen) as well as outlining the many others that unambiguously affirm free will and man's natural (i.e. innate) ability to take heed to God's law; to fear God and seek to do what is right – Origen de Principiis Book III Chapter 1

22. Epistle of Ignatius to the Trallians chap. 11

23. Irenaeus against heresies Book V chap. 2 (3)

Chapter Three

Justification and the Faithfulness of Christ

*[Being the righteousness of God by the faithfulness of
Jesus Christ upon all who "believe"]*
Romans3:22

Not all presented in this chapter is a direct result of the spiritual
encounter that resulted in this book. Partly I am drawing together
the reflections of various theologians and traditions such as from
the Catholic side the Vatican II Constitution Lumen Gentium
(Light of the World) concerning the mystery of the Church
which outlined a more inclusive perspective on God's plan to
reconcile the world to Himself through the Church. The Council
had clearly been influenced (as was I) by the earlier reflections
of Bl. John Henry Cardinal Newman (1801-1890) especially his
understanding of the role of conscience as a universal means of
revelation and an impulse for individual "faith" and morality. I
also take on board the new interpretation of some within
Evangelicalism regarding the teaching of Paul on justification,
faith and works, referred to as the "New Perspective on Paul";
also that apostle's various references to "the faithfulness of
Christ" (*pisteos christou*) which had previously remained
indistinguishable in English and Latin translation from cognisant
faith in Christ. That theologically crucial distinction is now
reflected in some of the more recent Protestant English Bible
translations. For some years I had wondered why someone with
ten times my ability had not attempted to draw these strands
together to construct a workable and biblical theological schema:
one that indicated how people of good will outside the churches
benefit from the atonement of Christ and are ultimately to be
reconciled to God through Him. If such has been developed I am
not aware of it. What is presented here is I believe very much in
the spirit of Vatican II yet undermines some of the foundational

159

biblical theology of Augustine (but then so in effect did the Council with regard to the fate of those outside the Church), whilst from an Evangelical perspective my solution will be too philanthropic, sacramental and synergistic ever to be countenanced within their mainstream; thus nobody entrenched within a particular Christian tradition would ever be inclined to draw all the necessary strands together. Yet such a synthesis can now be made, and it is an essential piece in the biblical jigsaw which when taken alongside what personally speaking were entirely new concepts can now be completed.

The nature of justification and faith

Since the Eden incident, justification in the sense of being accepted by God (like Abel) as opposed to being under God's condemnation (like Cain) has been by faith as a result of grace through the trans-historical merits of Christ's faithfulness [*dia pisteos Christou*]. But what in this context do the terms justification, faith and grace mean, for much ink (and blood) has been spilt about each. Reviewing Hebrews chapter 11, I am quite clear that I understand what the Bible means by faith. Returning to some of my old Reformed text books on the subject, I am bemused as ever I was. They define saving faith along the lines of a "fiduciary apprehension of gospel mercy", or "the act of closing with Christ's offers of mercy", better understood to be a confident persuasion that Jesus Christ had died for me as an individual and that I was to trust in Christ's merits alone for eternal salvation. It was also deemed necessary by the truly Reformed to be convinced in one's mind of the deep depravity of man's nature, such a conviction, according to Louis Berkhov, being a necessary component of the intellectual element of saving faith[1] Yet reckoning in one's heart that one is devoid of any God-pleasing virtue is a hard *work* indeed requiring the undoubted *virtue* of humility. It is an intriguing circle but genuinely endeavours to be self-effacing and give all the glory to God; yet it is neither what Scripture means by "faith", nor will it suffice for gospel salvation, though it served to provide some peace and satisfaction for Luther's troubled conscience to believe that he would not be judged for his own life, character and legacy but (effectively) for the life and character of the One who was to be his Judge, whose personal justice he believed had been imputed to him. The disposition of moral impotency deemed necessary to respond to such a gospel can be a specious piety indeed, souring one's genuine regard and respect for those outside the faith; it certainly did in my case as my parents could have testified. More to the point it opposes Christ's teaching and the witness of such direct evangelism as exists within the New Testament. Perhaps most tellingly of all, the idea that to be accepted by God one needed to cease from one's own efforts to be righteous and rely on God's mercy and the merits of Christ had not been expressed in such terms by any second and third generation churches that had been founded by the apostles according to their surviving writings. Given the counter-intuitive nature of such concepts, that simply could not be the case if it had been the teaching of the apostles. As for the rest of the package, far from Christ's good works ever being credited to the believer's moral account, our acceptance into His Kingdom is dependent on whether we have practiced works of compassion towards "Christ", equating Himself as Son of Man with all those in need (Mt25:37-40). It is to be observed throughout Scripture that divine judgement, punishments and rewards pertain more to individuals' lifetime dealings with their fellow man rather than their perceived devotion to God (especially Mt25; 1Jn4:12,20); those who truly understand the nature of holiness will already discern why that might be.

So what *according to Scripture* is the true nature of saving faith? Firstly, regarding faith itself:

Faith is the assurance of things hoped for, the conviction of things not seen (Heb11:1ASV)

The subsequent verses in Hebrews give examples of how that faith was exercised by various people in the Old Testament, but given that justification, being the great gift of the Lord's passion functions at two levels, the matter needs to be considered at both the universal (common) and special covenantal levels, although this chapter will be focussing more on the former, being a new concept for many.

161

Effectual common grace and faith

Faith is man's positive response to God as He is in various ways revealed to the individual. At the universal level it is most definitively a positive response to conscience. Given that the human's spirit (not to be confused with the human spirit) is planted by God and will one day return to Him it would be surprising if it did not incorporate (so to speak) a blueprint for human behaviour and so it does: the law of God written on the "heart" (Rom2:15) which is also described (but sometimes mistranslated) as the light of Christ that enlightens every man coming into the world (Jn1:9 Greek). [It is hardly likely that St John writing in the late first century would be informing us that the Light (Christ) "is coming into the world" (some translations)]. The atheist and agnostic, whenever they perform an action they know to be right because it's right, not merely for the praise of others or to be accepted within society are effectively exercising faith, responding positively to God (actually to the will of Christ as *Logos*) as He has revealed Himself and His law (the principles of humane living and sound reason) in their conscience. In that instant, they are choosing to do a good for in their innermost being they sense it is good and should be practiced (cf. Rom7:22,23). It is not entirely altruistic for they receive inner gratification by performing it, for in their inner being they are concurring with a natural precept, ultimately an Eternal Law. It is no different from a Christian receiving a measure of peace when he knows he is being obedient to Christ's will; it is how conscience functions. In the language of second century Clement of Alexandria it is that *common faith* which lies beneath as a foundation that is built upon and consummated in those who come to faith in Christ[2]. The law is spiritual (Rom7:14) and so is the human spirit for it *is* spirit. But infused within a degenerative vessel which is ever inclined to concupiscence (worldly lust), the instincts of that earthly tent look to override the inner light of conscience. Having planted human souls in such a disordered vessel (Paul's "body of death" ultimately derived from fallen Adam) it is no surprise given God's compassionate nature that He has made both provision and allowance for the resultant human weakness. In terms of provision, at the greatest personal cost God has provided a means by which our inevitable failures and misconduct might be pardoned through reference to an atoning Sacrifice; and in terms of allowance He is prepared to accept someone as "justified" on the basis of their exercising faith by responding positively or "faithfully" to the divine light that He has provided to them. Such common faith or faithfulness [same word in Biblical Greek] is proven to be present when love (*agape*) is exercised, being a genuine concern and care for another person, which is the heart of God's law (Rom13:10). Since love is the efflux of faith (cf. Gal5:6 cf. Greek), faith must be present for that love (*agape*) to flow out from it; love and faith being quite inseparable[3], faith being the agent of love and love being the product of faith (Gal5:6 again). A person is justified within the Universal Covenant by responding positively to God's witness to them through creed or conscience regardless of the degree of accomplishment. Providing the person demonstrates *agape* they are accepted by God, for He knows that *agape* was derived from Him, being His Own nature (1Jn4:7). This aligns perfectly with Jesus's teaching in Matthew 25 concerning the sheep and goats. In serving the weakest of humanity through any act of compassion, the "sheep" are regarded as serving Christ Himself even though they have no personal knowledge of Him:

In truth I tell you in so far as you did this (act of kindness) to one of the least of these brothers of mine, you did it to Me (see Mat25:31-45)

It might appear to some that Jesus is here teaching justification by works. Not as such; Matthew25:31-45 is demonstrating justification through faith *with reference* to works. No mention is made of how consistently or perfectly the "sheep" showed compassion, they just demonstrated they possessed it and were justified by exercising it regardless of measure. They therefore demonstrated they *possessed the quality* called faith whose product is *agape*, being the essence of true humanity. On the other hand, faith alone if it be merely a passive belief, trust or reliance on someone or something is dead if it does not result in positive action; it can be possessed by devils (cf. Jam2:17-19).

The "sheep" had not been passive; they showed compassion because they had responded positively to their "heart" motivating them to act in such a way out of sympathy, empathy and to be at peace with themselves. Jesus was thereby affirming that final salvation is not all of grace for fruit must be produced, yet it is entirely *dependent on* grace since the "sheep" are accepted by exercising the quality called faith, being an innate faculty provided through common grace, rather than having perfectly fulfilled God's law or lived a sinless life. Thus at the universal level justification is granted on the basis of such common faith, being a positive response to conscience (the light of Christ in the spirit) evinced by compassion, through the kindly favour (grace) by which pardon for sin has been granted to all producing the fruit of faith through the all-sufficient merits of Christ's atonement.

Some Christians will regard such insinuations of God's loving kindness towards wider humanity as disturbing and heretical; others will have sensed in their bones that it could never really have been the case that many of their relatives, friends and work colleagues who did not share their particular faith were destined for eternal punishment but couldn't have supported such a hope from Scripture. What is affirmed here should provide such people with much joy, without detracting at all from the purpose and urgency of the gospel message. Indeed, if the stupendous nature and benefits of service in God's Kingdom also come to be appreciated, all and sundry may wish to force their way into it once again (cf. Mt11:12). That is why certain inessential mysteries of the Kingdom have been veiled through much of the gospel age even from the Church: so that the rich, the mighty, the proud and the glory-hunters might be detracted by the shame of the cross of Christ and humble cruciform service as His disciples; whilst the humble, the gentle, the poor in spirit and in material possessions who are rich in faith will be the true inheritors of the Kingdom and the Earth. It is the wisdom of God. But how does this broader benevolence come about; is not Jesus Christ and His atoning death the key to all human salvation? That is absolutely the case.

The two-fold benefits of the Atonement

We saw in chapter two that Abel was justified within an overarching Universal Covenant that has applied throughout history. Yet the "faithfulness of Christ" in the centre of history is indispensable to both the Old and New Testament periods; it avails for two ages and, since its occurrence within history, at two levels: the forensic and participatory.

*For the love of Christ constrains us; because we judge that if One died for all then all were dead. And He **died for all** that **those which live** should no longer live for themselves but unto Him which died for them and rose again (2Cor5:14,15).*

The Bible does not teach a "limited atonement" in which pardon for the sin of falling short of God's glory is exclusively provided to those elected to suffer and reign with the Atoner. It is insistent and consistent: all were dead so the One died for all and atoned for all (cf. 1Jn2:2). However, *"He died for all... that those which live..."*. He died for all but not all shall "live". For what *is* limited is those who will be saved by His life by coming to participate in it (Rom5:10). In terms of the atonement, God is reconciling the whole world to Himself by not reckoning their sins (2Cor5:19). Note also from these verses that *"those that live should no longer live for themselves but for Christ"*; it is and always has been the small minority who no longer live for themselves and their families but are truly devoted to the Saviour. Those who share my conviction that it is God's intention to restore the bulk of humanity must keep that reality in mind; such a hope must be reconciled with Scripture or it is mere wishful thinking. Yet so it can be, for peace, pardon and universal reconciliation has been made possible for all by the blood of the cross (cf. Col1:19,20) where Christ *became* sin (2Cor5:21 Greek). The sin of humanity was expiated at Calvary; not *my* sin, sin. That is consistently how Scripture presents the matter. Jesus had come in the likeness of sinful flesh so that sin (not the sinner!) in the flesh should be condemned (Rom8:3). But through His resurrection I as a Christian can be set free from the domination and bondage of sin by sharing in Christ's life. *"If*

165

the Son shall make you free then you shall be free indeed" (Jn8:36). So for the many, including those living before its historical occurrence (cf. Rom3:25) the benefit of the atonement is expiatory, annulling the penalty of universal sin; for the "few" (proportionately speaking) it is both expiatory and cathartic through sacramental participation (1Jn1:7). For the latter it cleanses from sin's guilt *and* power by being able to purify the soul and unite it with the life of Christ (Rom5:10; 1Cor6:17). For Jesus came to save His own people from their sins, not merely from the punishment for sinning (Mt1:21); they are to be cleansed *from sin*, not just the *guilt* of sin. Christ had offered Himself *"in order to ransom (Christians) from all their faults and to purify a people **to be His very own**, and eager to do good works"* (Tit2:14). Through such good works, the Church as God's instrument of salvation declares His saving intentions for the whole world through its message as well as by the lives of her individual members: *"abounding in love towards each other and all men* (1Thes3:12). Thereby the Church fulfils its commission to *"announce the Good News to every creature under Heaven"* (Col1:23); for when men and women acknowledge the rule of Christ (i.e. obey the gospel) they themselves become faithful stewards caring for the welfare of all that is set under them, being (for the moment) the natural world (cf. Heb2:8). In the spirit of St Francis of Assisi may this joyful news of the gospel be preached, if necessary even using words. He was alleged to have preached the Good News to animals and birds; the prophet Joel certainly did (Jl2:21-23).

God's royal priesthood: Elected through unmerited grace

In terms of those who are "appointed to eternal life" (Acts13:48) and brought into a living relationship with God in the present, fulfilling the role intended according to earlier prophecy exclusively for the Jewish nation, it is a matter of elective grace at the individual level just as it had been for Israel at the racial level. Those predestined to Christian salvation were chosen *to perform* good works and become holy, not because they had *performed* good works or were foreseen to be holy (Eph2:8-10). Their calling to participate in the royal priesthood of God for the

166

salvation of the world was therefore nothing whatsoever to do with personal merit; justification being a gift (Rom3:24). God gives to some the ears to hear and the eyes to see Jesus and proclaim with Peter "*You are the Christ, the Son of the living God*". If that has had happened to you then "*Blessed are you, for flesh and blood has not revealed this to you, but the Father who is in Heaven*" (cf. Mt16:17). So election and calling is God's work alone but thereafter the Christian having been pardoned and cleansed through baptism is required to run a course, maintaining holiness through the divine provision made available to him through the supreme gifts of grace provided in the Church *and* by exercising self-discipline. In spite of such a glorious and holy calling there can be no cause for boasting; and any who do boast or gloat would be showing themselves to be profoundly unholy, as well as ignorant of the fact that:

(God) is saving us and calling us to a holy calling, not on the basis of our works but according to His own purpose and grace that was given to us in Christ Jesus before the times of the ages (2Tim1:9)

That is, *our calling* is not on the basis of our works, yet we are to provide fruit in the form of good works; that is *why* we were called, to bring light, healing and truth to the world and become conformed to the image of Christ. Just as JHWE had chosen Isaac's physical descendants to form the nation with whom He would especially relate and prepare for Kingdom service, so through the fellowship of the secret it was disclosed that He had also foreknown and predestined individuals to be drawn from all nations to be set apart for sacral service in that same priesthood (1Pet2:9). That was the role and destiny consistently foretold in Old Testament Scripture to be for the Jewish nation as we shall now briefly review.

Israel – the intended light of nations

The physical descendants of Abraham and Sarah's union were intended to be the "holy nation" that God called to be His priesthood for the world. They would learn the ways of JHWE and thus be equipped to enlighten other nations. His exclusive covenant with them had been as follows:

*So now, if you are really prepared to obey me and keep my covenant, you (Israelites) out of all peoples **shall be my personal possession, for the whole world is mine**. For Me you shall be a Kingdom of priests, a holy nation. (Ex19:5,6)*

So in due course He gave them the Decalogue along with more detailed requirements concerning how they were to conduct themselves, set out in the Torah of Moses or Pentateuch which Scripture generally refers to as "the Law". It was to be their schoolmaster up until Christ, for contrary to the teaching of many, justification by faith in a Saviour was not disclosed even to God's chosen people before His coming, as a careful reading of Gal3:23-27 affirms. When Paul asserts in that passage that justification on the basis of the faithfulness of Christ for those who had exercised faith had "not yet been disclosed" (v23) he was not saying it had not availed for those Jews who had been faithful, but their instruction had always been to "keep Torah" not to acknowledge their moral impotence and trust in the grace and merits of the coming Saviour or suchlike as Augustine and later the Reformers had indicated. At the same time Paul was making it clear that no one had ever been justified by perfectly fulfilling the Law (v21); it had always been on the basis of Christ's faithfulness availing for those with "faith". Yet once that was disclosed, the Torah as schoolmaster would be *filled out* by the teaching of Christ, and with the enabling that would be provided through an interior participation with Himself and the Spirit, the children of God would come to obey what James referred to as the "Royal Law" of love for God and neighbour (cf. Jam2:8) and would do so in spirit and in truth rather than the deadness of the letter.

In the meantime, it is quite clear from the above quote from Exodus that the chosen nation was to be obedient to their covenant with JHWE if they were to occupy a land that He had promised to Abraham. The occupants to be displaced were the polluted seed pool of Canaan, the accursed son of Ham that we considered earlier. Their supplanters were to become a divinely disciplined and holy nation to act as a salvific bridgehead to the rest of creation (Dt4:5,6). It had never been intended that the whole world become Jewish, but neither was it destined for the cosmic waste-paper basket; many in the world would be enlightened by the Jews and come to revere JHWE. King Solomon, still exercising great wisdom at this point, having completed the building of the Temple prayed not just for his own people but the whole world:

*Even the foreigner, **not belonging to your people Israel** but coming from a distant country attracted by your name – for they too will hear of your name, of your mighty hand and outstretched arm – if a foreigner comes and prays in this temple, listen from Heaven where you reside, and grant all that the foreigner asks of You, so that all the peoples of the Earth may acknowledge your name and, like your people Israel revere You (1Kings8:41-43 New Jerusalem Bible)*

Note, those "foreigners" who would come to revere JHWE would not become a part of "Your people" to do so (v43). As for the Jews, the Covenant was entirely do-able, for moral perfection was not expected; provision being made for human weakness through the system of animal sacrifices. Such sacrifices were only a figure of the Eucharist to be established under the Covenant of Christ's Blood, but contrary to the understanding of many, the blood of bulls and goats did expiate the day to day inadvertent sin of God's people (e.g. Lev16:15-22), which is why JHWE commanded them to be performed:

*If through inadvertence you fail in any of the orders which JHWE has given to Moses... this is what must be done: If it is an advertence on the part of the community, the community as a whole will offer a young bull as a burnt offering as a smell pleasing to JHWE with the prescribed accompanying cereal offering and libation and a he-goat as a **sacrifice for sin**. The priest will perform the rite of expiation for the entire community of Israelites and **they will be forgiven** for it is an inadvertence (Num15:22-25).*

On the other hand, those who sinned wilfully would be treated as aliens and "bear the consequences of their guilt" (v31). So moving forward in time to some of Paul's polemics it was not

169

the case that Jews believed they had perfectly to keep Torah in order to be accepted by God; forgiveness for day-to-day sins was provided. Neither was it their "human initiative" or "pride" to endeavour to keep the Law but a response to divine teaching; indeed, JHWE wished they had tried all the harder to honour their side of the Covenant (Ex19:5,6).

The teaching of Hebrews

The writer to the Hebrews was not contradicting the above. He taught that although bulls' and goats' blood could purify the flesh (Heb9:13), it could not sanctify the soul by taking away sin and thereby cleanse the conscience (Heb9:13-14). Pardon for sin is one thing; cleansing from sinfulness is another; this has been an area of confusion for many. The shedding of an animal's blood under the Old Covenant enabled sin to be pardoned as we have just observed from the Pentateuch but it did nothing to progress the partaker towards moral rectitude (Heb10:1). The Old Law made no one perfect (Heb7:19); only the blood of Christ can "save to the uttermost" (Heb7:25) by *"purging the conscience of dead works so as to serve the living God"* (Heb9:14). [Note how the faculty of conscience directly impacts upon our relationship with God, i.e. our spiritual life]. One can also get confused by passages such as the first chapter of Isaiah where JHWE appears to indicate that He is sick to the back teeth with Israel's animal sacrifice offerings and their solemn ceremonies. But He had instigated them: what He required of His rebellious people was to cease doing evil, search for justice, discipline the violent, show justice to the orphan and compassion for the widow (Is1:16,17), *then* bring their sacrifices to the altar (see also Mt5:24 and Amos5:24). The nation of Israel had been JHWE's vineyard; He had looked for a crop of good fruit but was receiving only bad. He had looked for justice and righteousness amongst His people but observed only bloodshed and distress (Is5:7). What He assuredly did *not* observe were people "desperately seeking to keep the Law in order to justify themselves in His sight". That is complete nonsense as even a cursory reading of the Old Testament should affirm. God's complaint was their lack of effort to keep His Laws and be

170

faithful to Him and the prophets and kings he had appointed over them. Tracing the history of God's Covenant people through the Old Testament one cannot but be amazed at JHWE's patience and tolerance towards them. But there is a limit and His chosen people exceeded it. Paul, quoting Isaiah, says of his fellow Israelites:

All day long I have been stretching out my hands to a
disobedient and rebellious people (Rom10:21)

As with our first parents, privileged individuals had been given their opportunity for a glorious inheritance but wilfully defaulted. Of course, this was in accordance with God's foreknowledge, and a "Plan B" (from our perspective, not from God's) was firmly set in place. His Son was always going to be at the centre of His salvific plans; the supporting cast may have to be changed. God's purpose and aim remained the same: the long-term salvation of the world through the redeeming action of His Son, the Saviour of the World (1Jn4:14), supported by a people God would give to Him (Jn17:6) to be cleansed from their sinfulness through His blood (Mt1:21). These were no longer restricted to the Jewish race:

*And with Your blood you bought people for God **of every race**,*
language, people and nation and made them a line of kings and
priests for God, to rule the World (Rev5:9-10 New Jerusalem
Bible)

So in the fullness of time, the Son of God, takes on our humanity, teaches whoever will listen about the Good News of the Kingdom, and disciples a group of twelve men to lead His work after Him, knowing He was shortly to die, be resurrected and ascend to Heaven. He shed His precious blood, acting out *within* history the righteous act by which Adam's sin had been nullified *throughout* history (Rom3:25). As Scripture also testified:

And He himself is the propitiation for our sins, and not for ours
only, but also for the whole world (1Jn2:2)

Propitiation (*hilasmos*) is provided *for the whole world*. Some Christians may be uncomfortable with propitiation (God-appeasement), but anyone who has a loving nature is distressed and offended at the sight of wickedness, cruelty and depravity, as was righteous Lot in Sodom (cf. 2Pet2:7). A god who is indifferent to these activities would show himself to be remote, unfeeling and devoid of love; a deistic divinity. Since God is none of those things His vexation at the world's wickedness requires appeasing. His Son's sacrificial act of love for humanity at the Place of the Skull acts as a perpetual sweet-smelling savour (Eph5:2) as from the rising of the sun to its setting it is constantly re-presented to the glory of His name through the sacrifices offered by His assemblies in East and West who have remained faithful to His will. Expiation, by which Christ's death alleviates man's guilt through the payment of a penalty, applies to all to whom it was promised in the proto-evangelium, being those remaining justified within the inclusive and universal Covenant of life by demonstrating they are of God (i.e. fully human) and not the seed of Satan (cf. Gen3:15). Expiation is a forensic term: it acquits from guilt the penalty having been paid. Purging or taking way (Greek: *aphairein*) sin is another matter and was not possible before the historical Act of Love enacted at Calvary (cf. Heb10:4). Through the fellowship of the secret this means of sanctification was unexpectedly granted to both Jews and Gentiles (cf. Acts26:18) who are baptized into Christ and partake of His Body and Blood, by which they can experience eternal life. That misunderstood quality is something which was "*with the Father*" (i.e. hidden in God) and has now "been manifested to us" (1Jn1:2). Jesus speaks of it as a "well of water springing up inside us" (Jn4:14); rarely if ever does it refer to "going to Heaven when you die". So infrequently is that concept mentioned that some groups who claim to believe the Bible reject the idea of the soul going to Heaven altogether, believing that people have no consciousness after death until the resurrection. But Jesus confirmed that the thief next to Him on the cross would that day be with Him in paradise, and Paul wrote that he would sooner be absent from the body and present with the Lord (2Cor5:8; cf. Phil:23); not that he wished to be naked, that is in the spirit, but what he most desired was to be clothed upon with his "house" which is from Heaven (2Cor5:2); that is not his heavenly home but his resurrection body. As is emphasized within the teaching of the Eastern Orthodox Church, the spirit being separated from the body at death is a disorder – a result of the Fall. Adam had not been created with the intention of his soul/spirit becoming separated from his body and joining the angels; man was intended to relate to God on *terra firma.*

Divine theology

It is possible that the very servants of Satan may be transformed into ministers of righteousness and become greatly revered amongst the righteous (cf. 2Cor11:14,15). But there is a benchmark that can be applied if they happen to be theologians or spiritual teachers in the Church and it is JHWE's own assessment of Himself:

"I AM who I am: the God of tenderness and compassion, slow to anger, rich in faithful love and constancy, maintaining his faithful love to thousands, forgiving fault crime and sin, yet letting nothing go unchecked, punishing the parent's fault in the children and in the grandchildren unto the third and fourth generation (Ex34:6-7 New Jerusalem Bible).

That is God's nature; these are His judgements which are evidently right and just and in accordance with human reason, by which I mean they are exactly how we would expect a loving and just God to behave in judgement. There surely can be no better theologian than God Himself, so if anyone presents a markedly different picture, he is no theologian at all however revered he may be; more likely he is of the devil. We may be mystified by God's *ways* at times, but this is a Being that we as human beings can truly love and adore as well as fear; not just for His grace and mercy *towards us* but because He is genuinely good from the perspective of those created after His own likeness. JHWE is forgiving, tender and compassionate just as a saintly human is uniformly tender and compassionate, only more so. Like a good parent He will have a special affection for His own (or His Son's) immediate family but will show generosity and kindness to all, for *that is His nature*. As such He makes full allowance for the human weakness unavoidably inherited at birth; toleration being a vital ingredient of love as any parent

173

will know, yet He will come crashing down on those who wickedly offend those He loves. He will take vengeance on behalf of His people (cf. 2Thes1:6); being all who fear Him and seek to do justice in accordance with the revelation they have received from Him. Truly, we shall praise God with uprightness of heart when we have learnt of His righteous judgements.

Who may approach God?

Many Christians effectively believe that a godlike perfection in righteousness is the prerequisite for a relationship with God or to "enter His courts in eternity" after physical death. Since such cannot be humanly achieved they believe such perfection must be credited to a person's moral account through an act of grace. It is linked to the thoroughly illogical notion we have just been considering that because God who is Love personified is also holy, He will not relate in any positive way to anyone less holy than Himself. If that were true it would be the antithesis of love and holiness as God Himself has defined those qualities, as well as opposing what we know from our own human and Christian experience. It also challenges historical and scriptural reality in terms of the relationship JHWE had with His prophets and kings. The holier a person is the more acceptable and forgiving he is of other's faults and shortcomings, especially those of weaker humans; he also tolerates the foibles and is tender hearted towards those lower order creatures over which he has care and oversight, as is the case in man's stewardship of the animal kingdom. These are not mere human foibles or sentimentality but a reflection of the divine quality of love, holiness and noble condescension that God Himself possesses and has imparted in measure to those made in His image; and in the Christian these qualities are being perfected through association with His Son. Such is the imparted "love of the Father" (cp.1 Jn2:15) and it is not an entirely soft and cuddly affair either, for incorporated within such a disposition comes an increased sensitivity and intolerance towards the cruelty, deceit and wickedness of others, especially towards those weaker than themselves. God and those who partake of His holiness are also well able to differentiate between pure evil on the one hand and the imperfection of

174

human weakness on the other; such are tolerant and compassionate towards the one yet invariably incensed by the other. Search the Scriptures - this is the reality of God's relationship with His people. JHWE had shown incredible patience towards the human weaknesses of His servants yet does become angry when they wilfully disobey Him or particularly test His patience. Likewise Jesus with His disciples: review His dealings with Peter on the one hand and Judas on the other. This has nothing to do with "imputed righteousness", this is our God; it is the outworking of His holiness. Those humans who possess the imparted love of God (which is akin to holiness) likewise are tolerant but do not remain impassive when they encounter cruelty, injustice or deception; they are filled with righteous anger and a strong desire that the perpetrators either relent or are swiftly brought to justice. However, the Christian, more than others, *can* retain a measure of serenity concerning the judicial considerations knowing that vengeance is the Lord's and He will repay the perpetrators; yet they will certainly feel a sympathy and empathy for the victim of injustice or cruelty, and if they do not they are neither loving nor holy, indeed barely human at all. Christians who already partake of the divine nature develop an instinctive and intuitive theology which senses the very nature of God. Such thereby discern the quality and outworking of divine love and holiness for they are (in measure) already partaking of it (Heb12:10b). Contrary to the perverse teaching of some (the usual suspects) it really is the same "stuff": God's holiness is like a saintly human's holiness, only deeper; His compassionate love is like human compassionate love, but perfected; they are the same in nature: Love is love; Holiness is holiness; it is a question of measure, not nature. Such is evidenced by the life and times of Jesus of Nazareth who perfectly reflected God's moral character *even whilst in human flesh* as we shall demonstrate in the next paragraph.

Adding to such misconceptions, Christianity has imported a Hellenistic perspective concerning how man is to relate to His Creator through eternity. Albeit unintentionally, it can demean the comprehensive divinity of Jesus as Son of God and Son of Man. At least one of His immediate disciples fell into the trap: *"Show us the Father and it will suffice us"*, pleaded Philip.

*"Have I been **with you so long** and yet you have not known Me, Philip? He who has seen Me has seen the Father"* (Jn14:9). Note here that Jesus is referring to Himself as he had appeared in His earthly ministry - (Have I been with you so long, Philip?). The incarnated Jesus and His Father have the same nature – that fact alone turns much traditional theology on its head. For Jesus had never been the "compassionate face of God", He was the very image (*eikon*) of God: the incarnate Word. "But is not God the Father a consuming fire?" some might ask. Well indeed, that is rather the point (Heb12:29); as with the sun, it is one thing to bathe in its warmth, another to approach it or be absorbed into it. God is pure spirit and has awesome power, creating and sustaining an immense universe; the devil himself appears before God when the Latter permits it and they communicate together (Job1:6-8), whilst the likes of Abraham, Moses and Elijah, according to St Paul, may not enter His immediate presence (1Tim6:16). So it is not really a question of whether "one's righteousness can avail in His presence", Satan's certainly didn't but he is an awesome being and a powerful authority in his own right (for the moment) as arch-angel Michael acknowledged when refuting with him (Jude 8,9). But for puny man, the Father Himself dwells in a *"light that no man can approach, whom no man has seen nor can see"* (1Tim6:16). Yet man can know communion with the Godhead even now through the Son and the Spirit who are equally holy yet communicable; apart from which man's eternal destiny is not to be "lost in God" but to resume his existence as a physical entity in union with the Man who is God's true Son. *"For in Him dwells the fullness of the Godhead bodily and (man) is complete in Him who is also the Head of all principality and power"* (Col2:9, 10). The Christ (anointed King) is also the Judge of humanity; God the Father judges nobody but has committed the matter entirely to His Son (Jn5:22). It follows that the kind of people who were accepted, albeit sometimes rebuked yet clearly loved by Jesus during His earthly ministry will be accepted by Him at that judgement and rewarded according to their works; the difference being that when He appears in His unveiled glory those in whom Jesus was profoundly offended (e.g. Mt23:33) will there and then be *"consumed with the breath of His mouth*

and destroyed with the brightness of His coming" (2Thes2:8). These are the children of the devil (chapter six).

Yet it is certainly the case that only the "pure in heart" may see God (Mt5:8) but that is not a requirement to possess the triple holiness of the Divine Glory; Solomon was told by JHWE he would be blessed provided he walked in "innocence of heart and in honesty" as had his father David (1Kg9:4); it is that childlike purity required for those who are to enter the Kingdom, not the inviolable perfection of God Himself, for He is superior to His creatures in every way and will continue to be so. (He is God, after all). So a measure of holiness is required even now to be in a living relationship with this glorious Son through internal communion, for He does become spatially intimate with the Christian (Col1:27). Such is not possible within this sin-prone mortal body of ours without both the forgiveness and cleansing of sin through baptism, without which one cannot be raised to eternal life (i.e. have communion with the Source of Life). But nor can such be sustained without the ongoing cleansing of the blood. For in shedding that blood Christ had provided "*purification through Himself*" (*di heautou katharismon poiesamenos* Heb1:3). Once again, this verse deceives through translation in many versions, implying that the sins of the believer were purged at Calvary. "*Katharismon* (purification or cleansing) is a noun, not a verb. The New International Version more accurately translates the verse as "(Christ) provided purification for sin" which is a very different matter, for we have to avail ourselves of such; pardon is one thing, purification another. The same applies to 2Pet1:9: this time *katharismou* is in the genitive, but of course it is still a noun. These verses are telling us that Christ provided a means of purification through His atoning death. The body, soul and divinity of Jesus must be received into ourselves ("come under our roof") so that as we continue to cooperate with Him He purges post-baptismal sins and progressively heals the soul. Such a purification was not provided until the shedding of that blood (Zech13:1; Mat26:28) and as God well knew and intended, although the Good News of Jesus's Lordship was to be announced to all, relatively few would rise to the challenge of discipleship and so come to benefit from it. Yet Jesus had said: "*If I am lifted up, I will draw all people to myself*" (John 12:32) and Paul was later to confirm that it was God's intention to reconcile the whole world to Himself; not holding their faults against them. All is resolved once the three soteriological categories are acknowledged and it is understood that those who are called to be Christ's "little flock" (Lk12:32) are those whom He sanctifies, disciples and spiritually empowers to play a priestly role in a vastly broader healing and reconciling process:

*It is all God's work; He reconciled us (Christians) to Himself through Christ, and he gave us the ministry of reconciliation. I mean God was in Christ reconciling the world to Himself, **not holding anyone's faults against them**, but entrusting to us the message of reconciliation (2Cor5:18-19)*

We have shown that God's reconciliatory strategy for the world has been to work from within; firstly, reconciling a particular grouping to Himself (the seed of Isaac) to act as a bridgehead to the rest, who in turn would come to admire their wisdom and even their laws (Dt4:5,6). Through Israel's failure resulting in the fellowship of the secret, that preparatory stage has itself been sub-divided and therefore extended by a realignment of personnel. Consequently, we are still in the process of assembling the priestly enlighteners that are replacing the race of Israel, not in the process of fulfilling Old Testament prophesies in a "spiritualized form"; and so shall the secret of God be brought to pass in accordance with the Good News he has brought to His servants the prophets.

Peter drops a further clue to the mystery when he refers to the Church both as a peculiar people and as a "nation" (Greek: *ethnos*). He is drawing on an Old Testament prophecy to summarize the nature and purpose of the Church; a purpose the prophets had expected to be fulfilled by others who were an *ethnos* in the more usual sense of the word:

*But you (the Church) are a chosen generation, a royal priesthood, a holy nation, His **own special people** that you may proclaim the praises of Him who called you out of darkness into His marvellous light (1Pet2:9 New King James Version; cf. Ex19:6):*

178

But this time there is no conditional clause as there was with the previous participants (Ex19:5). Christ and His Spirit have promised to see this one through to its completion: individuals may default for sure, but not the entire people (the Church).

The scope of God's salvific plans

*"(I pray that you) may be able to comprehend with all the saints what is the **width and length and depth and height** – to know the love of Christ which passes knowledge" (Eph3:18,19 New King James Version).*

It has for most of the gospel era passed knowledge that Christ's love and sacrificial death has made it possible for all who fear God and endeavour to walk in accordance with the light they have received to be accepted by God and in due time be received into His eternal Kingdom. Only about a third of the world's population is even nominally Christian; about the same proportion as a century ago. There are now more Muslims than Catholic Christians and nearly as many Hindus. It is an historical fact that a very small percentage of people inhabiting the largest continent on the planet have been Christian, but we can be assured God loves Asians as much as anyone else; He is no respecter of persons but is preparing them to serve His Son and ultimately be united to Himself in His own way. Those who through elective grace are offered the challenge to suffer and serve with Christ as part of His mystical Body on behalf of their human family are called to a life of self-discipline and self-denial. Those prepared to sacrifice much in this life gain much in the next (Mt19:29). That is intuitive to all with religious faith. Christ's disciples must *"lose their own life that they might save it"*. For them *"to live is Christ and to die is gain"*. The pros and cons need to be weighed up before making the commitment to Christian discipleship. That is not something you are ever likely to hear from the pulpit, but it is the teaching of the Master, which needs to be examined carefully in its context (Luke14:28-33). Jesus's caution will appear curious to many because they do not know *what the gospel is for.* Those who have grasped what I have been writing will recognize that Christian discipleship is not the means of avoiding an eternity in Hell (for that would scarcely need weighing up) but is the response of those called to eternal life and godliness (2Pet1:3). So those who by the help of the Spirit and applying all the means of grace rise to such a challenge will be greatly compensated (cf. Col3:24), being the sons of the resurrection (Lk20:36; Phil3:11) who are to be raised up at Christ's coming (Jn6:39,40,44,54). In terms of who will be raised, Polycarp an immediate disciple of St John understood that we will obtain the first resurrection *"if we do His will and walk in His commandments and love what He loved, keeping ourselves from all unrighteousness, covetousness, love of money, evil speaking and false witness[4]*. Achieving such a role in the Kingdom of God is not easy *"for many I say to you will seek to enter and will not be able"* (Lk13:24). Yet for those who can accept it, the Master's yoke is easy and His burden is light and they will find rest for their souls. Disciples of Christ act as the advance guard; those who have fore-trusted (Eph1:12 *"proelpikotas"*) in advance of His coming to the praise of His glory. They are the first-fruit of His creation (Jam1:18) to show forth the praises of Him who has called them out of darkness into His marvellous light (cf. 1Pet2:9). Christians are Christ's own purchased possession; not just those who will be liberated as the children of God (Rom8:21) but the firstborn of those children (Heb12:23 Greek), set apart to act as intercessors on behalf of the whole human family, for such is the role of the firstborn (cf. Ps89:26-27). The firstborn almost by definition will be the minority; the rest are on the broad road to *"apoleian"* (Mt7:13), by which the Greek conveys the meaning of being cut off from something vital and being "lost"; *"for the Son of Man came to seek out and save those who were 'lost'* (same word)". What they have lost or been cut off from is vital indeed: *"zoen"* (life), that is the Life for which they were created being a two-way relationship with God that only the narrow roadsters can experience whilst in mortal flesh.

As we have already seen "salvation" in the full gospel sense was not available for the people of God in the Old Testament. There was no fountain available for sin and uncleanness (Zec13:1). The forensic benefits of the atoning Sacrifice are trans-historical; the participatory benefits cannot be. Old Testament saints could

180

be pardoned on account of the later shedding of the blood of Christ as represented by the offering of bread and wine by the mysterious timeless priest of JHWE, Melchisedec (cf. Heb7:3). Effectively he did for the world what the Church does now as God's priesthood at the Eucharist, but unlike the latter those under the Old Covenant could not *themselves* be spiritually nourished by His body and blood for they could not partake of it. Those who think otherwise do not comprehend the letter to the Hebrews (especially 9:14,15 &10:1,2 & 13:11,12) and are denying the teaching of Christ:

*Whoever eats my flesh and drinks my blood lives in me and I live in that person... This is the bread that **came down from Heaven**; it is not like the bread our ancestors ate: they are dead, but anyone who eats this bread will live forever (Jn6:56&58 New Jerusalem Bible).*

Clearly the spiritual food and drink in question did not "come down from Heaven" until the Son of God was incarnated. Internal healing and spiritual empowerment was not possible for the faithful Jew until Christ physically shed His blood on the cross so that the Gift may be engrafted and *"the whole spirit, soul and body may be preserved blameless at the coming of our Lord"* (1Thes5:23). This is what it is to be *"saved to the uttermost"* (Heb7:25), requiring access to the Sacrament by which the body, soul and divinity of Christ is united to our spirit (cf. 1Cor6:17).

The Church as priesthood for the world

Through the sacramental mystery, the Sacrifice at Calvary is prolonged, actualised and re-presented in pure form for the benefit of the participants and for the glory of the Father who continues to delight in his Son's faithful act of obedience to death through His love for humanity. *For every chief priest is appointed to offer gifts and sacrifices, so it is necessary that this One also has something to offer* (Heb8:3) which is Himself as Victim; an offering in which the whole Church participates. Although the Passion has been accomplished - "it is finished", the Church implements its achievement to advance the salvation

181

of the world and for the sanctity of the faithful. Savours are not inclined to linger yet that historical sacrifice is perpetuated through the offering of the Church to act as a sweet-smelling savour (Eph5:2), propitiating God's displeasure at the world's sinfulness and justifying all those who "fear God and do justice". Each member of the faithful acts as a priest by joining in the offering of the Eucharist, receiving the sacrament in prayer and thanksgiving, offered in the hands of the celebrant, who *in persona Christi* acts as High Priest of the New Covenant, approaching the holy altar to offer the pure gift with incense (cf. Mal1:11). The Church as a spiritual House and a holy priesthood offers up spiritual sacrifices acceptable to God by Jesus Christ (1Pet2:5).

Yet if the Church be a priesthood it cannot possibly be offering sacrifices exclusively for itself. It exists for the benefit of those *"who are ignorant and have gone astray"* (Heb5:1,2). The Church as that priesthood shares in the sacrificial offering with her Head. Those outside her therefore must potentially benefit; not just from her enlightenment and good works within wider society but through her priestly intercession and sacrifice. Once this is understood, it resolves many biblical tensions and explains the broader reconciliatory picture painted particularly by Paul and articulated by the Catholic Church fifty years ago at the Vatican Council. Yet that propagation left several unresolved biblical-doctrinal tensions regarding the context of the Church in God's broader plan for reconciling the world, at least one of which was noted at the time. The late Bishop BC Butler, a pre-eminent participator of that Council, being a convert from Protestantism and renowned Biblical scholar made the following observation on the Council's constitution *Lumen Gentium* (chapter two):

*"Church is more closely examined under the single image of the people of God. **But the biblical tension of the chapter appears already** in the first paragraph, in which God's plan of universal salvation through the association of all men in this People (the Church) is set over the biblical assurance that the **one sufficient ground of acceptance with God is not membership of God's people but that one should "fear God and work justice"***

Acts10:34. Such fidelity to the Bible leads on to a doctrine of "belonging to the Church", which though is nowhere elaborated in the Constitution, is very much richer and more plastic than the rather rigid doctrine of Church membership emphasized by Pope Pius X11".

Whilst replacing the concept of "Church membership" with the more tenuous idea of "belonging to the Church" may be potentially richer (providing anyone can spot the difference) it still does not explain how people who fear God and shun evil (Job 1:8) are accepted by God through association with the Church. According to this disclosure their acceptance (justification) is not directly linked to association with the Church but through their incognisant association with the cross of Jesus Christ who has atoned for the sin of the world. But that leads to an *indirect association* with the Church which is God's royal priesthood making present that historical Sacrifice. So people of good will can be regarded as being "in association with this People" as they benefit in an expiatory (guilt removing) and propitiatory (God appeasing) sense from the sacrifice that the Christian faithful as God's exclusive nation of priests offers on the world's as well as its own behalf at the Eucharist. Of course, only those partaking of the Host may benefit in the full salvific or "soul-healing" sense, for which reason they say, *"Lord I am not worthy that you should enter under my roof but only say the word and my soul shall be healed"*. Likewise, as Jesus offered His Body for the good of the Church so the believer having been spiritually nourished by partaking of that Body may in turn offer his own body as a living sacrifice (Rom12:1), primarily to God but also to benefit the world. Though already raised to heavenly places in Christ (Eph2:6) and destined for a glorious inheritance, like His Master before Him he is to offer his life in the body in humble service for the good of humanity. Just as Christ came not to be served but to serve, so the Church is currently serving with Him; She will one day be a Monarch as the Bride of Christ but for now, far from "ruling with Christ" she is His suffering Body, Servant to the world.

As far as I can see all doctrinal and biblical tensions become resolved once the historical misunderstanding concerning the

183

outworking of original sin and the bi-fold nature of the benefits of the atonement are acknowledged. I appreciate the Catholic Church's reluctance ever to acknowledge doctrinal error: it pertains to her ecclesiology, particularly to her understanding of the boundaries of her own infallibility (which could only be infallibly determined if she were wholly infallible which she does not claim to be). Yet the Church's ability to have fulfilled her historical and universal primary obligations is not compromised, for the Lord has never ceased to gather a people to Himself so that from the rising of the sun until its setting a pure sacrifice may be offered to His name. As universal sacrament, the Catholic/Orthodox Church (West and East) has ensured that the fullness of sacramental provision necessary for gospel salvation has been provided, such that the ones called out to be the people of God may be supplied for divine service now and through eternity.

The Dogmatic Constitution pertaining to the mystery of the Church from which I have quoted also asserted that "*whoever knows that the Catholic Church was made necessary by Christ but refuses to enter or remain in it could not be saved*". But the reality is, for example here within the UK or in the USA for historical reasons, there would be very few if any currently outside the Mother Church who would believe in their heart and conscience that the right thing for them to do right now is to go along to their local Catholic Church to receive catechesis. They are not being disobedient; it is simply not in their mind. The same Dogmatic Constitution also made it clear that non-Christians are not all bound for Hell:

*Those who through no fault of their own do not know the gospel of Christ or His Church but who nevertheless seek God with a pure heart, and moved by grace try in their actions to do His will as they know it **through the dictates of their conscience** – those too may obtain eternal salvation (Vatican II Lumen Gentium 16)*

The Vatican II Dogmatic Constitution "Lumen Gentium" (Light of the World) also confirms God's acceptance of those who fear God through their observance of Judaism and Islam; "rejects nothing that is true and holy" within Hinduism and Buddhism, for the Council recognized the common seminal soteriological root present in all religions. But it also acknowledged God's gracious intentions towards those without any religious faith at all:

*Nor shall divine providence deny the assistance necessary for salvation to those who without any fault of theirs have not yet arrived at an explicit knowledge of God and who, not without grace, **strive to lead a good life**. Whatever good or truth is found amongst them is considered by the Church to be a preparation for the gospel and given by Him who enlightens all men that they may at length have life. (Vatican II Lumen Gentium 16)*

The statement is necessarily vague concerning *how* such may come to "receive life". The "divine assistance for salvation" and "grace" must be distinguished from the celestial variety provided through the Covenant ratified in Christ's blood (Lk22:20) or else we deny the efficacy and essentiality of the Church's sacraments. Yet it is indeed the case that these people of goodwill are "not without grace", nor have they been "denied assistance" for they have been given a spirit provided with a conscience as a link to the divine by which they may discern a sense of right and wrong; and whenever they seek the right they are effectively exercising "faith" by positively responding to the divine revelation within them (deferring in effect to Christ Himself who provided such illumination). Anything such people do which is not entirely self-centred or sinful in itself is derived from "faith", for anything that is not of faith is sin (cf. Rom14:23). It follows therefore that any action that is loving, kind, gentle or patient, against which there is no law, must be of faith derived from a measure of grace. For without the divine help provided by conscience one would do no good at all whilst in this mortal vessel, for its own intrinsic impulses entirely consist in self-gratification (Rom7:22,23).

The Eucharist – our sanctification

Those who respond positively to conscience demonstrate they are "of God" as opposed to being out of or derived from (*ek*) the Wicked One. I can say that from over half a century of personal

185

observation the former group appears to be the great majority of the people I have ever known. However, agnostics and those of other faiths cannot be presented *"faultless before the presence of His glory with exceeding joy"* (Jud1:24). That requires one to become a disciple of Jesus Christ and a partaker of Jesus Christ to become conformed to His image. One must draw on His spiritual life-force by eating His flesh and drinking His blood, for *"whoever eats Me will draw life from Me* (Jn6:57). Receiving this Sacrament might be likened to the body's blood flowing through the heart and being renewed and cleansed by it: spiritual life is renewed and refreshed by participation in the Eucharist. Yet it is no mechanical process even for those regularly attending this means of grace (as is regrettably evident as one observes the life of some participants): faith is required just as it was when Jesus was physically present on Earth by those who would be healed by Him. According to the pupil of the apostle John (Ignatius) this Sacrament is the medicine of immortality; yet it is more even than a salve it is a Saviour (i.e. a Person). The Eucharistic meal possesses the body, blood, soul and divinity of Christ, not through the magic of a priest but by the Holy Spirit imprecated by him acting in the place of Christ. One must have faith to regard it as such if one is fully to benefit from its transforming power for one is not merely receiving medicine for the soul but a Person to relate to it. The analogy within the liturgy recited communally by the participants refers to the idea of Christ "coming under our roof", drawing on the Roman Centurion's words to Jesus in Luke 7:6. That Gentile soldier sponsored by his Jewish friends (v3) did not feel worthy that the Saviour should enter His home *"but only say the word and my servant shall be healed"* (v7). In the Eucharist, unworthy though we are, the Lord does come into our eternal spirit's temporary home, but what shall this sacred Guest find there? He has come to heal the soul but what is His *modus operandi*? Does He as it were get on with it whilst we get on with our lives, or does He not also wish to engage in a more meaningful communion? *"Behold I stand at the door and knock. If any man hears my voice I will come into Him and will sup with him, and he with Me"* (Rev3:20). As will be seen from the context, that invitation is not evangelistic, it was addressed to Christians (in

Laodicea). So "supping" in this context is not just eating but communing together and reasoning together (cf. Is1:18). Some might prefer a kind of spiritual oil-change: being mystically sanctified as one goes about one's daily business. Not so if one receives His body and blood with faith, for that mutual "supping" will be transformative; it is all very challenging and intimate: Jesus Christ wishes to unite His spirit with ours and thereby empower us and remain with us to direct those life-changes that are needed for our inner sanctity. St Paul makes some astonishing statements none more so than his allusion to the fact that just as a believer who joins his body with a harlot becomes one flesh with her, so "He that is joined to the Lord is one spirit" (1Cor6:16,17). Hence priest and people exchange the greeting: "*God be with you*" - "*And with your spirit*" (cf. Gal6:18). He is received not *by* faith but *with* faith: it is not faith alone for He must be received. Indeed, Christ is received at the Eucharist regardless of the faith of the priest or the recipient *[ex opere operato]*, yet it needs to be said that the fruits of the sacrament very much depend on the disposition of the one receiving it, remembering its purpose is not to deliver the many from Hell but to sanctify those being prepared for glory (not a place or realm but a shared inheritance with Christ). But "*How can this man possibly give us His flesh to eat?*" (Jn6:52). Such were the mutterings of certain Jewish unbelievers in Jesus's day; and as a result of a certain ecclesiological catastrophe many otherwise faithful Christians have been asking the same question for five hundred years. The answer pertains to a profound mystery which is not scientifically explainable, which is what we sometimes find when the Holy Spirit is at work; for not many rationalists get far explaining "*creatio ex nihilo*" or the feeding of the five thousand either. Its heart is an interior union with Christ: "*He who eats My flesh and drinks My blood abides in Me and I in him*" (Jn6:56). Such are the participatory benefits of the Atonement for those incorporated into the Body of Christ from which are dispensed the mysteries of heavenly grace.

Yet all people of good will shall be subjects of God's eternal Kingdom:

*The sun will be turned into darkness and the moon into blood before the Day comes, that great and terrible Day. All who call on the name of JHWE will be saved for on Mt Zion will be **those who have escaped**, as JHWE has said, and **in Jerusalem a remnant whom JHWE is calling** (Joel2:31-32; ch3:4-5 in some versions)*

The location and logistics will have changed for as ever it is necessary to apply the Dual Perspective Principle to this Old Testament prophecy. The secure Jerusalem remnant will be the called, chosen and faithful gathered to Christ; those escaping on the mountain equate to those calling on the name of the Lord for mercy. Only the former shall have been prepared to receive an immediate inheritance and intimate association with the Bridegroom at His coming (Col3:24) whereas in view of the corrupting nature of original sin the unsaved soul will be tarnished for it cannot be made whole except Christ had first been admitted to the vessel. Even disembodied and re-clothed in an incorruptible body, a soul (the real person) will not by nature be disposed, disciplined or formed in the ways of righteousness to serve in intimate communion with the Lord of Glory, for everyone must enter eternity as themselves or else it is not their life. Nevertheless, the joyful prospect that all are to be subjects of God's eternal Kingdom providing they have evinced "faith" through love (cf. Mt25:40) and that they will be forever re-united with those they have loved and lost is the inevitable corollary to an understanding of the "fellowship of the secret".

Special grace and faith

Common grace has been provided to all, and those who are of God co-operate with it, endeavouring to live uprightly and in accordance with sound reason, taking heed to conscience and producing the saving fruit of compassion (cf. Mt25:40). The *"exceedingly abundant grace which is in Christ Jesus"* (1Tim1:14) is a gift freely provided for the last two thousand years to those whom God has called to form the sacred assembly of the firstborn (the Church) as part of His adapted strategic plan to reconcile the scattered seed of God. Coming to share His nature and being called to suffer with Him in the present so that they may reign with Him in the future (2Tim2:12), these elect individuals are meant to be a blessing for the whole human family, for that is the privilege and responsibility of the firstborn, just as their Master and Saviour is in turn the Firstborn amongst them:

For whom He did foreknow, He did predestine to be conformed to the image of His Son that He might be the Firstborn among many brethren (Rom8:29 King James Version)

The Creator's methodology is undoubtedly inscrutable, but in terms of His nature, **God is good, desires the long-term wellbeing of humanity and acts with fairness and generosity towards everyone.** So, in the religious sphere, individuals who are being prepared for a glorious future inheritance with Christ by being associated with Him in the present, are called in the meantime to self-sacrifice and divine chastening (Heb12:6); they are to offer their bodies as a living sacrifice with all the discipline and self-restraint that requires (cf. Rom12:1). Others order their lives as they see fit; they may well be able to say (or sing) at the end of their earthly lives, "*I did it my way*". Disciples of Christ will not have had that luxury, for they will have done it *His* way, the way of the cross (Rom8:17). Not many wise, not many mighty or noble are called, for God has chosen the foolish of the world to confound the wise so that no flesh should glory in His presence (cf. 1Cor1:26-29). Christians are drawn by the Father to Jesus Christ; go on to love Him; wishing to serve Him and enjoy close communion with Him for ever. To that end they are willing to forsake everything that detracts from that goal for they have discovered the Pearl of greatest price, have sold all to buy it (Mt13:46) and will go on to demonstrate their love for Him by keeping His commandments (Jn14:15). They are "justified", that is marked out in the present as accepted members of the redeemed community of Christ by exercising faith in Him and staying faithful to Him; there was no need, as some of Paul's detractors in the Galatian churches were insisting, for fulfilling the works (deeds) of the Jewish Law such as circumcision, fasting and the like.

189

Special Covenants in the context of universal enlightenment

Abraham is the father of faith as it pertains to an elective or exclusive covenant, but he is not the father of faith, period. Abel, Enoch and others had earlier been declared as justified, effectively within a Universal Covenant for there was no other in operation at the time. For given that Abel was "reckoned to be righteous" there must have been a covenant in operation for justification is always in the context of a covenant: if you do X, God will accept you as a member of a group benefitting from His gracious benevolence; if you fail to do X, He won't (cf. Gen4:7 Masoretic text); although as we have shown it is not so much a case of "doing", but "having" and "demonstrating" by "bearing" (fruit). God had spoken to Abraham directly; he believed God concerning His promise of a son in old age, and this was credited to him as righteousness (Rom4:3). But as is made clearer in Hebrews 11 (v8), it was Abraham's earlier obedience to God's call to leave his home country that first evinced his faith. This undeniably virtuous quality is also described in Scripture as "godly fear". Peter concluded on the matter once he had grasped that Gentiles were to be invited to gospel salvation:

*"I have **come to understand** that God has no favourites but that anybody of any nationality who fears Him and does what is right is acceptable to Him" (cf. Acts10:34,35).*

As a late second century Father expressed the matter: *"faith (is that) which of itself and from its own resources chooses at once what is best"*[5]. It is a positive response to God's will for humane living, truthfulness and integrity as it is perceived through a religious creed (if one has one) or the dictates of one's conscience. Through such common yet effectual grace, many will instinctively go on to perform acts of charitable love (*agape*) towards their fellow man. In so doing they confirm they are of God, since:

*Love (agape) is from God and **everyone who loves is a child of God** and knows God" (1Jn4:7).*

Anyone who acts according to conscience is responding positively to God's witness in their heart and mind (Rom2:15). For

Faith is man's response to God, who reveals Himself and gives Himself to man, at the same time bringing man a super-abundant light as he searches for the ultimate meaning of His life [Catechism of the Catholic Church #27]

Yet that "super-abundant light" will only be apprehended by those who through the will of the Father are drawn to Christ and His Church, both described as the "Light of the World"; the universal light enlightening all men coming into the world is the conscience, being the innate witness to God's guide to humanity for those made in His image (cf. Rom2:15). As with Abraham, it was not *how* positively he responded to God, it was *that* he responded positively that led to him being counted as righteous. Faith is a quality whereas works pertains to achieving a standard or compliance with statutes. Faith is a virtue for sure, but it has not been worked for or earned but simply possessed by nature and utilized. Certain Christians tend to be obsessed with "merit" or rather with its avoidance. Such a notion would have seemed perverse to those who had been instructed by the apostles or their direct appointees as one can read for oneself. For after all, what does the apostle Paul teach? – we are justified by faith; that is we are justified by a virtue; not by acknowledging we have no virtue; nor by the deeds of the Torah (circumcision and the like); nor by achieving an acceptable aggregation or positive netting out of good and bad deeds, but simply exercising the quality called faith; responding positively to the light of Christ, indeed Christ in Person if the Father reveals Him to us. If Pauline "faith" is not a virtue, then neither is hope nor love (1Cor13:13). Believing God's word about His Son and seeking to obey Him is meritorious; it does not have to lead to a swollen head. Nor will it for those who are being sanctified and are constantly aware they receive vastly better from God than they deserve, and never cease to praise Him and thank Him for it. Justifying faith always pertains to evincing the continued presence of a divinely provided quality by producing fruit. A tree that produces apples can be "marked out" or "be justified" as a valid occupant of an apple orchard regardless of the quality or quantity of the fruit, although it may need some pruning. One who is of God evinces the fruit of love to some measure; he can be justified, i.e. marked out in the present as a valid member of the human race, one who has retained his Creator's image, for God is love and man reflects His image and a measure of His glory (*eikon kai doxa theou* - 1Cor11:7). The children of the devil on the other hand are "*trees whose fruit had withered, now devoid of fruit, twice dead and plucked up at the roots*" (Jude12). Such may give a fortune to charity and the like, but it will be for the praise of man rather than through love for humanity or faithful reparation (cf. Lk11:41).

No cause for human boasting

The "natural faith" which those who are of God exercise is a formed faith; it results in action. Love or the lack of it is what separates the sheep from the goats. But unlike the perfect completion of a divine law of which man has become incapable, it could be no cause for boasting. As we have shown, it is simply the exercise, however feeble, of an innate God-given quality, which God counts as righteousness:

*What have you got that was not given to you? And if it was given to you, **why would you boast** as though it were your own? (1Cor4:7)*

The fact that a person is "justified" in the present does not mean they will not be subject to judgement in the future. Final judgement may involve chastisement or purifying but most especially rewarding (cf. Mt 12:36). Justification is a gift, not a wage or reward (Rom4:4, 5:18); final judgement *does* involve reward for it pertains to how that which has been freely provided has been utilized. In Paul's chronology the Christian has been reconciled and was justified by Christ's death but will be saved to fulfil his eternal destiny through participation in Christ's resurrected life (Rom5:10 Greek: note tenses). The apostle's perspective on final judgement (as opposed to justification) is summarized in the second chapter of Romans:

God will repay everyone as their deeds deserve. For those who aimed for glory, honour and immortality by persevering in good works, there will be eternal life, but for those who out of jealousy have taken for their guide not truth but injustice, there will be the fury of retribution. Trouble and distress will come to every human being who does evil- Jews first but Greeks as well; **glory and honour and peace will come to everyone who does good** *– Jews first but Greeks as well.* **There is no favouritism with God** *(Rom2:6-11)*

"Ah! Romans chapter two: difficult; difficult." On the contrary, the above is a passage of common sense theology; it is the rest of Romans that is difficult and has thoroughly confused much of Christendom for centuries. The apostle's references to justification throughout his *magnum opus* are not alluding to final judgement but to present covenantal membership. The issue Paul was seeking to clarify was this: under the new covenant ratified in Christ's blood, who is now to be marked out as a member of the community of the redeemed – the one who has been circumcised and outwardly fulfils the detailed requirements of the Law (Torah) or the one who has faith in Christ? That is the issue he is addressing in Romans and in his still more polemical letter to the Galatians: it was not a tirade against self-help moralism but a challenge to Judaic exclusivism and the humiliating shame such people associated with their justification being associated with the atoning sacrifice of a crucified Messiah rather than the signification of circumcision and Torah observance (the Law). Paul's antagonists were not "moralist", they were racist.

The potential need for final purification

The soul possessed at physical death is the soul which will either be resurrected or face Jesus at His coming if still around at the time. Paul's "vessel", "tent" or the "body of this death" is replaceable by a glorious new body; the soul/spirit we possess cannot be replaced for it is our identity. No one is to be "clothed in righteousness divine"; the Father already relates to His Son, both now wish to relate to human beings – the real us. All

193

Christians must stand before the tribunal of Christ *"so that each person can be paid back for the things that were done whilst in the body whether they were good or bad"* (2Cor5:10). Christians who after being baptized into the Faith wilfully continue to do wrong will be repaid accordingly. Every human being is to be judged impartially and rewarded according to their works (Mt16:27; 1Pet1:17), which *should* place the Christian at a very great advantage if he has taken heed to divine teaching, walked in the light and received ongoing cleansing in the blood of Christ. Yet the writer to the Hebrews warns even more starkly of the fallacy that Christians who continue to live sinful lives will escape condemnation; Christ's blood will not avail for them (cf. Heb10:26-29). It is difficult to interpret Jesus's parable in Matthew18:32-35 (the unforgiving debtor) in any other way than to mean that those who have been forgiven by Christ yet refuse to forgive others are to receive temporary punishment at death.

There is only ever one foundation the Christian can build his life on, which is Christ. However, he may build with gold, silver precious stones, wood, hay or straw, and the "Day" will reveal which it is because it will be tested by fire (1Cor3:11-13). God is described as a consuming fire; the Holy Spirit appeared as fire at Pentecost, so biblical fire is not always hurtful or destructive, but it purges and consumes the dross: that which is worthless. Every positive contribution a Christian makes to the building of God's Kingdom on Earth will be of lasting value for that is the nature of gold, silver and precious stones; but the rubbish will be burnt and the builder, having built on the right foundation but with the wrong materials will be saved, but as through fire (v15).

The Catholic Christian's assurance of salvation

As Scripture makes clear, perseverance in the Faith is not guaranteed. Taking Jesus's parable of the sower those who receive the seed on the stony ground receive the gospel with joy (and so clearly act upon it) but it does not last for they have no root in themselves; likewise, with those whose seed was sown amongst thorns and are distracted by the cares of the world and the deceitfulness of riches. This is an observable reality; it is not all of grace or else the seed would either be in good ground or snatched away altogether. Paul might appear to be contradicting this (and himself elsewhere) in Phil1:6, but he is referring to the Church of Philippi as a whole that he was confident God would continue the work He had begun in them, not necessarily every individual. God will never forsake the individual, but the latter may depart from God as all the apostles elsewhere testify. Yet personal assurance of salvation is attainable – communicated by the Holy Spirit witnessing with our spirit (Rom8:16); the Spirit being given to us to enable our hearts to become filled with love for God, and others (Rom5:5). I have come to understand Paul's reference to the "love of God poured out in the heart" as a genitive of origin. It refers not so much to God's love for us (a fact, but not the context here) or even ours for Him (hopefully true but only half the story); it pertains rather to the impartation of the divine quality of love (cf. Jn17:26) engrafted by the Spirit such that we come to love others more as God loves them (cf. 1Jn2:5). That is more clearly indicated where John refers a few verses later to those who are worldly not having "the love of the Father *within them*" (1Jn2:15). It is in the context of partaking of the divine nature by which we come to possess more of what God possesses: especially holiness aligned with love; God being love and thrice holy. Loving the Lord in our hearts, thrilled by His goodness and coming ourselves to possess "the love of the Father" towards the rest of humanity, we know we are being saved and heading for victory. So much for the subjective; assurance of salvation in Scripture is more often expressed in terms of actions rather than feelings:

Now by this we know that we know Him, **if we keep His commandments**. *He who says, "I know Him" and does not keep His commandments is a liar, and the truth is not in him. But whoever keeps his word, truly the love of God is perfected in him.* **By this we know we are in (Christ)** *(1Jn2:3-5 New King James Version).*

We know we have passed from death unto life **because we love the brethren**. *He who does not love his brother abides in death (1Jn3:14 New King James Version)*

Little children let no one deceive you: he who practices
righteousness is righteous, just as He is righteous (1Jn3:7 New
King James Version).

Truly, personal righteousness must wholeheartedly be pursued
and practiced (also Prov21:21). As for the reality of one's faith,
anyone may extol the Being who they believe is going to bless
them eternally; the test of love (and saving faith) lies elsewhere
(1Jn4:20). St John confirms that all who claim to love God will
demonstrate it by their love for humanity and by keeping God's
commandments (the heart of which is love for neighbour). That
is Christ's commandment and it is not burdensome (1Jn5:1-3).
So it is possible to become unshakably established in love for the
Lord, compassion for others and perseverance in the faith, but
that is not the experience of all Christians. Nowhere to be found
in Scripture is any assurance pertaining to salvation as Luther
interpreted it: "looking at Christ's perfect work and
appropriating it to oneself" or as Calvin tended to express his
understanding of saving faith: "standing in God's mercy" or
"attaining to God's free promise". I know: I used to look for
such textual support and once tried to preach on such a concept –
it's a hopeless cause for those who would be faithful to a literal
reading of Scripture. All references to being confident of one's
true standing pertain to personal behaviour (especially
philanthropy e.g. 1Jn4:12), walking in the light and attending to
the means of grace (cf. 1Jn1:7) or in the language of the
parables, bearing fruit.

Preparing for the creational renaissance

Speaking with regard to His people of the Old Covenant and
what they should expect at Christ's coming, to which we can
now apply "the dual perspective". The Lord of Hosts had
declared:

Behold, I will send my messenger and he will prepare the way
before Me; and the Lord whom you seek will suddenly come to
His temple, even the Messenger of His Covenant whom you
delight in ... But who may abide the day of His coming and who
will stand when He appeareth? For He is like a refiner's fire

196

and a fuller's soap. And He shall sit as a refiner and purifier of silver, and He shall purify the sons of Levi, and purge them as gold and silver, that they might offer unto the Lord an offering of righteousness (Mal3:1-3 King James Version).

The original messenger was John and the Messenger of the Covenant is Jesus, but in the event, He did not suddenly come to His temple and His appearance was in no way awesome (cf. Phil2:7); He did not cleanse and purge the Jewish priesthood through fire and the offering of Judah and Jerusalem did not become "sweet to JHWE as in former years" (v4), quite the contrary. Malachi is referring to an awesome event (for who shall abide it?) which has been deferred till the conclusion of the gospel age. At that time, refining and cleansing, for that is surely the purpose of the fire and soap may be required by some of God's covenant people if they are to serve Him as priests and kings in holiness; for through the fellowship of the mystery and the fellowship of the blood "the sons of Levi" will not now exclusively be Jewish (1Pet2:9). Even having been cleansed in the bath of regeneration (Tit3:5) and been sealed with the Holy Spirit does not ensure that the soul does not later become defiled. To be fit for service in God's Kingdom something more may be required for some. But many alive at His coming will have been made ready for such service through participation in the sacramental life of the Church, personal discipline and suitable preparation. For the process of salvation requires our effort and cooperation; Grace replacing grace (Jn1:16) as the Christian works out his own salvation with fear and trembling. In Pauls' words:

If you live according to the flesh you shall die, but if by the Spirit (sic) you put to death the deeds of the body you shall live (Rom8:13NKJ)

As in the earlier passage from Romans Two, the apostle is not here referring to covenantal acceptance (justification) which marks out in the present who are God's chosen people but how one's salvation is accomplished. But it is the human's spirit (Rom8:16) or "inner man strengthened by the Spirit" (Eph3:16) that puts to death the deeds of the body, not the Holy Spirit Himself as many would infer from this verse. It is "by the Spirit"

197

in the enabling sense, but "by the spirit" in the operative sense, so either translation is valid, but I suspect Paul intended the latter. For we cannot command or operate the Holy Spirit; *He cannot be a faculty.* The spirit is a part of us; the Holy Spirit is with us; the One witnesses to the other (Rom8:16). The Spirit is the God who guides (v14) instructing us to control our fleshly inclinations by responding to the inclinations of our inner man rather than the desires of the flesh. That is how we "crucify the old man" (Eph4:22) to preserve the soul (cf. Heb10:39). Paul's "old man" and "new man" is the before and after of that soul. The old man was being "*corrupted according to the deceitful lusts*" arising from the concupiscence of the "body of this death" or "flesh". Now through the means of grace and with the mind renewed both by the Spirit and divine teaching, the Christian is to "put on the new man". He himself has to do it: "*Therefore putting away lying, speak every man truth with his neighbour; be angry and sin not.*" Now the "new man" the heart, soul and spirit of the Christian can be recreated in righteousness and true holiness (v24). It is a virtuous circle: *Charin anti charitos* (Grace for grace). "*Assuredly the same spiritual grace that is equally received in baptism by believers is subsequently either increased or diminished according to our conversation and conduct*" (Cyprian)[6]. And all for one purpose:

For this is the will of God, your sanctification: that you should abstain from sexual immorality; that each of you should know **how to possess his own vessel** *in sanctification and honour (1Thes4:3,4).*

St Peter's teaching is in the same vein: the Christian has died to sin and now lives for righteousness, for by His stripes he is being healed (1Pet2:24). In the current age it is the soul that is healed through the sacraments, not the body, either physically (as a norm) or in terms of its moral inclination: *For if Christ be in you the* **body is dead** *because of sin but the spirit is life because of righteousness* (cf. Rom8:10). It would be facile for Paul to be asserting that the Holy Spirit is alive because of righteousness (*dia dikaiosunen*); He could never be other than alive or righteous; the Christian's spirit is alive because it is intrinsically sound and enlightened unlike the body which remains disordered and inclined to sin. The Christian is no longer under obligation to his degenerative vessel to satisfy its whims and desires but needs to deny them by his spirit which has been united to Christ. For, says the apostle, to be bodily-minded is death but to be spiritually minded is life and peace (v6):

Therefore, do not let sin reign in your mortal body so that you obey its lusts (Rom6:12)

If the Spirit were the Operator and salvation "all of grace", such an exhortation would be superfluous. Rather He is the Comforter and Facilitator – our spirit/will/inner man must apply itself, then the Spirit will aid us. The evidence for such a symbiosis is our fellow Christian: each believer does not achieve the same degree of sanctification in his lifetime and it is clearly not perfected in all. For the Christian is required to purify *himself*:

Having therefore these promises dearly beloved, let us cleanse ourselves from all defilements of the flesh and of the spirit, perfecting sanctification in the fear of God (2Cor7:1)

The Christian is to become "*teleioi*" in his own right, i.e. perfected[7] or complete; not by receiving an imputed righteousness but by personal effort and endurance (Jam1:4), perfected that is in love such that we become "*like God in the world*" (1Jn4:17).

Salvific synergy in the language of Jesus

Jesus makes it clearer still that those who are to enter the Kingdom of God need to discipline themselves:

*And if your foot should be your downfall, cut it off; it is better for you to enter into life crippled than to have two feet and be thrown into hell. And if your eye should be your downfall, tear it out; it is better for you to enter into the Kingdom of God with one eye than to have two eyes and be thrown into Hell where their worm will never die nor their fire be put out. For **everyone will be salted with fire - salt is a good thing** but if salt has* *become insipid, how can you make it salty again. Have salt in yourselves and be at peace with one another (Mk9:45-50).*

Jesus's teaching has a timeless quality and value, yet one must remember it was addressed to the fellow Jews of His day. Just as we saw Paul speaking of the necessity to put to death the deeds of the body by "crucifying the flesh with its passions and desires" (Gal5:24) so Jesus was referring to the need to control those bodily members relating to sight and action which might cause those expected to inherit the Kingdom (His fellow Jews) to fall into mortal sin, that is a sin that is serious enough to lead to spiritual death (1Jn5:16). But in the language of Jesus, there is no confusion about who is to exercise the control. For those of His people who physically die in a state of mortal sin would have to be salted in fire. Purgatory is not a place but a process, and I have come to understand is indistinguishable in Scripture from the "fire" of Gehenna; something that someone who seriously insults his fellow believer may be required to undergo (Mt5:22). The burning away of dross that will be necessary for purification cannot be measured in earthly time or degree; such concepts have led to deformed practices packaged as "indulgences", the perversion of which helped trigger Luther's revolt and were rightly condemned. *"As soon as the coin in the coffer rings, the soul from purgatory springs"* [attributed to Johann Tetzel, papal seller of indulgences]. Forsooth, who would *not* wish to be a Reformer in sixteenth century Europe? Seemingly spiritually insightful men pleading scriptural truths against the deformed doctrines and practices of the seriously corrupted monolith that was the Roman Catholic Church. Yet the unifying Spirit of Christ requires us to take a step back from all that and, utilizing the resources available to us in the digital age, undertake a pan-bimillennial review of church history applying the rationale I have set out in chapter five. Then, if the Spirit is behind this work, many may come to perceive what is required for the fractured Body of Christ to be healed at last (cf. Rom12:5).

The reality of Hell

Returning to the matter of where the soul may find itself after physical death, Hell (Gehenna) was a town located just to the South of Jerusalem; it was something of a dump – for rubbish that is, forever smouldering and smoking. It had once been a place where certain pagans and apostate Jews had sacrificed children and was deemed to be cursed. Nevertheless, Hell *is* a reality for Jesus clearly indicates that some after death will experience suffering in "fire", which I now understand (along with some early Church Fathers[8]) is as much to purify or "purge" (salting with fire) as it is to punish, and that is the context of Jesus's teaching in the above passage. It is better to keep one's body in check and "have salt in oneself" than for body and soul to require such salting (Mk9:49,50). Jesus and Scripture are quite unambiguous that all mortal sin apart from that against the Holy Spirit can be forgiven in this age and the next (Mt12:31-33). Confusion has arisen here from the fact that those (Christian or otherwise) who continually practice mortal sin will certainly not inherit the Kingdom of God:

Do you not know that wrongdoers will not inherit the Kingdom of God? Do not be deceived; fornicators, idolaters, adulterers, male prostitutes, sodomites, thieves, the greedy, drunkards, revilers, robbers – none of these will inherit the Kingdom of God (1Cor6:8-10)

As we are seeking to explain, "inheriting the Kingdom of God" is not referring to going to Heaven but to inheriting everything Christ is to inherit. Those who continue to practice the above will not be amongst them, even if incorporated in the Church. The one mortal sin that will not be forgiven as can be discerned from its context (Mt12:22-32) relates to knowing or sensing in one's heart that something is of God working through His Holy Spirit yet asserting it to be wicked or satanic as certain Pharisees did regarding Jesus's miracle which they maligned for their own ends in order to preserve their own status and traditions. This connection is made clearer in Mk3:29-30. One may well have challenged the working of the Spirit in ignorance, but what is done in ignorance cannot be the unforgivable sin which is why even blasphemy against Christ can be forgiven but not what is said against the direct working of the Spirit where that is perceived within the conscience (Mt12:32). In the current context those who are determined to defend a particular tradition against what they sense might be divine Light must tread very carefully for this damnable sin is a form of intransigence being an unwillingness to be persuaded of the truth by any means. Heretics and false prophets can be sincere but simply mistaken or deluded for which they will be humiliated and punished for their presumption, but those who directly revile or obstruct the workings of the Spirit are in still more danger. As for purgatory, final purification is an act of love, enabling morally damaged souls who have wilfully neglected their salvation to become fitted for the eternal glory of God's Kingdom, but clearly it is best avoided by having salt in oneself (Mk9:50).

"The fury of God's vengeance is profitable for the purgation of souls. That the punishment also which is said to be by fire is understood to be applied **with the object of healing** *is taught by Isaiah: The Lord will wash away the filth of the sons or daughters of Zion and shall purge away the blood from the midst of them by the spirit of judgement and the spirit of burning...* **The Lord will sanctify in a burning fire**. *[Origen - 3rd century]*[9]

Salvation for all?

1Tim4:10 is taken by some to imply the ultimate salvation of all humanity, God being described as "the saviour of all men, but especially those with faith". Likewise, Col1:20 affirms that God ultimately wishes to reconcile everything on Earth and in Heaven back to Himself. But Scripture also makes clear that the wicked as we have defined them are to be excluded from God's Kingdom and receive punishment in the age to come, which is as far ahead as one can have any clarity on the matter. The concept of universal reconciliation (absolute universalism) goes beyond current revelation but neither is it definitively refuted by it. The above quoted Origen who speculated on such matters believed such a notion and I can find no flaw in either his biblical or philosophical reasoning but cannot positively affirm the matter from Scripture. Such a possibility should have no impact

202

whatsoever on the choice of actions in this life, especially for those who believe Jesus Christ to be the Way, the Truth and Life and according to whom the fire of Hell which itself will have a role not just for an age but throughout eternity (Mk9:43) is a painful reality that is to be feared and avoided at all costs. Yet it should be evident from another passage in which Jesus refers to it that he could hardly be referring to eternal condemnation:

But I say unto you that whosoever is angry with their brother without a cause will be liable to judgement; and whosoever shall say to his brother Raca! (vain fellow or dunderhead) shall be in danger of the Sanhedrin; but whoever shall say "stupid idiot!" or "dullard" [Greek: moros] shall be in danger of Hell fire (Mt5:22).

So calling one's brother vain, a Jew may still go on to enjoy eternal bliss after a ticking off from the Sanhedrin, yet calling's one's brother a dullard, or in modern parlance one might say a moron *"more!"* he is in danger of eternal torment. Such all or nothing, black and white binary theology delights the Adversary since it distorts the equity of Jesus Christ, impugning His charity and truthfulness. The Son of Man has promised to judge humanity applying standards that accord with human reasoning; for it is *His own* reasoning. His standard of judgement will be in accordance with the standard we apply to others (Mt6:14; 7:2). Given the gradation of insults outlined in Mt5:22 and the fact that Jesus is quite adamant about the reality of punitive fire, it must be referring to a need for final purification for those who grossly insult and belittle a fellow Jew. It should be evident by now why Jesus referred only to the Sanhedrin and not the Church at this stage in His teaching. Of course, for the Christian such a sin can be wholeheartedly repented of in life and be forgiven. Each individual's whole life or legacy is to be evaluated at final judgement and rewarded accordingly (Mt16:27), for that is how an equitable and loving person exercises judgement. Mature Christians will instinctively know these things for they have the same mind-set as the Judge (1Cor2:16); which is why they are to be entrusted to judge men and angels (1Cor6:1-4). The context of those verses in Corinthians (taking fellow-believers to court) can only be

203

referring to a definite juridical function, not "putting to shame others who have not accepted Jesus as saviour" as some would dissemble, for that has nothing to do with the ability to exercise judgement or settle a dispute with a fellow believer, which is the context. Jesus was also explicit: when He takes His Throne of Glory at the renascence, the twelve disciples whom He told would *"have a Kingdom conferred upon (them) as My Father has conferred upon Me"* (Lk22:29) will sit on twelve thrones and judge the twelve tribes of Israel. That will be the kind of activity some of God's people are to be involved with, and those fitted and rewarded with the greatest responsibility, like the faithful apostles will have the privilege of working in close communion with the current Joy of Heaven; indeed, some will be very close indeed (Mt20:23).

"Aionian" Punishment

Even where Hell or punishment is specified to be "eternal" in the Latin Vulgate or English translations, the Greek text has *"aionian"*, referring to an age – and there are to be numerous ages (e.g. Gal1:5 & Eph3:21 Young's Literal). Young's Literal always translates *"aionian"* as "age", whilst the Bible-gateway Greek Interlinear does not translate it at all. The folly of more typical translations becomes apparent in Luke16:9 where Jesus appears to be encouraging His disciples to make friends with the dubiously wealthy so that when they fall on hard times their wealthy friends may be able to welcome them into their "eternal dwellings". Rather, the Lord is referring to the dwellings pertaining to the current age (*tas aionious skenas*). This is evident from the context, for in the previous verse He had said that the sons of this age (*huioi tou ainos*) are more prudent in financial matters than the sons of light, hence the fabulous real estate. Likewise, in Mt28:20: "Low I am with you until the end of the *aionos*". Here, translators have no choice; *"aionos"* cannot mean "eternity" for it doesn't end, so it has to be translated as "age". *"Aion"* (Strong G165) *can* refer to eternity, although as already demonstrated, there are to be numerous ages. Its cognitive adjective *"aionos"* (Strong G166) pertains to a quality either relating to a particular age or unrestricted by time. So "*ainos life*" is available to the believer now but may fairly be translated as "eternal life" for that pertains to its quality (experiencing God's presence Jn17:3), and it also happens to be everlasting. The same principle cannot be applied to punishment, although when it is specified as "*aionas ton aionon*" (ages of ages) as it is for the beast and false prophet (Rev20:10), that certainly implies an exceedingly long and indefinite period of time. There is much debate on this matter on the internet and we won't add much more to it here. The Book of Enoch, regarded as inspired and genuine by several early Fathers, describes final judgement in more detail and confirms that punishment is never eternal, even for the worst fallen angels. Nevertheless, Enoch *was overwhelmed at its severity* in the case of such creatures, more specifically the Gen6:1 brigade (the fallen watchers). Likewise, it indicates that powerful and privileged evil humans will suffer to a multiple degree for the misery and pain they have caused to others. The translation from Greek in the Ethiopic version of Enoch also falls into the trap of not distinguishing between "an age" and "eternity". The folly is clearest in 69:9 regarding "*the men who sin from eternity to eternity up to the present day*"! It is also wise to ignore the various sub-headings provided by the translator based on his own contextual interpretation; not least when reviewing the chapter which I believe is referring to the medieval corruption in the Church and the apostasy that sprang from it (ch93 – weeks 6&7 cf. ch104:10). As with all pre-apostolic prophecy, one would need to apply the dual-perspective principle considered earlier with Enoch's prophecy for the Temple being realized within the Church, a key phrase being "and in it a man shall ascend" (v8). Unlike the Church in the middle ages, the Temple was not torn apart by a man arising from its own ranks but by an external political force (consider also En90:32-36)[10].

Enoch's account of final judgement asserts that an individual's status and suffering during their lifetime is taken into account, as does the only reference to individuals' experience in Hades[11] in the New Testament: the rich man and Lazarus, the text of which requires careful attention. Much to many a hellfire preacher's chagrin, the only stated criterion distinguishing these two men was that one had had a life of ease and comfort whilst the other had been poor and wretched (Lk16:25). It can be deduced from vv27-31 that the rich man was suffering partly because of the way he had utilized his wealth; failing to show care and compassion for miserable beggars like Lazarus. Yet no reason is given why Lazarus should be comforted after his death other than that he had experienced a life of poverty and sickness; thus had he been salted (cf. Mk9:49). The rich man and Lazarus's "compartments" in Hades are just two of the four compartments or "hollows" referred to in Enoch chapter XXII for those who are interested. The various locations and their environments take account of whether the unrighteous received judgement in their lifetime: the rich man in the gospel clearly had not (Lk16:25). The redistributive and compensatory aspects of judgement at death are also emphasized in the letter of James who exhorts the oppressive rich to weep and howl for the miseries that are to come upon them (Ja5:1), and by Jesus, particularly as recorded by Luke:

How blessed are you who are poor; the Kingdom of God is yours. Blessed are you who are hungry now: you shall have your fill. Blessed are you who are weeping now; you shall laugh (Lk6:20,21).

Whereas -

Alas for you who are rich: you are having your consolation now. Alas for you who have plenty to eat now: you shall go hungry. Alas for you who are laughing now: you shall mourn and weep (Lk6:24,25).

I now understand this to be partly a question of redistributive justice but that it also relates to the role and necessity of human suffering (salting) explained in the theodicy (chapter seven). Luke's interpretation of Jesus's teaching needs to be taken alongside Matthew's emphasis on more spiritual and moral qualities: poverty of spirit, hunger for righteousness, kindness, compassion and purity. For a lousy crook may be poor but is not fitted for God's Kingdom. So, life experience, moral and spiritual integrity and especially how one has treated the poor with whom Christ as Son of Man personally identifies will determine how one fares once Christ's Kingdom is consummated. It will be a Kingdom in which the status of many will have altered (Mk10:31). The age to come will not be concerned with clouds, harps or spiritual wafting but the administration of Christ (*oikonomian* Eph1:10), when all things in the heavens and on the Earth are placed under Him and the kingdoms of this world become in a functional sense the kingdoms of our Lord and His Anointed (Rev11:15). As for those who are called, chosen and faithful:

He who overcomes, and keeps my works unto the end, to him I will give power over the nations. "He shall rule them with a rod of iron; they shall be dashed to pieces like the potter's vessels". As I also have received from my Father; and I will give him the morning star (Rev2:26-28 New King James Version).

It is to be observed that whenever Jesus specified the nature of a reward for loyal service, it is nearly always expressed in terms of levels of authority or responsibility, which is hardly indicative of a spiritualized egalitarianism (e.g. Lk19:15-27; Lk22:28,29). Such applies to those who already have great responsibility in the Church:

Who then is the wise and trustworthy servant whom the Master placed over His Household to give them their food at the proper time? Blessed is that servant if his Master's arrival finds him doing exactly that. In truth I tell you, He will put him in charge of everything He owns (Mt24:45-47 New Jerusalem Bible).

The last phrase rules out the idea that this can be referring to a local church leader; it must refer to one man - the leader of the Church. All who are to be the Spouse of Jesus Christ and heirs to His Kingdom must reasonably expect to be involved in His activities, which are bound to involve exercising authority:

*For unto us a Child is born; unto us a Son is given; and the government shall be upon His shoulder. And His name will be called Wonderful, Counsellor, Mighty God, Everlasting Father, Prince of Peace. **Of the increase of His government and peace there will be no end**, upon the throne of David and over His Kingdom, to order and establish it with judgement and justice from that time forward, **even for ever** (Is9:6,7)*

207

If one is foolish enough to believe that Jesus Christ is never more to rule or reign then neither will the elect and vice versa, for they are affirmed in Scripture to be as Husband and wife, ever in each other's company. The concept that the Jesus people are to judge, rule and enlighten others is not restricted to Revelation, it is evident in Old Testament prophecies (especially Daniel) as well as the gospels and epistles, but will have made little sense to those who believe that only those chosen as Christ's Bride are to escape perdition. That may well be why the earlier referred to hedonistic chiliasts of Augustine's time perceived the millennium of Christ's rule as party-time for the elect of God rather than a time of healing, correction and enlightenment for the unsaved world; but then a grasp of these issues has been deliberately veiled through the centuries for reasons considered below. The qualities required for those who are already reconciled to God as His children are faithfulness, humility and self-discipline. That is why Jesus taught that it is next to impossible for the rich and powerful of this age to enter the Kingdom of God (Mk10:25), for they simply don't have the humility and believe they have too much to lose. If only they knew what they would have to gain, which (again) is why these indications of future glory are so obscure; they are to be the reward of faith (Heb11:6b). Relatively few from the higher ranks of society have come to gospel salvation: the weak and foolish of this world are to put to shame the wise and mighty (1Cor1:26,27). That is the way God has chosen to work and it still is (Mt11:25). It is so that no man will boast in God's presence: the world's strong and mighty will have nothing to swagger about for they will have been eclipsed by the weak and lowly; and the lowly will not boast because they will readily acknowledge they have been ransomed, healed, restored and elevated through God's enabling grace. Apart from which, those who have become holy are not given to boasting; they regard it as abhorrent.

People of good will

This perfectly apt description utilized by the Catholic Church will appear too vague for many as it was for me, and this chapter has sought to identify and define such from Scripture. As is the case for the Christian, their eventual deliverance from the bondage of sin to be united to God will have been made possible by divine grace and the redemptive work of Jesus Christ, for these are the *core elements of all human salvation.* We have asserted that people of good will can and do participate even now in the building of God's Kingdom, for anyone who seeks to reconcile and bring peace between nations, families or individuals is acting like a child of God (Mt5:9) and anyone who contributes to alleviating the plight of the poor and needy will be judged as having succoured Christ Himself (Mt25:45). Anyone who accepts and acknowledges someone righteous as righteous is accepted as righteous himself (Mt10:41). Those who pursue truth and justice for its own sake show themselves to be of the Truth (cf. Jn18:37b). Indeed, anyone who desires from the heart to do anything good and acts upon it is demonstrating they will one day adore Jesus Christ, the summit and perfection of all that is good.

The universal benefits of Christ's faithfulness

In order to be clear from Scripture how Jesus Christ's unlimited atonement (1Jn2:2) avails for those outside the Body of Christ it is necessary to understand what Paul was saying in Galatians 2:16, firstly by discerning how it should be translated by reference to the Greek interlinear and Young's Literal translations:

*Having known that a man is not declared righteous by the works of the Law but **through the faithfulness of Christ**; we (Christians) **believed in Christ Jesus** that we might be declared righteous **by the faithfulness of Christ** and not by the works of Law (Torah), wherefore no flesh shall be declared righteous by the works of the Law (Gal2:16 from Greek).*

209

Christ's faith or faithfulness (*pisteos ieosou christou*) is a subjective genitive, referring to Christ's own faithfulness as is unambiguously the case in the similarly constructed "faith(fulness) of Abraham" (Rom4:16); whereas reference in the same verse to "*eis Christon Iesoun episteusamen*" concerns an individual's faith in Christ. The apostle affirms in the next chapter that personal faith in Christ is required to become a son of God (Gal3:26). Applying this distinction to Gal2:16 (above) resolves the earlier translation's triple tautology and shows how Christ's faithfulness in terms of His saving work on humanity's behalf benefits those who do not have a personal knowledge of it yet instinctively fear God and "attend to moral discipline" as we earlier observed some early Fathers refer to the matter. For Jesus had said of those who experienced His ministry: "*If I had not come and spoken to them, they would not be guilty of sin, but now they have no excuse for their sin* (Jn15:22), incidentally affirming that Adam's guilt is not assigned to his offspring, they "merely" inherit his carnal body, for "*if I had not spoken to them they would not be guilty of sin*". Countless billions who have lived have not benefitted from hearing a faithful account of Jesus's teaching and the Good News of His Kingdom. Many of the Church Fathers before Augustine's assertions recognized that man in his natural state, although unable to raise himself to eternal life had effectual free will to choose and practice what is just and in accordance with sound reason[12]. Likewise, man may equally choose or be persuaded to reject the light of Christ provided to all men and become a godless and intransigent "unbeliever", devoid of faith and susceptible to sifting (cf. Lk22:31,32). I have referred to Romans1:17 several times for it summarizes what Paul is saying regarding Christ's faithfulness and human "faith". I will use one of the better translations in this instance, the New Jerusalem Bible:

For in it (the gospel) is revealed the saving justice of God; a justice based on faith and addressed to faith. As it says in Scripture, "Anyone who is upright through faith will live" (Rom1:17 New Jerusalem Bible)

The faith (Greek LXX) or faithfulness (Hebrew Masoretic text) upon which the justice of a human can be reckoned "out of faith" is Christ's faithfulness (*ek pisteous*), i.e. His perfect obedience to death which benefits all those with "faith" (*eis pistin*). "*Ek pistous eis pistin*" being literally: "from faith to faith". This is "the righteousness of God", i.e. His covenant faithfulness and saving justice toward those who fear Him. We have shown that in the universal sense the object of faith is something innate, which is Christ's implanted witness to the truth operating through the conscience. Jesus described the little children who were brought to Him as "*little ones who believe in Me*" (Mt18:6) and the context (v2) makes it absolutely clear that Jesus is not on this occasion referring to His adult disciples that He also sometimes describes in such a way; nor could He possibly be anticipating those infants who would go on to "receive Jesus as their personal Saviour" or become baptized Catholics, for it was an inclusive observation concerning all young children who were placed into His loving embrace (Mt19:14). Their "belief in Jesus" was hardly a sophisticated Christology for His own disciples had scarcely grasped who He was at that stage; it therefore can only refer to what was innate to all very young lives – the internal witness of the light of Christ (the Word/Reason – Greek: *Logos*) their Creator and moral Guide diffused within their spirits and consciences, guaranteed in their case not (yet) to have been obscured or distorted by the lusts of the flesh or impurities of the mind.

The fate of unbaptized infants

In that context, it is to be observed that The New Advent Catholic Encyclopaedia asserts the Roman Catholic Church's traditional view that unbaptized infants must be excluded from Heaven in view of their understanding (largely but not entirely through Augustine's influence) of the forensic dimension to original sin, which is in error according to this disclosure as well as from the long-standing perspective of the Orthodox Catholic Church. The 1992 Catechism of the Catholic Church is more accommodating, *"entrusting (unbaptized infants) to the mercy of God... who desires that all men should be saved; and Jesus's tenderness towards children which caused Him to say, "Let the children come unto me and do not hinder them" allows us to*

211

hope there is a way of salvation for children who have died without baptism". There is indeed "a way of salvation" for these young children and it relates to a universally atoning sacrifice which nullified Adam's guilt for his descendants (Rom3:23,24; 5:18), not to mention the compassionate nature of Jesus their Judge from Whom little children scarcely need to be protected. The French theologian par excellence of the Reformation John Calvin, drawing on his favourite Church Father's sentiments went still further asserting that the eternal misery in Hell the unbaptized who die in infancy must experience was not primarily for Adam's sake but because in themselves they were "odious" and *"an abomination to God"; their very natures being a seed-bed of sin*[13]. He had been equally forthright about God's instinctive hatred for fallen humanity: *"Without controversy, God does not love man out of Christ"*[14], by which token Christ should have hated the human beings He encountered in His ministry or else He is not His Father's Son. For veiled glory does not distort nature, and as we have already shown, contrary to many of the theological systems being critiqued, Scripture affirms Father and *incarnated* Son to be identically disposed towards humanity (Jn14:9 cp. Jer9:24).

But I return to Romans1:17, for it is the verse which prompted Luther's particular breakthrough in his understanding of justification by faith without reference to works: the Old Testament Scripture that Paul is quoting is Habakkuk 2:4 which should be examined in context:

See, the enemy is puffed up; his desires are not upright but the righteous person will live by his faithfulness (Hab2:4 New International Version)

I am not a Hebrew scholar and those who are do not agree on its translation, but the above is consistent with the context. To understand better what Habakkuk (and Paul) meant by the righteous "living by faith/faithfulness" we need to turn to Ezekiel:

If a wicked man turns from all the sins he has committed, keeps all My statutes and does what is lawful and right, he shall surely live; he shall not die. None of the transgressions that he had *committed will be remembered against him; because of the righteousness he has done he shall live… But when a righteous man turns away from his righteousness and commits iniquity and does according to all the abominations that the wicked man does, shall he live? All the righteousness which he has done shall not be remembered **because of the unfaithfulness** of which he is guilty and the sin which he has committed, because of them he shall die. (Ez18:21-24)*

Thus says the Lord (through Ezekiel); this is justification by faith as Paul understood it. Examine carefully: why does the man who was initially wicked come to live? – because he repents and does what is right. Why does he repent? – because he senses it is the right thing to do and will gain God's approval. What standard of righteousness must he acquire? – that is the wrong question; he is to be justified by exercising faith, not accumulating works. It is clearer still in the second case: the righteous man who turns to wickedness. Firstly, according to God's own assessment he used to be righteous (not perfect, righteous); then he turns to wickedness as a result of which he dies. Why does he die? – *because of his unfaithfulness* (v24). Standards are not the issue, faith or faithfulness is. Personal merit applies either way, so it is not a case of "acknowledging moral impotence and trusting in God's mercy". God's mercy is however involved, demonstrated by the fact that He recognizes human weakness and justifies a man through the exercise of his faithfulness in seeking to do what is right to please Him; not by achieving perfection or some arbitrary standard of obedience. This is God's mercy and grace in action as Paul understood it: it was **not a new concept** which is why he quoted from Habakkuk (Rom1:17), but for those who are to be justified within the new exclusive covenant ratified by Christ's blood, the new focus is Christ Himself and His law of liberty (James' "Royal Law") rather than Torah; *that* was the novelty.

References in the Old Testament to "uprightness" or people who are "righteous" are not referring to moral perfection but a life of integrity or "faithfulness". JHWE's verdict on His servant King David was that he had walked before Him in "innocence of heart and in honesty" (1Kg9:4). That is not moral perfection or

213

"imputed righteousness", but purity of heart that we considered earlier in the context of becoming like little children. In the account of Paul's ministry recorded in Acts, Lydia the purple-dyer (16:14) and numerous other Gentiles were recorded as God-fearing folk before they responded to the gospel (17:4). But many Protestant Bible translations (e.g. New International Version) choose to insert a comma at Rom1:18 where Paul is talking about God's retribution being revealed against men "," who suppress the truth by their wickedness and go on to be sexual perverts (v27), rotten, greedy, malicious, envious, murderous, treacherous, spiteful (v29), libellous, slanderous, God-haters, rude, arrogant, rebellious to parents (v30), brainless, loveless and pitiless (v31). Many translators make this out to be Paul's description of humanity by means of their punctuation (v18). The apostle is not here referring to all mankind or indeed all Gentiles, rather he is drawing and linking together various Old Testament scriptural texts which highlight a particular group's wickedness to set out a typically Jewish critique of the pagan world and the inevitable consequence of idolatry. He recognized that many Gentiles, though not possessing the Law, do by nature the things contained in it in response to their conscience (Rom2:14). The context of his tirade against ungodly Gentiles was the previous verse (17) that those who are righteous live by their faith whereas the ungodly do not, hence: *"We are sure that the judgement of God is in accordance with the truth against those **who commit such things**"* (Rom2:2).

He continues in the next two chapter of Romans to challenge the Jews who would go on to pass judgement on these Gentiles but who behave in a similar way yet take comfort in their heritage. He employs a similar method of critique, linking together passages from Scripture, in these instances where God's own people are being chastised. Take these excerpts from Romans3:10-18 – "not one (Jew) is upright, no not one (v10); not one of them does right, not a single one (v12); their feet are swift to shed blood (v15); there is no fear of God before their eyes (v18) etc. etc. What was the apostle intimating? – that no Jew ever feared God or ever did anything right? Of course he isn't, and likewise with his depiction of the Gentile nations in the previous chapter. It is a literary technique to adduce universal sinfulness, i.e. that all are under the reign of sin (Rom3:9); he is not intimating that it is in everyone's nature to act in the depraved manner described in these concatenated prophecies. It is those who as individuals suppress the truth God has revealed to them through their conscience who are to come under condemnation (1:18). The fact that references to "righteous" individuals in the Old Testament does not indicate perfection or "Christ's own righteousness being imputed" can also be demonstrated from verses such as –

*If a righteous person **turns from their righteousness** and does evil, they will die for it (Ezek33:18 New International Version).*

A "righteous person" as Scripture defines them can fall into sin and die for it; clearly therefore it is their earlier righteousness that was being referred to (also Ezek18:24). David, king and psalmist asked JHWE to "judge him as *his righteousness and integrity* deserve" (Ps7:8). That was his own righteousness: but in Psalm 32, probably penned after his grievous sin against Uriah to gain his wife Bathsheba, he says "*I confessed my offence to JHWE and He took away my guilt and forgave my sin*" (v5). For "*blessed is the man to whom JHWE **imputes no guilt** and in whose spirit is no deceit*" (v2). God forgave his sin, accepted him as righteous or vindicated him because he confessed it from a pure heart, although he was punished through the death of Bathsheba's son (2Sam12:14) which caused him great grief. That is the only sense in which "righteousness is imputed" (e.g. Rom4:11+22); it is not God's own Righteousness but His declaration that an individual or group are vindicated and accepted by Him, or in the formulation of the Psalmist God no longer imputes guilt to them for a specific offence. Had David not confessed such a mortal sin, his spirit would have been tainted; his guilt would have remained as would his broken communion with His Lord and the Spirit that he enjoyed as anointed king. Likewise, under the New Covenant forgiveness of a sin that leads to "death"; mortal sin as opposed to venial sin (1Jn5:16) requires the sacrament of reconciliation to restore "life", i.e. fellowship with the divine:

215

If we confess our sins He is faithful and just to forgive our sins and cleanse us from all unrighteousness (1Jn1:9 New King James Version).

That is not simply to acknowledge that one is a sinner but relates to the confession of a specific sin and making reparation for it as required (cf. Jn20:23).

The role of works in justification

I have covered this to an extent already but in view of it being at the heart of a longstanding error I shall review it again briefly, this time to show how Paul's assertions perfectly cohere with the teaching of James. The background to Paul's polemic against "deeds of the Law" in Galatians was that some Jewish converts to Christianity were insisting that Christians needed to be circumcised in accordance with Jewish Law to be justified or marked out as a Christian in God's sight. *"You foolish Galatians: Having begun in the spirit, are you to be made perfect by the flesh?* (Gal3:3) And again:

Did you receive the Spirit by works of the Law (i.e. circumcision etc.) or by the hearing of faith? (Gal3:2)

Those who complied with this false teaching, Paul declared, had "fallen from grace" (Gal5:4) for as he had preached to Jews and God-fearers at Antioch in just about the only reference to "justification" within the evangelistic preaching of the New Testament:

Through (Jesus), justification from all sins which the Law of Moses was unable to justify is being offered to every believer (Acts13:38b/39)

Often when Paul is referring to the Law, he is referring to the Torah, God's Covenant Charter for His people, for in Philippians3:6 he declares that in terms of righteousness based on the Law he was "faultless". He was not being ironic or saying he never sinned but claiming that he had perfectly observed all the physical requirements to be marked out as a Jew, such as circumcision, dietary restrictions and the like, that some Galatian converts were saying were essential for Christians to observe to be justified before God. No, said the apostle, we are justified by faith in Christ, not the works of the Law (Torah). If righteousness came through the Torah then Christ had died in vain (Gal2:21). The Jews also, he said, had approached the Law in the wrong way. It is not that they should not have personally striven to keep the Torah (God help us all, yet that is what many believe Paul to be saying), rather that they had sought to be regarded as righteous "as it were by works rather than faith" (Rom9:32), by which he meant they relied on "the deeds of the Law" – the fact they were circumcised and observed dietary and sacral regulations (cf. Gal4:9,10) to be marked out as the genuine children of Abraham and heirs to the Promise as opposed to being *circumcised of heart*, being those who deny the disordered desires of the body so as to serve God (cf. Col2:11). For the letter of the Law kills but the spirit (of the Law) brings life (2Cor3:6):

But now we are freed from the Law (Torah) that being dead wherein we were held that we should serve in newness of spirit and not the oldness of the letter (Rom7:6 King James Version)

The spirit of the Law focusses on love for our fellow man:

*For the **entire Law is fulfilled in keeping this one command** "Love your neighbour as yourself" (Gal5:14 New International Version; see also Rom13:8)*

This re-affirmed Jesus's teaching that at the heart of the Old Testament Law and Prophets was the inculcation of kindness and treating others as one would wish them to treat us; that is the Teacher's own summary of the Law and the prophets (cf. Mt7:12) with which Paul concurs. God's Law was something about which the psalmists frequently eulogised (especially Ps119, by far the longest) for true human living expressed in fear of God and concern for fellow man was at its heart. Paul's critique was never aimed at those Jews like King David who delighted in the Torah and had earnestly sought to keep it, but those individuals, especially leaders who were bogged down in the minutiae of rules, regulation and liturgy (and indeed had added to them), laying impossible burdens upon their fellows,

217

whilst entirely neglecting the weightier matters of social justice, mercy and love. Nevertheless, to keep the Law perfectly in letter and spirit was impossible for anyone and **had never been the basis of justification**. If acceptance before God were on such a basis, then the Law would indeed be something to fear and hate for it would condemn us all. The point that Paul wished to make in the context of the gospel was that the Torah had now become redundant for "i*n Christ Jesus neither circumcision nor non-circumcision avails anything but faith operating by love*" (Gal5:6 King James Version). But James makes it quite clear that works (or deeds) are relevant to (or referenced within) the process of justification, but unlike Paul, he is not referring to the outward requirements of the Law (Torah), but the practical outworking and evidence of formed faith:

How does it help, my brothers, when someone who has never done a single good act claims to have faith? (Ja2:14)

And again:

You believe in one God; that is creditable enough, but even the demons have the same belief, and they tremble with fear. Fool! – do you not realize that faith without works is useless? (vv19,20).

St James goes on to the give examples of how Abraham and Rahab the harlot were justified by their actions. He concludes:

You see now that it is by works and not only by believing that someone is justified (Ja2:24).

By that he means there needs to be a reference to works, i.e. to see that fruit is produced confirming the faith to be "formed"; it is not really the works themselves that justify but the faith from which they spring. The devils have a passive fiduciary faith (they believe God exists and Christ is His Son) but no fruit: they are not justified. James is not contradicting Paul, who was addressing the problem in the churches initiated by the Judaic exclusivists that Peter had also had to deal with in Jerusalem that were insisting that Christians be circumcised and keep Torah (Acts15:7-11). We know Paul is referring to the Torah when he speaks of the Law in this context from Galatians3:17, where he says that the Law was given 430 years after God's Covenant with Abraham. James would entirely agree with Paul that only perfection would suffice if justification were on the basis of perfect obedience to the Torah, and then it would no longer be by grace, it would be a wage (Rom4:4). Likewise, Paul would agree with James when he insisted that nobody can be justified without the good deeds that flow out from faith, showing that it is "formed". For deeds in the form of kindness and compassion are not merely the evidence of faith, *they are its efflux*. Expressed another way there cannot be love (*agape*) without formed faith being present, for love flows out from faith; they are effectively a part of the same (Gal5:6). James affirms with Paul, the Jewish Law has been replaced for the Christian by the Royal Law of "Love for neighbour" (Jam2:8), a law by which Christians are to be judged (v12). It is a law of the spirit rather than the letter and it is also written in the heart. Paul regarded himself as being outside the Law, yet at the same time under a law; that of Christ (1Cor9:21). Anyone who shows kindness to his "neighbour" is justified by faith within the Universal Covenant being a "doer of God's law" as both James and Paul have re-envisaged it (Rom13:9,10); and that applied to many Gentiles who did not have the Law (Torah) but are a law to themselves (Rom2:14) which they endeavour to obey, whereas as we shall see, some do not - chapter six.

Ubi caritas et amor, Deus ibi est

Wherever love and charity are to be found within human society, God is there. Love according to the blessed apostle is the fulfilment of the Law (Rom13:10 and Gal5:14), and of the three cardinal virtues being faith, hope and love, love is the best (1Cor13:13). In terms of the individual: where love is demonstrated "faith" is behind it, but it does not necessarily result in hope for the future; that requires an informed faith, being a definite creed. St John manages to summarise the essence of Christian theology and anthropology in a single verse:

Love is from God and everyone who loves is a child of God and knows God. Whoever fails to love is not of God because God is love (1Jn4:7b,8).

219

Love is the beating heart of Johannine *and* Pauline theology, i.e. *"agape"*, compassionate love: the essence of true humanity and the essence of God (cf. Jam5:11). But in terms of a creed, what right did these apostles have to re-envisage the Torah as being fulfilled by acting in the spirit rather than in the detailed observance of laws and ordinances? Every right now that Jesus had abolished in His flesh the enmity, the intimidating Law of commandments contained in ordinances (Eph2:15). For the righteous requirements of the Jewish Law are now fulfilled by those who no longer live to gratify the flesh but live in accordance with the dictates of their spirit (cf. Rom8:4) by which they are bound to exercise love and so fulfil James' "Royal Law": that is what it means to be spiritually rather than carnally minded. The "common law" revealed to all through the conscience within the spirit is intuitive; the Royal Law that the Christian is to live by is not opposed to reason but goes beyond it: "Love and respect those who deserve respect" is the instinct of the human spirit guided by the conscience; "love and pray for those who hate and despitefully use you" is the instinct of the Royal Law written in the heart of those whose spirit no longer contains merely a seed of truth to enlighten it but is fully in union with *Logos* (cf. 1Cor6:17; Jn1:1). The first response is acceptable human behaviour, the second is worthy of the saint. It was to be the Way for those who were expected to be the Kingdom people (i.e. the Jews), and that was the context of Jesus's teaching for most if not all His ministry. He had come to make complete or fill out the Law not to abolish it (Mt5:17 cf. Greek); for the Law says "Do not kill" but He says "Do not hate without a cause". The Law says "Do not commit adultery" but He says "Do not even lust after a woman in your mind". The Law made allowances for hardness of heart and permitted divorce (Mt19:8); Christ's law says the sons of the Kingdom can do better for the Spirit will write these new principles upon your heart and He will aid you. The Law had pertained to the letter; Christ's law pertains to the spirit and mind also. The Decalogue was filled out by the teaching of Christ; it was not "fulfilled" by proxy so as no longer to be a requirement for the Christian, for the doers of the law are finally to be justified, not the hearers (Rom2:13). Those who belong to Christ instinctively love God and their neighbour or they are none of His; they therefore ***do fulfil the law*** in spirit and in truth – "*the righteous requirement of the law being fulfilled in us who do not walk according to the flesh but according to the spirit*" (Rom8:4). Servants obey commands out of duty but those who have become the "friends of Christ" (Jn15:15) are acquainted with their Master's business and obey Him out of love. Such may be a new interpretation to many, but it is what it I have been shown and it works: the teaching of Jesus, Paul and the other apostles acquire perfect coherence once the re-interpretations and various linguistic ameliorations presented in this package are taken on board. How do I know that? – by reading the New Testament with reference to the Greek over and over again. I have subsequently found this perspective on Christ and the Law to be more in line with the teaching of the ante-Nicene Fathers through the additional verification process referred to in the introduction, most especially in the case of Irenaeus, who was hardly a maverick but a staunch defender of the catholic faith as it had been received from the apostles. He had personally come under the tutelage of Polycarp who in turn was an immediate disciple of the Apostle John. Not that the other ante-Nicene Fathers contradict my assertions in this area, but second century Irenaeus not only affirms Christ's aforementioned filling out of the Decalogue[15] but also the purpose and context of gospel salvation within a broader providence, natural law, free will, the primacy of the Roman See, the restoration of physical creation at the Parousia, a tripartite anthropology, the utilization of Enoch as an important reference source and the "Elijah" to come. These have been cross-referenced where they occur in the book. Irenaeus of course was but one man but note what he writes concerning the *uniformity of essential doctrine* in the second century Church:

The Church having received this preaching and this Faith although scattered throughout the whole world yet as if occupying one house carefully preserves it. She also believes these points of doctrine just as if she had one soul and one and the same heart and proclaims and teaches them and hands them down with perfect harmony as if she only possessed one mouth. For the churches which have been planted in Germany do not believe or hand down anything different, nor do those in Spain

221

or Gaul. . . But as the sun, that creature of God is one and the same throughout the whole world, so also the preaching of the Truth shines everywhere and enlightens all men that are willing to come to a knowledge of the truth.[16]

Such a depiction of doctrinal uniformity may be somewhat exaggerated, but equally it could not have been the case that the essential doctrines concerning the nature of faith and salvation could have uniformly be in error given that each of the churches he refers to could trace its origins just a few generations back to the apostles. They cannot all have interpreted Paul's teaching wrongly yet none of their surviving writings support the Reformers' distinctive teachings on faith, works and law or indeed the distinctive teachings of Augustine concerning one dimensional grace, the rejection of a positive role for natural law and the innate viciousness of humanity that the Reformers had drawn upon, some of which had become embedded in Catholic doctrine (e.g. regarding unbaptized children). It is not that all the second century churches will have agreed on the essentials through a sublimity of biblical exegesis, it is because a good number of these assemblies will have been founded and superintended by the great apostle to the Gentiles himself or his direct appointees. These leaders knew what Paul was talking about because they or their leaders *had heard him* and talked to him; they did not have to rely entirely upon his pastoral epistles that even his fellow apostle Peter observed were hard to understand and misunderstood by many (2Pet3:16). Of course, such an historical affirmation cannot be provided for all *my* assertions, for as Origen had observed, certain mysteries were left to be explored and resolved over the course of the Church's pilgrimage; but I say again that cannot apply to the means of obtaining eternal life through Jesus Christ which was made clear from the start and has always been adequately set forth within the Apostolic Church in East and West, at least in terms of the "how" (i.e. what is required for salvation), if not the "why" and "wherefore", such as the context of gospel salvation within broader providence and the nature of mankind's future participation with the Godhead.

Returning to the role of the Law, Jesus's reference to His filling it out has been partially confounded by the fact that contrary to earlier teaching (Mt5:18) given in the context of the Jewish nation inaugurating the Kingdom, Jesus went on to nullify the jot and tittle of the Torah by erasing and "taking out of the way" the written decrees through his death on the cross (Col2:14). In so doing He liberated His would-be followers, breaking down the barrier between Jew and Gentile in the process (Eph2:14). Physical circumcision and the legal particularities of Torah observance had been replaced by a spiritual law that is to be obeyed from a circumcised heart (cf. Rom2:29); one that delights in God and cares for neighbour. All Christians would claim to love God yet: "*No man has seen God at any time but if we **love one another**, God dwells in us and His love is perfected in us"* (1Jn4:12). So as John is indicating, genuine philanthropy is the test of godliness; less so the ability to eulogize concerning the God whom one thinks has shown one undeserved mercy; a devil would be inclined to do that if he mistakenly believed such had been granted him, yet he would retain a hateful and heartless perspective towards the rest of humanity, and thereby would we know him. Those who are from God instinctively demonstrate compassion and goodwill towards their fellow man, especially those in need (a.k.a. Jesus Christ - Mt25:40). Augustine believed such charity should be exercised "in serenity" rather than an emotional empathy. Those who are moved by compassion to help others he believed lacked wisdom. He concluded on the matter: "*There is no harm in the word 'compassionate' when there is no passion in the case*"[17]. I think not: it is noble enough for the individual to endure misery without complaint but those who remain unmoved by another's pain or distress are either evil or dead. Jesus Christ provided the pattern for genuine stoicism: silent resilience in the face of personal suffering and abuse; yet filled with heartfelt (literally bowel-felt) compassion (Greek: *esplanchnisthe*) towards others who were in need (Mt9:36, 14:14, 15:32). His Father's character even as it is revealed in the Old Testament reveals both passion and compassion; His nature that we are to emulate (Eph5:1) is thoroughly animated in the face of human wickedness, cruelty, injustice, lies and hypocrisy: He does not exhibit a placid, deistic indifference to these matters but is filled with righteous anger, as was often expressed through His prophets (e.g. Jer6:11). Yet equally He is compassionate towards those who fear Him and who suffer through the wickedness of others and has promised to punish the latter firmly and proportionately, recompensing the offended at the expense of the offender (cf. Is59:18). Some might imagine such passion and punishment to be inconsistent with perfect love; on the contrary it as an essential aspect to it. Godly wisdom (which can bear an uncanny resemblance to common sense) and those who have God's own heart will rightly discern these matters; for contrary to the teaching of the Reformers, Scripture positively encourages the use of human analogy and perspective when seeking to understand God's nature and the equitable way that He responds to us (Mt6:12 & 7:11, Lk11:5-8). Sound reason is not to be confused with worldly wisdom or rationalism ("if I don't see, sense or understand it I won't believe it"). The Christian can well discern these differences for he exercises faith, living according to Kingdom principles for eternal glory rather than worldly gain in the present. Luther would have profoundly disagreed with much of this; he further reinforced the epistemological duality of his monastic Patriarch Augustine perceiving God's Character to be entirely incomprehensible to human reason and His person quite remote: *We are here; God is there; we are this; God is that.* But the God of the Bible is "*the God who in Christ is reconciling all things to Himself, whether things on Earth or things in Heaven*" (2Cor5:18) and the Christian may add: "*we have the mind of Christ*" and "*Christ in me, the hope of glory*" - how remote is that? Apart from which, meaningful communion cannot take place where mutual love is not at its heart. Fear, awe and gratitude are insufficient; we need to understand the mind and heart of our Lover; and so we can, being one spirit with Christ (1Cor6:17). God may truly be loved because He is already intimate to us (as Christians) and it will be perceived that *God is good* even from a human perspective once some crooked theology has been straightened. Likewise, God will not just show mercy, but love and delight in the members of His human creation in whom the character of His Son is being formed. Such people need not be "hidden in Christ" or "robed in His righteousness", they themselves are to be like Him (1Jn3:2). Such authentic communion is the reason God created humanity in the first place, as well as to help administer His universal rule. As Christ Himself taught, those who come to love Him are loved by the Father for their *own* sake, not merely the sake of His Son (cf. Jn16:27).

The gift of justification

In terms of everyman's standing before God, the fact that *agape* love is needed in evidence does not detract from the fact that justification is a gift from God (Rom3:24), for all that is required to receive it has already been provided! In the universal case, it is the ability to love (1Jn4:7), with faith as its operant. Like the breath in his body, a young child possesses *agape* from birth and like that breath it flows out from his God-given spirit in the very process of being human as he bonds with his mother. So whether we were justified on the basis of human faith working through love or simply by the ability to breathe air it would be a free gift and nothing to boast about. At the exclusive covenant level regarding who is in Christ and who has yet to be reconciled to Him, the marker is faith and allegiance to Jesus indicated by incorporation within His Body through baptism. The instrumental cause of Christian justification (faith confirmed by baptism) could never be a cause for boasting; the meritorious cause certainly is (Gal6:14): that was the slow and agonising execution of the Son of Man as a sufficient atonement for the sins of the world. So acceptance within a covenant is unmerited, but co-operation and faithfulness are required to stay within it and continue to benefit from its blessings. In the words of a third century Father (Cyprian): "*It is a slight thing to have been able to attain anything; it is more to be able to keep what you have attained; even as faith itself and saving birth makes alive, not by being received **but by being preserved**; nor is it the actual attainment but the perfecting that keeps a man for God... hence 'Behold thou art made well, sin no more lest a worse thing come unto thee*[18]. Such has always been the catholic faith.

225

Abraham – Father of the first *elective* covenant

Just as Cain and Abel being the first siblings to be born of woman were representative players in the Universal Covenant, Ishmael and Isaac are such for the new embedded elective covenant established through Abraham. The difference here is that unlike Cain, Ishmael was not disqualified by his actions, he just wasn't selected in the first place, which of course cannot apply to the inclusive universal Covenant into which all are admitted but some later default. Ishmael had been circumcised by his father Abraham and blessed by God (Gen17:20) but Sarah's son Isaac was elected to inherit the promises given to his Father Abraham. However, God continued to relate favourably to Ishmael (Gen21:20). He was still accepted within the Universal Covenant of life as potentially were his descendants. Others outside or preceding the elective covenant specifically referred to as righteous in the Old Testament include Abel, Enoch, Noah, Lot, Melchizedek and Job. As for the Christian:

*You brethren, **like Isaac**, are children of promise (Gal4:28)*

And you sisters and brethren, if baptized, are in the elective covenant that replaced Abraham's and you are there by grace alone. Others like Ishmael are loved by God but not elected to that exclusive family predestined before the foundation of the world to form the community in which the education and spiritual resources are provided for individuals to become holy and faultless in love before God through Jesus Christ (cf. Eph1:4,5). That is the Church, priesthood for the world, brought forth by God's will to be His first-fruits for the created universe (cf. Jam1:18).

The postdiluvian blessing upon fallen humanity

All who came out of the ark to populate the world after the universal flood were blessed by JHWE (Gen9:1). Of the sixteen seeds and nations stemming from Noah's grandsons (Gen10), only the seed of the youngest son of Noah's youngest son was cursed for his father Ham's sake, and his name was Canaan (Gen9:25). His seed would go on to practice great wickedness

226

as they did in Sodom and Gomorrah and would become contaminated with the Anakim/Raphaim giants (e.g. Deut2:21, Num13:32-33), the offspring of unions between satanic beings and humans who occupied the Canaanite territories, a notable being Og, the Amorite King of Bashan famous for his oversized bed (Deut3:11). I don't remember him from my Sunday School days, but these are no more fairy stories than Noah and the Ark: they are scriptural and archaeological realities, referred to by some of the very earliest Church Fathers[19]. From these giants came the unclean spirits that roamed the world and were prevalent in Jesus's day. Again, the book of Enoch fills out much of the detail here for it pertains to the Gen6:1 incident concerning the fallen watchers. This polluted seed pool needed to be eliminated, which explains the wholesale extermination of men, women *and children* in seven of the Canaanite nations God's elect nation went on to inherit, although some of these demonic hybrids continued up to the time of David (e.g. 1Chron20:4-8 cf. Hebrew interlinear). At the other end of the spectrum, the children of Israel stemmed from Arpachshad being the firstborn of Noah's firstborn Shem. So for illustrative purposes (it is dangerous to extrapolate), one of the sixteen postdiluvian ancestral lines was cursed, stemming from the lastborn son (Canaan) of Ham who had exposed his father's nakedness, one was the elect patriarchal line stemming from the firstborn son of Noah's firstborn son leading down through a line of firstborns to Abraham; whilst the remaining 87.5% of Noah's grandsons (i.e. 14 of the 16 postdiluvian national patriarchs) retained the blessing imparted to Noah and his family on leaving the ark but were not the elective line of firstborns (Gen9:1). There is also a motif evident here pertaining to the firstborn being the line of special blessing. This can be traced back to Adam's son Seth; firstborn by default, his two elder brothers Cain and Abel having been respectively disqualified (reprobate) and murdered. Seth's firstborn was Enosh, the first to evoke the Lord (Gen4:26). The re-occurring phrase within these genealogies is in the format: "*When X was a certain age he fathered Y. X lived for so many years and went on to father (other) sons and daughters*", only the firstborn son ever being named (Gen5). After Enosh came Kenan, then Mahalalel, Jared,

227

Enoch who "walked with God", Methuselah who outlived his son Lamech, father of Noah, dying within a year of the Flood. There is no reason not to take the patriarch's ages literally, especially in view of Gen6:3. The same motif continues with the Church and her Head. The "Firstborn of all creation" is Jesus Christ (Col1:15); the firstborn of God's children are the elect, who collectively are described as "the Church of the firstborn ones" (Heb12:23 cf. Greek). Under the Old Covenant with Israel, the firstborn son was always consecrated unto the Lord (Ex13:2). The firstborn sons are typically designated to sanctity and kingship, and through them are the whole family blessed.

In terms of the New Covenant, Luke provides an account of how non-Jews were for the first time to be beneficiaries of the Covenant of Promise. This was revealed to St Peter through a vision and led to his meeting with the Gentile Roman centurion Cornelius (Acts10). He and his household were described in verse 2 as devout, God-fearing, generous and prayerful. It will be noted from verse 4 that this Gentile non-Christian's good works and prayers had been accepted by God. Cornelius was already participating in the cause of God's chosen people "giving generously to Jewish causes". The case of Cornelius is the clearest example in the New Testament of a non-Christian who feared God, acted in accordance with his conscience and was accepted in God's sight (Acts10:35). But he can hardly have been unique: Acts2:5 refers to the devout men living in Jerusalem from every nation under Heaven, who assembled on Pentecost, the Feast of the First-fruits, when the Holy Spirit descended on the disciples. In Paul's sermon to a mainly Jewish assembly at Antioch, he addresses them as follows:

*Men and brethren, sons of the family of Abraham, and **those among you who fear God; to you** the word of this salvation has been sent (Acts13:26).*

Of course, many pagan Gentiles came to believe in Him too, but the point being made is that Jesus and the apostles acknowledged that many who had not yet responded to the gospel were devout, decent and God-fearing, and if we if interpret Paul's teaching as indicating otherwise we are mistaken (also Acts17:4). The fact that God does not set humanly

228

unattainable standards of perfection but delights in human integrity and efforts to please Him was the starting point for the Book of Job as He addresses Satan, the arch-calumniator of human nature:

Did you pay any attention to my servant Job? There is none like him on the Earth: a sound and honest man who fears God and shuns evil (Job1:8)

Yet not all who come to Christ are God fearers, there are also many scoundrels; such was I and *"such were some of you, but you were washed, you were consecrated, you were justified in the name of the Lord Jesus and by the Spirit of our God"* (cf. 1Cor6:11). Some who practice wickedness God punishes by hardening their hearts all the more, whereas with others who appear to be hell-bent on self-destruction or like Saul of Tarsus before his conversion are misguided fanatics, the Lord may show mercy (Rom9:18); yet we may be assured that He would never harden the hearts of those who fear Him, for He loves them.

Conscience as an object of faith

I have referred to conscience a great deal for it is the eluded medium of effectual common grace and pertains to the spirit (also eluded). The Blessed John Henry Cardinal Newman, a nineteenth century Evangelical convert to Catholicism and humanly speaking the greatest influence in my own spiritual journey described the conscience as "the aboriginal vicar of Christ"[20], serving the natural law, which in the absence of a personal knowledge of Jesus Christ is, in Thomas Aquinas's words *"the impression of a Divine Light within us, a participation of the eternal law in the rational creature"*[21]. As such, conscience as the "universal revelation" of God, anterior to the Gospel and *"supreme over all other human faculties"* provides everyone with *"a clear and sufficient object of faith"* (Newman again)[22]; for faith is simply man's positive response to what has been revealed to him from God, be it innately through the conscience or religiously through a Creed. Through it one discerns the nature of right and wrong and senses a benefit in practicing the former to be at peace with oneself. Newman observed that "*the cardinal and distinguishing truth that conscience teaches is that God rewards the good and punishes the wayward*"[23]; again, a facet of faith as the Bible defines it (Heb11:6). Its very existence is the consequence of the fact that the human spirit has been created in God's image and enlightened by Christ. That is why the majority who have a working conscience experience a tension between their immaterial soul/spirit and the body in which it is temporarily housed which has a separate law or governing principle engrained within it (Rom7:23) being concupiscence. That vessel is drawn to worldly lust like a magnet for unlike the spirit it houses which is from God, it was conceived in sin and was "shaped in iniquity" (Ps51:5). But by habitually taking heed to the dictates of conscience, the soul/spirit is effectively relating positively to something, in fact Someone superior to itself; hence a man is regarded as exercising faith in God and so he is graciously justified through the merits of Christ's atonement.

Paul states that the conscience bears witness to God's moral law, which is engraved in our hearts (Rom 2:15 Greek). "*To obey conscience is the very dignity of man, and according to it he shall be judged*". So teaches the catholic faith[24]. The New Jerusalem Bible recommended for Catholic readers is one of the fewer translations that correctly conveys the meaning of this section of Paul's letter regarding the role of this faculty:

*When Gentiles, not having the Law, still through **their own innate sense** behave as the Law commands, even though they have no Law, they are a law **for themselves**. They can demonstrate the effect of the law engraved on their hearts, to which their own **conscience bears witness**; since they are aware of various considerations, some of which accuse them, while others provide them with a defence. (Rom2:14-16a New Jerusalem Bible).*

"*Heautois eisin nomos*" (v14) is literally "a law *to* themselves" but Paul does not mean this in the negative English colloquial sense of being lawless or doing things in one's own way. As is perfectly clear from the context he means that many Gentiles, not possessing and therefore not observing the Torah did by nature the things contained within it, such as care, concern and consideration for their fellow man. And so they become a law for themselves as the New Jerusalem Bible correctly relays and the Apostolic Fathers largely understood. That is the result of the divinely implanted faculty, which at any particular time we describe as being either clear, such that the individual can find no reason for self-reproach, or guilty in which the person feels a sense of self-condemnation and shame. However, in the category of people to be focused upon in chapter six, conscience has "withered away" (1Tim4:2) or become fatally corrupted (cf. Tit1:15) such that the person loses that most vital and noble part of their humanity, and with it any remaining interior semblance of the divine image. Such become absolute unbelievers and godless for the internal witness (seed) of Christ has departed from them; they effectively opt out of the human race, for love (*agape*) is definitive to being human as well as reflecting the image of God who is pure goodness, for He is *Agape* (1Jn4:8).

Self-respect - not pride

The sense of satisfaction a person may receive from doing the right thing is regarded by certain Christians as a sin in itself. On the contrary, it is how conscience functions in man, which is why Paul writes that he as a natural man was gratified (Greek: *sunedomai*) by the law in the inward man (Rom7:22). It is quite perverse for people like myself in the past to regard such a sense of self-worth as pride. It demonstrated a hyper-critical view of my fellow man and was in stark contrast to Jesus's perception of the matter as is reflected in his recorded teaching and dealings with humankind, where to those who can discern it He makes a very marked distinction in attitude and approach towards sinners in general and those He specifically describes as "children of the devil"; a term also utilized by the apostles John and Paul. The sense of peace and satisfaction a person may receive when acting in a humane way towards someone in need, far from being sin is a reciprocation of the divine faculty of conscience; for God delights in human acts of kindness and efforts to comply with the moral code He has engrained within man's spirit; He regards it as faith. Truly, if I had known what this meant: "*God*

231

delights in compassion and not sacrifice", I would not have condemned the guiltless (cf. Mt12:7). It is evident from the various English translations that some have misunderstood that verse to be referring to God's mercy towards sinners and His willingness to dispense it (e.g. Amplified Bible & King James Version). Most modern translations have rightly perceived the matter, for as is clearer from the context of Hosea 6:6 from which Jesus quotes He is here referring to God's delight in human philanthropy and the exercise of compassion towards others whereas He is less concerned with their religious activity. Of course, any who go around bragging about their kind deeds have had their reward for clearly the deeds were not primarily performed out of compassion but to impress others; that is not of faith but of the flesh. Most people would acknowledge in their heart and to anyone who enquires: "I simply did what I sensed I should do as a fellow human being". Such is the outworking of justifying faith in the context of the Universal Covenant.

The proportionality of divine punishment

Wherever in Scripture punishment for sin is quantified, it is typically specified at double the offence; a principle applied quite literally in the Law of Moses (e.g. Ex22:4,7,9). Likewise, in the Prophets, God's rebellious people pay double for their sins (Is40:2, Jer16:18) as at the universal level do the wicked (Jer17:18, Rev18:6). "Double" need not be taken literally but it is indicating that God's punishments are *proportionate* and therefore finite, for $nX \neq \infty$ (where n is the multiple and X is the offence). Eternity therefore could never be a function of proportionality; even so, applying such a principle it is no surprise that Jesus said of a few: "*it had been better for them if they had never been born*", especially those who through a total absence of "faith" have defaulted from the Universal Covenant and whose actions have brought untold misery to numerous lives. Such will pay a heavy price for their rebellion and for injuring those God loves.

Pauline anthropology and its moral outworking

The moral predicament for those outside the Church concerns their inherited disordered nature and the struggle the unaided human's spirit has in controlling it. The non-Christian's plight is best summed up by Paul in this passage in Romans, which I have amplified in brackets for it is at the heart of misunderstandings concerning the human condition:

For we know that the law (of God – implanted in the conscience) *is spiritual but I* (by nature and composition) *am of flesh sold into bondage of sin* (through Adam's disobedience). *For what I am doing I do not understand: for I am not practicing what I would like to do but I am doing the very thing I hate. But if I do the very thing I do not want to do, I agree with the law, confessing that the law is good, so now no longer am I the one doing it, but sin which dwells in me.. For I know that nothing good dwells in me,* **that is, in my flesh** *– for the willing (*to do good*) is present in me, but the doing of the good is not: for the good that I want I do not do; but I practice the very evil which I do not want. But if I am doing the very thing I do not want, I* (i.e. my soul/spirit the real me) *am no longer the one doing it, but sin that dwells in me. I find then the principle that evil is present in me (being) the one who* **wants to do good** (showing at heart I am a good person), *for I joyfully concur with the law of God in my inner man* (affirmed by my conscience and the peace I receive when I do what is right*), but I see a different law (*the triple concupiscence*) in the members of my body (*as processed through the brain*) waging war against the law in my mind* (i.e. the conscience – c.f. Rom2:15) *and making me a prisoner of the law of sin which is in my members. Wretched man that I am; who will set me from the body of* **this** *death? Thanks be to God (it is) through Jesus Christ our Lord! So then, on the one hand I myself with my mind am serving the law of God, but on the other, with my flesh the law of sin* (Rom7:14-25 New American Standard Bible with my highlighting and amplification in brackets)

This passage perfectly fits the model of anthropological dualism presented in chapter two through revelation, for it was previously quite alien to me, and if others have proposed it I am not aware of it, albeit we have shown that some of the earliest Fathers came to a similar view. Paul goes on in chapter 8 to confirm that the inability to practice what is right through enslavement to the opposing law of the "*somatos tou thanatou toutou*" is **not** the state of affairs for the Christian, who is enabled by the Holy Spirit so that he is "*not living in accordance with the flesh but in accordance with the spirit*" (Rom8:4 Greek). Apart from which, Paul says at the start of the passage the person he was depicting as himself was "in bondage to sin": he therefore cannot be referring to the Christian; this passage is not describing the Christian – it is man by nature. For -

*You (Christians) however live **not** by the flesh but by the spirit (or Spirit), since the Spirit of God has made a home in you (Rom8:9a)*

Clearly, the person the apostle depicts as himself in the passage is living by the flesh: he desires good but fails to practice it because he gives in to the lusts of the body (the flesh). That is not Paul the Christian or else he would be contradicting his own teaching. Of course, possessing the Holy Spirit demonstrably does not ensure that one never follows such desires or else no Christian would ever sin. The inward struggle continues for the Christian to control his bodily passions, but with the power of the Holy Spirit, he can keep them in check:

We have no obligation to the flesh to be dominated by it. If you do live in that way you shall die, but if by the spirit you put to death the habits originating in the body, you will have life (Rom8:12,13 New Jerusalem Bible).

The mortifying of the "worldly" habits originating in the body is further aided by the renewing of the Christian's mind, being enlightened by Christian teaching (providing that is sound), and the Christian's spirit is in mystical communion with Christ's spirit (1Cor6:17) so has the potential to over-ride the desire of the flesh and carry out what is pleasing to God:

*Be not conformed to this world, but be transformed by the **renewing of your mind**, that you may prove what is that good and perfect and acceptable will of God (Rom12:2 New Jerusalem Bible)*

This mystical union of spirits also affirms the tripartite nature of man, for whilst Christ can have intimate fellowship with our spirit He surely cannot become one with our "soul" or else we become as sinless as Christ, indeed we would become Christ. For the soul is what we are; it is what is being "saved to the uttermost" within the "tent" or "vessel" that is our temporary sin-prone body. In spite of that mystical union of spirits and the presence of the Holy Spirit the soul has to overcome the desires of the flesh. The non-Christian on the other hand does not have the "*grace of our Lord Jesus Christ aiding the human's spirit*" (Gal6:18) to help control the impulses of the flesh; nor the teaching of the Church and Scriptures to train his mind.

Those insistent on the Reformer's concept of "total depravity" or wishing to support Augustine's interpretation on which it was built will make a case that this passage from Romans 7 (or part of it) must be depicting Paul's inward struggle at or after his conversion for they would not accept that anyone who is not a Christian could desire what is good or wish to be in accordance with God's law. But every account of the Apostle's post-conversion life and ministry shows him to be a thoroughly spiritual man who declares himself to have "*lived in all good conscience before God up to this day*" (Acts23:1), someone whose behaviour set a pattern for his converts to imitate (1Cor4:16; 11:1). Speaking of himself and his fellow workers "***our exalting is in the testimony of our conscience*** *that in godly sincerity and purity, not in fleshly wisdom but in the grace of God we have conducted ourselves in the world*" (2Cor1:12). This is hardly the testimony of one who was still the "chief of sinners" that Evangelicals tend to latch on to (1Tim1:15); that had been in the context of what he had referred to two verses earlier concerning his pre-conversion attempt to rip apart the infant Church of Jesus Christ; that was in the past. He also described the Christians in the Roman churches to whom he was writing as "*full of goodness and filled with all knowledge*" (Rom15:14) whereas he described many of the Christians in the Corinthian churches as "fleshly" or "carnal" (1Cor3:3). It is the same Holy Spirit in Corinth as in Rome: the same Spirit, but different spirits and different mind-sets. It is therefore quite inadequate to regard the Church (as once did I) as an "assembly

235

of justified sinners"; there are many of these in the world thanks to the faithfulness of the One who died (yea, even for His enemies). The people consecrated to Him are intended to be like the Roman Church of Paul's day which we have just observed the apostle delight in: an assembly of those who had been and indeed would be sinners, but like the seed that fell on the good ground are noble of heart (Lk8:15), zealous for good works and bearing much fruit (cf. Tit2:14). They seek to imitate the Apostle Paul, who *"disciplined his body like an athlete, training it do what it should"* (1Cor9:27), whilst *"pressing towards the mark for the prize of the high calling of God in Christ Jesus"* (Phi3:14); endeavouring to attain to God. Such was the language and expectation for those chosen for Christ as expressed by the apostles *and their successors through the earliest centuries*; truly, a theology of glory.

No peacocks in Heaven

Some protest that the concept of co-operating with grace and earning a reward would have Christians "strutting around Heaven like peacocks". They simply do not grasp that this is not how holiness works, and only the holy will be rewarded in such a way. The saintly and Christ-like will indeed be ennobled; but being Christ-like means to be like Christ who was the antithesis of a strutting peacock; meek and lowly of heart. And *"when He is revealed, we shall be like Him"* (1Jn3:2). The divine quality of holiness is the moral cognate to love as Paul defines it in 1Cor13: *"Love does not parade itself and is not puffed up"* (v4). For example, if you have God's love in your heart and you see a lowly person or an animal in need, you are not inclined to strut around them with thoughts of superiority; you are filled with compassion to help them. Such meekness of spirit and genuine condescension is the nature of love (*agape*) and likewise the nature of holiness; these are the refined instincts of those who already partake of the divine nature. The holy also delight in honouring and submitting to those who are honoured above them, as was evident regarding Jesus towards His Father during His earthly ministry (My Father is greater than I - Jn14:28), and Prophet John with regard to the One he was heralding (He must

236

increase, I must decrease). Additionally, worldly pride arises in part from the disordered nature of our mortal vessel (the body of death). This is discarded at death and will be thoroughly renewed at resurrection. Those inclined to strut with pride have not received the imparted love of the Father; they are morally and spiritually deficient and will one day be recognized by all to be so.

The beauty of holiness

On the other hand, those who come to share Christ's nature and holiness are destined to shine forth as the sun in the Kingdom of their Father (Mt13:43). Once frail children of dust, through obedience to the gospel they will have drawn life from the Saviour (Jn6:57) and placed their necks under His yoke (Mt11:30) so that through self-disciplined obedience He might be formed in them. For God's healing plan for the world was to purify a special people who would be devoted to His Son and the pursuit of good works:

*For the grace of God has appeared **for the salvation of the human race** teaching us to deny ungodliness and worldly lusts to live sensibly, righteously and devoutly in the current age, anticipating the blessed hope and Shekinah of our Great God and the appearing of our Saviour Jesus Christ, who gave Himself for our sake so that we should be **delivered from lawlessness** and be purified as a **specially chosen people for Himself** burning with zeal to do good works. This is what you (Titus) are to say, rebuking with authority; let no man despise you (Titus2:11-15 from Greek)*

Note, such was what the apostle Paul had instructed Titus **to *say*** to the churches; it is worth keeping this in mind when we shortly consider how the Faith was passed on to the successors of the apostles. The purpose of the people chosen for Christ being devout and devoted to doing good, apart from their own salvation and eternal reward was to bring light and healing to the world that God loves and intends ultimately to reconcile to Himself. The scale of His restorative plans is reflected in Luke's description of Christ's second coming: "*Chronon*

237

apokatastaseos panton" - the time of the restoration of all things (Acts3:21), the precise nature and course of which Scripture has only very sketchily outlined, which we will now review briefly in the next chapter.

Notes: CHAPTER THREE

1. Louis Berkhov – Doctrine of soteriology (elements of faith 2a(1)) p503 Banner of Truth

2. Clement of Alexandria (A.D.153-217) The Stromata Book V chap. 1

3. in particular: Irenaeus against heresies Book IV chap. 13 (paras 1 and 2)

4. Polycarp – Epistle to Philippians chap. 2

5. Clement of Alexandria - Exhortation to the heathen chap. 10

6. The Epistles of Cyprian – Epistle 75 (14)

7. e.g. Ignatius (AD30-107) epistle to Philadelphians chap. 5

8. See Origen De Principiis Book II chap. 5 (3) re purpose of God's punishment for healing and correction

9. Origen de Principiis Book II chap. 10

10. Book of Enoch: R H Charles version utilized

11. The Jewish understanding of Hades or Sheol (wrongly translated "Hell" in some versions) was the place of the dead which was divided into various compartments for the wicked and righteous. According to Rev20:13-14 this is not a permanent arrangement.

12. e.g. Irenaeus against heresies Book IV chap. 37 para 1

13. Calvin: Institutes of the Christian Religion Second Book chap. 1 para 8

14. Ibid. Third Book chap. 2 para 32

15. in particular: Irenaeus against heresies Book IV chap. 13 (paras 1 and 2)

16. Irenaeus against heresies Book I chap. 10 para 2

17. Augustine – "On the morals of the Catholic Church" chap. 27

18. The Epistles of Cyprian – Epistle 6 (2)

19. e.g. Athenagorus (A.D. 177) A plea for the Christians chap. 24

20. John Henry Newman (Letter to Duke of Norfolk - 1875)

21. Thomas Aquinas (Gousset: Theol. Moral.,t.i. pp24 &c).

22. J H Newman "Grammar of Ascent" pp117-118

23. Ibid. pp390-391

24. Conscience: Gaudiam et Spes n.16.

Chapter Four

The Restoration of All Things

[*chronon apokatastaseos panton* - Acts3:21]

*For it pleased the Father that in (Christ) all the fullness should dwell, and by Him **to reconcile all things to Himself**, by Him, whether things on Earth or things in Heaven, having made peace by the blood of His cross (Col1:19,20 New King James Version)*

This much shorter chapter anticipates the time when the Kingdom of God, inaugurated through the Church is realized in the presence of the One *"whom Heaven must keep until the universal restoration comes which God proclaimed speaking through His holy prophets"* (Acts 3:21). As a result of the secret hidden in the Father concerning the reconstitution of God's people and the dispensation set apart to establish it, Paul confirms that it is the *next age* that is in a meaningful sense "the Kingdom of Christ" (2Tim4:1). In this age the implementation of Christ's reign on Earth is confined to His Church for only she acknowledges Him as Sovereign and observes His Royal Charter. Luke confirms that it is at Christ's coming that the restoration promised to Israel by the Old Testament prophets truly comes about in the world (Acts3:21). Paul speaks again of this consummation in Ephesians:

God made known to us the mystery of His will, according to His kind intention which He purposed in Him with a view to an administration suitable to the fullness of times; the summing up

241

of all things into Christ, things in the heavens and things on the Earth – in Him (Eph1:9,10)

Reference to the Greek Interlinear Bible clarifies that Paul is envisaging an administration that Christ will be heading-up or gathering together into one (*anakephalaiosasthai oikonomian*). As the New International Version and New Jerusalem Bible have appreciated, verse 10 is saying that at the end of this age *all things* (not "all things in Christ") are to be placed under Christ's Headship. Paul refers again to this concept of final restoration in his letter to the Church at Rome, placing it in the context of their current predicament; not just for the Christian but the whole of creation:

*For I consider that the sufferings of this present time are not worthy to be compared to the **glory that will be revealed in us**. For the earnest expectation of the creation eagerly waits for the revealing of the sons of God (huion tou theou). For the creation was subjected to futility; not willingly **but because of Him who subjected it** in hope (that) the creation itself will be delivered from the bondage of corruption into the glorious liberty of the children of God (teknon tou theou). For we know that the whole creation groans and labours in birth-pangs. Not only (they) but **we also who have the first-fruits of the Spirit**, even we ourselves groan within ourselves, eagerly waiting for the adoption, the redemption of our body (Rom8:19-23 New King James Version).*

This passage is prone to mistranslation for it does not fit either traditional Catholic or Reformed apocalyptic expectations whereas the major theologian of the second century (Irenaeus) who will have been acquainted with the immediate successors of the Apostles well understood the matter: "*It is fitting therefore that the creation itself, being restored to its primeval condition should without restraint be **under the dominion of the righteous**, and the apostle has made this plain in the epistle to the Romans when he thus speaks: 'For the expectation of the creature awaits the manifestation of the sons of God'*[1] . With the notable exceptions of the King James Version and New King James Version, there is also a reluctance to translate "*huion tou theou*" as "sons of God" in verse 19. Paul and Jesus as recorded by Matthew (5:9) alone use the expression "sons of God" to refer to elect humans. As can be seen above, the apostle refers to "sons" (*huioi*) and "children" (*tekna*)" within the one cohesive passage implying two distinct groups. The "sons of God" (angelic and human) will be revealed to creation who in turn will receive liberation as children of God. "Sons of God" intentionally has regal overtones. Christians are certainly numbered amongst God's children – the Spirit confirms it with their spirits (v16); the *sons* of God are those being led by the Spirit of God (v14) who share in Christ's sufferings and will share His glory (v17).

This is the greater of the two restorations I referred to earlier, the lesser being the restoration of Christendom to prepare for it. Then shall the whole Earth be seen to be full of God's glory (Is6:3) and the outcomes depicted in Old Testament prophecies will at last have been fulfilled. Here is an example of such a prophecy from the Book of Isaiah that, like all other Old Testament prophecy, bi-passes the inauguration of the Kingdom through the Church and envisages the joyful events of its fulfilment, which align with Paul's depiction in Romans when *"the whole of creation is brought into the same glorious freedom as the children of God* (Rom8:21): Highlighting will be explained below

And there shall come forth a Rod from the stem of Jesse

And a Branch shall grow out of his roots.

The Spirit of the Lord shall rest upon Him,

The spirit of wisdom and understanding

The spirit of counsel and might

The spirit of knowledge and the fear of the Lord.

His delight is in the fear of the Lord

And He shall not judge by the sight of His eyes,

Nor decide by the hearing of His ears;

But with righteousness He shall judge the poor,

And decide with equity for the meek of the Earth

He shall strike the Earth with the rod of His mouth,

*And with the breath of His lips **He shall slay the wicked***

Righteousness shall be the belt of His loins,

And faithfulness the belt of His waist.

The wolf shall also dwell with the lamb,

The leopard shall lie down with the young goat

The calf and the young lion and fatling together;

And a little child shall lead them.

The cow and the bear shall graze;

Their young ones shall lie down together,

And the lion shall eat straw like the ox.

The nursing child shall play by the cobra's hole

And the weaned child shall put his hand in the viper's den.

They shall not hurt or destroy in all My holy mountain,

*For the **Earth shall be full of the knowledge of the Lord***

As the waters cover the sea (Is11:1-9 New King James Version).

I have highlighted the aspects of this prophetic revelation that are especially relevant to the subject of this chapter. In summary:

i) The Man appointed to judge humanity is meek and lowly of heart (Mt11:29). He will apply the standards He indicated during His earthly ministry, which will be understood to be reasonable from a human perspective (cf. Mt7:2);

ii)The gospel of the Kingdom is Good News both for the poor in spirit (the contrite ones) (Mt5:3 reflecting Is66:2) and those who are materially poor (Lk4:18, Lk6:20 reflecting Is61:1). The account of the respective fates in Hades of the rich man and Lazarus confirms the redistributive aspect of judgement in favour of those who have suffered poverty and hardship in this life (Lk16:25) with whom the Saviour and Judge has always personally identified (Mt25) and towards whom He will be especially merciful;

iii)The wicked as defined in my chapter six will have no positive role in the new order and will be physically removed from Earth. *"These shall incur punishment of age-long wholesale ruin from the face of the Lord and the glory of His strength"* (2Thes1:8,9 cf. Greek)

iv)The faithfulness of Christ (*pisteos Iesou Christou)*, in particular His atoning death for sin will have been the primary means by which humanity is able to benefit from the restoration;

v)The restoration will be as much physical as it is spiritual incorporating both a renewed Heaven and a renewed Earth; humanity reconciled to itself and God; the animal Kingdom at peace with itself and benign towards man as its caring overseer.

Jewish expectation of the restoration

God's first choice people will have understood from prophecies like this that a divinely appointed king would come effectively to restore the Davidic dynasty, ushering in a time of peace, justice and security, which would naturally be focused around the race of Israel. What they will not have expected, even though His death could be understood retrospectively as being foretold in the Fourth Song of the Servant (Isaiah53) is that their longed-for messiah would be executed, resurrected and returned to Heaven leaving the Jewish nation still under the control of its political oppressors. Our Jewish fathers in the faith would quite reasonably have expected the political aspects of prophecy to have been fulfilled for after all *it is what their Scripture and ours affirms*. Even the preacher of righteousness who was sent by God to "prepare the way of the Lord", having himself been placed in prison became disillusioned or confused enough to ask:

Are you the coming one or do we look for another? (Lk7:20)

Jesus's reply to John's disciples who had visited his prison raises more interesting points and throws further light on the present and future context of what Matthew calls "*basilean ton*

245

ouranon" – the reign or kingdom of the heavens; whilst Luke and Mark, referring to precisely the same concept use "*basileain tou theou*" – the reign or kingdom of God:

So He replied to the messengers, go back and tell John what you have seen and heard: The blind receive sight, the lame walk, those who have leprosy are cleansed, the deaf hear, the dead are raised, and the Good News is proclaimed to the poor (Lk7:22 New International Version)

From this, the imprisoned prophet was meant to understand that the Kingdom of God/Heaven was in the process of initiation. It is clear from Jesus's response and indeed from His ministry that this Kingdom was not exclusively about the saving of souls but also physical healing and social justice; in other words a healing of the whole person and entire society. Symbolically at least, it represented the overthrow of Satan, the one responsible for leading the world astray (Rev12:9) as well as being responsible for physical sickness (e.g. Lk13:16, 2Cor12:7) and more mysteriously, the one who holds (i.e. has been granted) the power of death (Heb2:14.) and harnesses the souls of the wicked (cf. Mt13:39, 15:13). So until Satan is placed out of harm's way, God's Kingdom would not be fully realized.

More specifically Jesus had told John's messengers: "*the blind receive sight, lepers are cleansed, the deaf hear, the dead are being raised and the Good News is preached to the poor*". This was evidence that the Kingdom of God was underway: this is what it would be like when Israel's God came to reign on Earth (cf. Isaiah 52:7): the healing of souls for sure, but also the healing of bodies, the whole society and ultimately the whole world. But that is clearly not how it has panned out. The miraculous healing activity has not really been in evidence since the end of the apostolic age. The fate of "the chief of this world order" was indeed sealed on the cross (cf. Jn12:31) but the fulfilment of his demise was deferred, for he still deceives its people such that they are more inclined to worship Mammon than JHWE (Eph2:2 cf. Jn12:31; 1Pet5:8; Jam4:7). The nature of the Kingdom is further clarified, though not for some, by a statement of our Lord, which I have quoted using Young's Literal Translation:

And from the days of John the Baptist till now, the reign of the
heavens doth suffer violence, and violent men do take it by force
(Mt11:12)

Contrary to the understanding of one Reformed commentator on
the Bible-gateway, "violent men taking the Kingdom by force"
is not intended to be positive. It is not speaking of those
"violently apprehended by a sense of their lost estate" or
"violently in love with Jesus" (so, John Gill). Jesus was referring
to what John Baptist had earlier had to contend with when he
was less than over-welcoming towards some who had come to
him for baptism:

Brood of vipers! Who taught you to flee from the wrath to come?
Bear fruits worthy of repentance! (Mt3:7b-8a).

These were some of the Sadducees and Pharisees who had come
to be baptized in the name of the coming Messiah, believing it
would as the prophet said, give them final immunity from the
punishment they deserved. Also envisaging that a new Kingdom
was to be established and seeing themselves as top dogs within
the current arrangement they will have wanted a piece of the
action. The Jews had expected the Old Testament prophecies to
be fulfilled through an administration to be established by God's
anointed one (not necessarily a deity), and that he would
physically stay at the helm whilst these glorious predictions were
realized. The Jews' mission was to be a light to the nations. N T
Wright has made the observation that the long awaited Kingdom
did "*not look like Jesus's contemporaries had imagined… it*
would not endorse their particular agendas"[2] But to be fair to
Jesus's contemporaries, all OT prophecy had consistently
assured God's chosen race that their universal salvific mission
would not be achieved without divine intervention. Professor
Wright proposes that the surprising turn of events (regarding the
apparent subversion of Old Testament prophecy) was in view of
Israel's faithlessness in her role as the means of bringing
salvation to the world, and that that role was instead being
fulfilled by the one true and faithful Israelite Jesus[3]. Of course,
Israel's infidelity and failed mission is beyond dispute but that
was a part of the prophecies that were being subverted! For
Israel had just been assured that "*her warfare has now ended,*

247

*her iniquity had been pardoned; she had **already received**
double for all her sins"* (cf. Is40:2-5 King James Version). You
will note that that was in the context of the coming "Elijah"
(John the Baptist) who would *"bring back many of the Israelites
to the Lord their God; reconcile fathers to their children and the
disobedient to the good sense of the upright, preparing for the
Lord a people fit for Him* (Lk1:16-17)." What lay behind the
prophetic displacement was not the thoroughly anticipated failed
historical mission of Israel for which we have just seen she had
paid the price and been forgiven, but what Jesus came to refer to
as "this faithless and perverse generation": the generation of the
Baptist, Jesus and the apostles, who even after His ascension to
glory rejected the apostolic witness to His Kingship (cf.
Acts13:46). It was not that Jesus Himself was fulfilling the
mission of Israel as the "true faithful Israelite" (although He was
that and much more); the prophecies had been subverted by the
fact that the Church had been formed to replace Israel as
priesthood for the world (1Pet2:9). Jesus Himself superseded
the Temple and the Mosaic Covenant to provide a new and
living way by which those who were now to make up "His
peculiar people" could be spiritually united with Him and
sanctified to serve as kings and priests within that Kingdom. He
had become the surety of a better covenant (Heb7:22) with the
Torah being replaced by the Royal Law of love for neighbour
(Jam2:8) written on tablets of flesh in the believer's heart
(2Cor3:3); whilst the blood of bulls and goats had been replaced
sacramentally by something far more precious to be appointed
for sprinkling (Heb12:24 cf. Greek), which not only remits sin
and pardons but has power *to cleanse the conscience from dead
works to serve the living God* (Heb9:14). That was the Good
News, but there was also a downside. In terms of where we
currently are within the restructured metanarrative we must be
content with what theologians refer to as:

An inaugurated eschatology

The cleansing, restoring and reconciling of creation depicted in
the eleventh chapter of Isaiah's prophecy featured above is *not
to be realized* within the dispensation that immediately succeeds

it. The Kingdom of God is arriving in two stages; the rolling together of eschatological events having been both re-ordered and re-structured. According to Isaiah, when the promised redeemer arrived, the wicked were to be dealt with (i.e. got rid of); the remaining people are chastened but brought to peace with their God and each other, the animal Kingdom is tamed and at peace with itself and us, and God's Holy Mountain, generally taken to refer to Jerusalem, is safe and secure under its divine Head. Moreover, the whole Earth is filled with the knowledge of God for the Lord would have become King of the world. Zechariah concurred:

*When that day comes, living waters will issue from Jerusalem, half towards the eastern sea half towards the western sea; they will flow summer and winter. Then **JHWE will become king of the whole world**. (Zec14:8-9a New Jerusalem Bible)*

That is Biblical eschatology realized and it corresponds in scope and shape to Paul's eschatological expectations set out in Romans 8:21-25. But, of course, they relate to what is to be established after Christ's return, not in the current age. Christ is presently represented by His mystical Body, and not yet as royal Consort but suffering Servant (like Israel). She endeavours to establish Kingdom principles whilst preparing herself and the rest of creation for the coming of Her King and theirs, who is also the Judge of all. But not until Jesus Christ commands His angels to bind the prince who continues to have power over sickness and death, destroys his power-base and removes his agents (Mt13:49) will the universal restoration be realized. The eradication of the wicked cannot be subsumed within the current mission of the Church, it has been postponed (cf. 2Thes1:8). The world, the Church and especially God's beloved nation of Israel must continue to wait patiently, for what has been subverted for the greater good has not been forgotten (cf. Rom11:15). Such is the "inaugurated but yet to be realized" nature of the Kingdom of God as we currently experience it. It *is* inaugurated being present in mystery through the Church, intended to function as a Counter-Kingdom. For acknowledging Christ as her Sovereign Head and observing His Charter, she is to exercise authority quite differently from the kingdoms of this

249

world both in terms of her self-governance and outreach. For just as Jesus's Kingdom was not of this world; likewise, the Church's dominion is not derived from this world order *or else her servants would crusade through the world and seek to convert it by force* (cf. Jn18:36).

Everyone incorporated within the Church through baptism can be said in a sense to be "in the Kingdom of God". Yet Paul had warned Christian disciples at Derbe, *"we must all experience many hardships before we enter the Kingdom of God"* (Acts14:22); and as Jesus indicated, it is easier for a camel to go through the eye of a needle than for a rich man to enter it. He also told His would-be disciples **carefully to evaluate the cost of discipleship**, like someone intending to build a tower or a king about to go to war (Lk14:28-33). That could hardly be referring to obtaining Church membership, receiving a sacrament or making a profession of faith; rather it is the assessment to be made by those who are to enter pilgrimage as a learner of the Christ. Such who are called, chosen and remain faithful will be fitted for Kingdom service in eternal partnership with the One before Whom every knee must bow, whether on Earth or in the heavens or under the Earth (Phil2:10) when He is shortly revealed as Lord of all. That would be the context of the resurrection and imperishable crown for which Paul strove and disciplined his body like an athlete so as not to be disqualified (1Cor9:24-27). It would be achieved through personal self-discipline aided by grace, but hardly "grace alone" - *"**Strive** to enter (the Kingdom of God) by the narrow gate, for many I say to you will seek to enter and will not be able"* says Jesus. The irony is that those who take up the challenge of the gospel and in Paul's words, *"aim for glory and honour and immortality by persevering in good works so as to obtain eternal life"* (Rom2:7) will find that as they take the Master's yoke upon them and learn from Him, He is gentle and lowly of heart, and they will find rest for their souls (cf. Mt11:29), whilst at the same time being fitted for glory.

This chapter has been distinctly short for Scripture does not detail precisely *how* Christ will restore all things or the exact nature of His people's involvement in it; only that it will be set in motion at His coming. Those who prophesy must do so according to the measure of faith (Rom12:6) so I claim to know nothing beyond what Scripture has at least implicitly indicated. It is not necessary to know more detail at this stage and as I explain elsewhere such would compromise the role of faith. What does become essential is a united understanding of the Good News message (the gospel) within the churches so that a suitably *unified witness* can be provided to the world. To achieve that will be anything but a painless process, as indeed will be the case at the regeneration of creation that shall follow it - the great and dreadful Day of the Lord (Mal4:5)[4].

Notes: CHAPTER FOUR

1. Irenaeus against heresies Book V chaps. 32,33 para1 and chap. 36 para 3; and with regard to the restoration of the animal Kingdom chap. 33 para 3

2. "What St Paul really said": NT Wright chap. 10 Lion p179

3. Ibid: chap. 6 Lion p106

4. I utilize Protestant Bible chapter and verse referencing where these occasionally differ from Catholic editions, usually in the Minor Prophets. This excerpt is referenced as Mal 3:23-24 in the New Jerusalem Bible for example.

Chapter Five

Progressive Revelation

[with particular reference to God's restorative plans for creation]

The chapter subheading might be regarded as the Bible's "dark matter"; yet not in any sinister sense, quite the contrary. In cosmology that term refers to mysterious mass that scientist hypothesize must exist, being inferred by its gravitational effects on visible matter. Yet it cannot be observed through telescope or through radiological measurement even though it is believed to constitute around 85% of the total matter in the universe. Unless and until this phenomenon is understood, then neither will the origins and workings of what is more clearly detectable within the universe be settled. Likewise, with Scripture: the "visible matter" is not the totality of God's plan for His creation but concerns His stratagem for the reconciliation of the world to Himself and the key structures and players within that plan. The fuller picture is alluded to in Scripture but only matters directly relating to the key human agencies involved within the reconciliation (Israel and the Church) have been illuminated. Yet until quite recently that sub-plot has been mistaken for the whole salvation story. That has distorted an understanding of the whole (divine providence) whilst not preventing the salvific recruitment and enlightenment operation within it proceeding according to plan. *For God did not send His Son into the world to condemn the world but that through Him the world might be healed* (cf. Jn3:17). The whole matter has been in accordance with God's stratagem for the Church and the world, being "progressive revelation".

Natural law – the dark matter of Scripture

Given the divine intimation that all humanity was ultimately to be restored and come to understand the truth (1Tim2:4), it was necessary, especially following the breakdown in relationship between man and his Maker depicted in the Eden incident that man be given some awareness of the Creator, how he should relate to his fellows and manage the creative order set under him. This was to be by means of natural law, a concept referred to indirectly by St Paul and accepted to a substantial degree by the Catholic Church, particularly through the influence of thirteenth century Thomas Aquinas and his formulations on the primary and secondary precepts of natural law, and nineteenth century John Henry Newman's reflections on universal revelation and the role of conscience, the latter having a substantial impact on the Second Vatican Council's articulation of broader benign providence in the 1960s. Many Evangelicals on the other hand will be turned off if not positively repulsed by the concept of "natural law" playing any part in human salvation. Yet the description is something of a misnomer for it pertains to *divinely provided* precepts within man that enable him, even in his fallen state, to discern good from evil and endeavour to choose the former for his own well-being and everyone else's. Yet it is more than that for it pertains to what is spiritual, even the essence of Christ Himself, and I have come to understand can be directly associated with His atoning death; since that avails at the forensic level for all who respond positively or "faithfully" to such precepts (for not all do - next chapter). It provides an object of faith, independent of special revelation through a religious creed, for God foreknew that the Christian message would become confused and distorted, indeed entirely obscured for many through historical cultural and religious formation. Natural law is not unconnected to Christ himself, involving as it does an underlying faith in *Logos* (cf. Jn1:9 King James Version) by which little children can do no other than "believe" in the Saviour (Mt18:6 – note the context in verse 2: it is *not* referring to His disciples). All this should not be so surprising given that *all things*, not least the precious human soul, were created by the pre-incarnate Christ *as Logos, through* Him and *for* Him (Col 1:16). Amongst the earliest Church

254

Fathers such as Justin Martyr and Clement of Alexandria, natural law was likewise expressed in terms of the divine *Logos* (Word) whom they recognized had provided every age, race and each individual with seeds of divine truth – the "*Logos spermatikos*" so as to lead everyone to some knowledge of God and His law, however fragmentary; indeed Origen also regarded the seed of reason provided to all men equipping them with a degree of wisdom and a sense of justice as the essence of "Christ", as did Justin Martyr[1] , and as we have just indicated did the incarnated Word Himself. Those, Justin believed, who entirely disregard the internal light of Christ and "do not conform to right reason" would be punished in fire at their death[2]. From such a perspective Christianity does not supersede natural law but rather builds on it. Even pagan literature, philosophy and mythology contain wisdom that could be regarded as a preparation for the gospel, and that is exactly how St Paul utilized it. He drew upon a Greek poet Epimenides and a Greek philosopher Aratus in his sermon in Athens (Acts17:28 below), but firstly in addressing a pagan audience in Lycaonia, the apostle states:

We have come with Good News to make you turn from these empty idols to the living God who made sky and the earth and the sea and all that these hold. In the past He allowed all the nations to go their own way; but even then He did not leave you without evidence of Himself in the good things He does for you: He sends rain from Heaven and seasons of fruitfulness; He fills you with food and your hearts with merriment. (Acts14:15-17 New Jerusalem Bible)

So unlike His chosen people of the Old Testament whose inexcusable idolatry was not tolerated and was punished severely, God permitted primitive people to "go their own way" in terms of their search for God, hoping as Paul said that they would recognize the **goodness of His nature** through the natural provisions made for them. According to the apostle's natural theology, God expected primitive man to grope after Him and find Him to an extent:

And He has made from one blood, every nation of men to dwell upon the Earth, and has determined their pre-appointed times

255

and the boundaries of their dwelling so that they should seek the
Lord in the hope that they might grope for Him and find Him,
though He is not far from each one of us, for in Him we move
and have our being; as also some of your poets have said, "For
we are also His offspring" (Acts17:26-28 New King James
Version)

This was in response to the Athenian pagans setting up an altar
inscribed "To the unknown God". Paul concluded his message:

Truly these times of this ignorance God overlooked but now
commands all men everywhere to repent (Acts17:30 New King
James Version)

We see how God had overlooked or given the wink (King James
Version) to primitive man's idolatry. Paul affirms that God had
been willing to tolerate past sins; He was not as it were bound to
Himself to punish them, and that was in part due to His Son's
atonement for the totality of human sin in the middle of history
(Rom3:25,26). Contrast this with how the Lord dealt with His
own people Israel:

You alone have I intimately known of the families of the Earth.
That is why I shall punish you for all your wrong-doings
(Amos3:2 New Jerusalem Bible)

Christians must surely take note: "*You are my chosen people:*
that is why I will punish you for your wrong doing". For when it
comes to judgement, God has no favourites; on the contrary He
has always made generous allowance for the unenlightened
(Acts17:30) but expects a higher standard from those who have
been privileged to be acquainted with His decrees and have a
personal knowledge of His Son; for such have been given
inestimable privileges, resources and opportunities for a glorious
inheritance. *How shall we possibly escape if we neglect so great*
a salvation? (cf. Heb2:3). *How much worse a punishment will*
those deserve who have trodden underfoot the Son of God and
have counted the blood of the covenant by which he is sanctified
as a common thing and so outraged the Spirit of grace?
(Heb10:29). For the Lord shall judge His people (v30 – *not*
"vindicate" them e.g. Catholic New Jerusalem Bible). As for the
rest, He has not left them entirely in the dark; so the irreligious

are neither entirely without excuse nor indeed hope. Yet it is not only pagans who sometimes need to be reminded how good and gracious JHWE is to all; His own servant Jonah the prophet longed for wicked Nineveh's destruction. JHWE rebuked Him:

Why should I (JHWE) not be concerned for Nineveh, the great city, in which are more than 120,000 people who **cannot tell their right hand from their left, to say nothing of all the animals** *(Jon4:11 New Jerusalem Bible)*

"I knew this would happen", complained the prophet after the city had been spared; "I knew you were a tender, compassionate God, slow to anger rich in faithful love, who relents about inflicting disaster. I'm so miserable I just want to die" (cf. Jon4:2,3). This man should have been a theologian, but to be fair the latter have an excuse, it is called Holy Scripture. That is especially cryptic concerning God's wider providence (the dark matter) as a result of which the Catholic Church, having been set back centuries in this regard particularly by the theology of the fearsome Augustine, has only very recently come to apprehend or at least articulate the length, breadth and height of divine magnanimity, whilst many other Bible believing Christians do not perceive the matter at all, still confident and strident in their assertion that those not elected to Christian salvation are to be damned. The really good news (God's hidden purpose and context of the Church) would appear to have been saved for last. Such is the procession of progressive revelation regarding providence, but it has also applied to an understanding of the nature of the inheritance of the elect which has been obscured and overly spiritualized in part through the influence of Neoplatonism:

(May God) give unto you the spirit of wisdom and revelation in the knowledge of Him; the eyes of your understanding being enlightened that you may know what is the hope of His calling and **what are the riches of the glory of His inheritance in the saints** *(Eph1:17,18 King James Version)*

257

The Father of lights

As well as the light of reason and conscience, the loving Creator also works through His Holy Spirit in the gifts and talents He provides to mankind, for *"every good gift and every perfect gift is from above and comes down from the Father of lights* (Ja1:17). These gifts are not all religious in nature. The Father of lights can reveal something of Himself and His benign providence in music, art, poetry and many aspects of human endeavour; for our weakened, currently fragmented Church cannot be relied upon to shed light into every community or nation – our Lord utilizes other methods. Any great artistic creation or composition that inspires or elevates the mind is likely to have been the result of its human creator being themselves "inspired". So anyone who genuinely admires and appreciates such work is honouring and welcoming something of God into his heart; for everything that is truly worthy, every good and perfect gift has derived from Him. In modern society, any play, book or television drama that challenges people's prejudices and encourages a more considered, open-minded or compassionate way of life is a preparation for the gospel. Even gifted comedians bring sunshine to brighten the tedium and drudgery that can be a substantial part of many people's lives. And it was God, not the devil who provided wine to gladden the hearts of men (Ps104:15) for as we have just observed St Paul affirm, our loving Creator wishes His human creation to be happy (Acts14:16-17); holy too if possible for only then can we know true happiness. Any artistic outpouring that creates a sense of longing and wonder that people would not otherwise experience helps to create the void which ultimately can only be filled by God Himself. Science and learning are also gifts from the God who would not only have all men to be saved (healed and restored) but come to know the truth (1Tim2:4). The prowess and self-discipline of the top sportsperson as well as being admirable in itself is also analogous to gospel salvation, certainly as St Paul perceived the matter:

*I press towards the mark **for the prize** of the high calling of God in Christ Jesus. Let us therefore, as many as be perfect be thus minded (Phi3:14:15)*   And:-

258

*I discipline my body **like an athlete**, training it do what it should. Otherwise I fear that after preaching to others, I myself might be disqualified (1Cor9:27)*

At the natural level of revelation, something of God's providence and power are seen in the magnificence of creation and in the more wholesome aspects of human talent and industry described above, to which much could be added. The Christian is assuredly not to "despise everything that is sensible" (i.e. pertaining to the senses) as Augustine had asserted[3]. These are gifts from the Father of lights to humanity to be appreciated and cultivated; for sure, not to be embraced as if they themselves were the culmination of beauty or joy, for such apotheosis is to be discerned through them not in them.

Special revelation

The Catholic Church affirms that natural law and human reason play a positive and preparatory role in man's search for God; human reason is not antithetical to divine revelation, indeed is a part of it; yet these faculties are insufficient of themselves to bring individuals to the kind of intimate relationship God ultimately wishes to have with the creatures made in His own image:

By natural reason man can know God with certainty on the basis of His works. But there is another order of knowledge, which man cannot possibly arrive at by his own powers: the order of divine Revelation. Through an utterly free decision, God has revealed Himself and given Himself to man. This He does by revealing the mystery, his plan of loving goodness, formed from all eternity in Christ, for the benefit of all men (Catechism of the Catholic Church – chap. 2)

And God having chosen to work from within, used *a people* (Israel succeeded by the Church) to enlighten and reconcile *the people* (the world) to Himself. That process was initiated when God revealed Himself to Abram and made him Abraham – the father of many nations, by whom all peoples of the Earth should ultimately be blessed. From his seed would spring the nation of

259

Israel, intended to become the priestly people of God. For them, divine revelation would no longer be restricted to what could be determined innately or by observing creation. God would reveal Himself and His requirements more precisely by means of the Law and Prophets. He would even reveal His name: JHWE – "I AM who I am", and something of His awesome power and purity through His presence in the Holy of Holies. Later and more openly, God's personality and loving purposes for humanity were witnessed, albeit briefly and to a privileged few, through the incarnate Word Himself:

*The **Word was made flesh** and dwelt among us, and we beheld His glory, the glory as of the only Begotten of the Father, full of grace and truth...And of His fullness we have all received and grace for grace (Jn1:14,16 King James Version).*

Now, through the New Covenant initiated by Christ's blood, God's saving truth is known more fully through the Church and her Scriptures. For this holy, universal and apostolic Church is the mystical Body of Christ on Earth; His flesh and bones (Eph5:30) being Christ the first-fruits (1Cor15:23), the instrument of His saving and redemptive mission. The Spirit guides her and progressively leads her into all truth (John16:13). A further progression of understanding continues in the Church through the centuries, but there can be no entirely new revelation which surpasses or in any way seeks to correct the initial revelation itself, but only its interpretation. For the foundation has once and for all been laid by Christ and His apostles and forms the scriptural and oral deposit of faith which the Church must guard and teach; the faith having once-for-all been entrusted to God's holy people (Jude3):

*Yet even if revelation is already complete, it has **not been made completely explicit**; it remains for the Christian faith gradually to grasp its full significance over the course of the centuries* [Catechism of the Catholic Church #66].

For that "completed revelation" incorporated some clear instruction essential for the functioning and mission of the Church, much of it provided in verbal form, but also a less vital package of mysteries for the Church to unpack during the course of its long journey of discovery. No contributor to the canon of Scripture utilizes the word "*musterion*" more than the apostle Paul. A mystery from the human perspective is necessarily a secret or partial veiling from God's perspective, the Greek word encompassing both aspects. There is the mystery of godliness (1Tim3:16), the mystery of the Kingdom (Mk4:11), the mystery of the Church (Eph5:32), the mystery of the gospel (Eph6:19), the mystery of the faith (1Tim3:9) together with the four particularly relevant to this exercise: the mystery of lawlessness (*anomias* - 2Thes2:7), the fellowship (or dispensation) of the mystery, being the unforetold nature of Gentile inheritance and its implications to wider providence (Rom11:25, Eph3:9; Col1:27), the mystery of Babylon (Rev17:5) and the final mystery of God, which I believe pertains to His hidden providential intentions towards His earthly creation, the disclosure of which brings sweetness to the mouth but bitterness in the gut. (Rev10:1-10).

The unavoidable need to deconstruct

In terms of new revelation, the most that can now happen is that what has already been revealed in Scripture may become better understood, but something being "better understood" is indicative of a deficiency or misunderstanding in the past, and that is certainly the case regarding divine providence. The Spirit's progressive enlightenment both within the Catholic and Protestant churches has invariably resulted in a keener awareness of God's gracious magnanimity towards humanity, challenging the harsh and narrow perspectives of the mighty Augustine as well as that of the Reformers. In the context of ecclesiological re-integration if that is to occur, these Spirit-derived new perspectives must be underpinned from Scripture. Inconveniently that involves deconstructing the biblical theology that was foundational to the original doctrinal understanding. In terms of the Catholic Church, either the Holy Spirit has been misinterpreted at Council fifty years ago or Augustine (in particular) had substantially misread Scripture; thankfully it is the latter. A major part of the current process is to demonstrate that the broader scope of God's salvific plans that has been

261

revealed through the Spirit's working on the mind of the churches was there in Scripture all along; it is just that it was not perceived. This is not a problem; this is progressive revelation; this is God's timing. This I understand to be a disclosure concerning God's munificent intentions towards His earthly creation, which together with a unified understanding of the gospel is required to enable "*those who will be living in the day of tribulation when all the wicked and godless are to be removed*"[4] to have suitable opportunity to prepare.

The boundaries of new revelation

Biblical scholarship has come a long way since the time of the early Fathers and indeed since the middle-ages; nor is Holy Spirit's enlightenment restricted to Catholic scholars as the latter readily acknowledge. The exegetical skills of earlier theologians cannot invariably be considered superior to that of later scholarship for that is a contradiction of the progressive revelation principle, evinced by an indisputable and entirely authentic development of doctrinal understanding and devotional practices through the centuries. The Holy Scriptures like the Kingdom can be likened to a storehouse of treasure from which may be brought out new things as well as old (cf. Mt13:52). But Augustinian monk Brother Martin Luther went quite beyond authentic development and further still beyond the bounds of reason when he made the following remarks about the Church Fathers in one of his "table talks". If he were right it would mean that nobody in the Church or any breakaway Christian movement for the previous thousand or more years had understood or could sensibly articulate the means by which one could be delivered from perdition:

"OF THE FATHERS OF THE CHURCH"

Behold what great darkness is in the books of the Fathers concerning faith; yet if the article of justification be darkened it is impossible to smother the grossest error of mankind... Augustine wrote nothing to the purpose concerning faith for he

262

*was first roused up and made a man by the Pelagians, in striving
against them. I can find no exposition upon the Epistles to the
Romans or Galatians **where anything is taught pure and aright**.
Oh what a happy time have we now in regard to the purity of the
doctrine, but alas we little esteem it.* [Martin Luther Table Talk #
DXXX Marshall Montgomery Collection – translated William
Hazlitt]

I trust I have already demonstrated why such a proposal is
farcical. Why, does one think God would be so perverse as to
deny the world, the Church or any known assembly separated
from her any instruction on the means of salvation for over a
millennium? For none of the known Christian sects that had
separated from the Catholic Church understood "saving faith" in
anything like the thoroughly counter-intuitive way Luther
conceived it, yet if he were right they could not have escaped
perdition unless they had. For, said he: *"It is certain that a man
must utterly despair of his own ability before he is prepared to
receive the grace of Christ"*. When I was directed to this and the
other 27 paradoxical theses articulated at the Heidelberg
Disputation and the attempt to justify them from Scripture, my
heart, mind and conscience affirmed them to be the doctrines of
devils, demonstrably contrary to the teaching of Christ in the
Gospels. Yet such theological paradoxes are effectively the
foundations upon which Protestant Evangelicalism has been
built, so we need to examine them in a little more detail. I have
reproduced the list below:

*28 THEOLOGICAL THESES - presented by Martin Luther and
Leonhard Beyer to a meeting of the Augustinian order at
Heidelberg on 26th April 1518: [my highlighting]*

Introductory Statement: *"Distrusting completely our own
wisdom, according to that counsel of the Holy Spirit, "Do not
rely on your own insight" (Prov. 3:5), we humbly present to the
judgment of all those who wish to be here these **theological
paradoxes**, so that it may become clear whether they have been
deduced well or poorly from St. Paul, the especially chosen*

*vessel and instrument of Christ, and also **from St. Augustine, his most trustworthy interpreter** ".*

*1 The law of God, the most salutary doctrine of life, cannot advance man on his way to righteousness, **but rather hinders him**.*

2 Much less can human works, which are done over and over again with the aid of natural precepts, so to speak, lead to that end.

*3 Although the **works of man always seem attractive and good**, they are nevertheless likely to be mortal sins.*

*4 Although **the works of God are always unattractive and appear evil**, they are nevertheless really eternal merits.*

5 The works of men are thus not mortal sins (we speak of works which are apparently good), as though they were crimes.

6 The works of God (we speak of those which he does through man) are thus not merits, as though they were sinless.

*7 **The works of the righteous would be mortal sins if they would not be feared as mortal sins by the righteous** themselves out of pious fear of God.*

8 By so much more are the works of man mortal sins when they are done without fear and in unadulterated, evil self-security.

9 To say that works without Christ are dead, but not mortal, appears to constitute a perilous surrender of the fear of God.

10 Indeed, it is very difficult to see how a work can be dead and at the same time not a harmful and mortal sin.

11 Arrogance cannot be avoided or true hope be present unless the judgment of condemnation is feared in every work.

*12 In the sight of God **sins are then truly venial when they are feared by men to be mortal.***

*13 **Free will, after the fall, exists in name only,** and as long as it does what it is able to do, it commits a mortal sin.*

14 Free will, after the fall, has power to do good only in a passive capacity, but it can always do evil in an active capacity.

15 Nor could free will remain in a state of innocence, much less do good, in an active capacity, but only in its passive capacity.

16 The person who believes that he can obtain grace by doing what is in him adds sin to sin so that he becomes doubly guilty.

17 Nor does speaking in this manner give cause for despair, but for arousing the desire to humble oneself and seek the grace of Christ.

18 It is certain that man must utterly despair of his own ability before he is prepared to receive the grace of Christ.

19 That person does not deserve to be called a theologian who looks upon the invisible things of God as though they were clearly perceptible in those things which have actually happened (Rom. 1:20; cf. 1 Cor 1:21-25),

20 he deserves to be called a theologian, however, who comprehends the visible and manifest things of God seen through suffering and the cross.

21 A theology of glory calls evil good and good evil. A theology of the cross calls the thing what it actually is.

22 That wisdom which sees the invisible things of God in works as perceived by man is completely puffed up, blinded, and hardened.

23 The law brings the wrath of God (Rom. 4:15), kills, reviles, accuses, judges, and condemns everything that is not in Christ.

24 Yet that wisdom is not of itself evil, nor is the law to be evaded; but without the theology of the cross man misuses the best in the worst manner.

25 He is not righteous who does much, but he who, without work, believes much in Christ.

26 The law says, do this, and it is never done. Grace says, believe in this, and everything is already done.

27 Actually one should call the work of Christ an acting work (operans) and our work an accomplished work (operatum), and thus an accomplished work pleasing to God by the grace of the acting work.

28 The love of God does not find, but creates, that which is pleasing to it. The love of man comes into being through that which is pleasing to it.

As our limited patristic analysis has shown, the above would have been anathema to those who received the Good News from the apostles or their immediate appointees. Such cannot possibly have been *"the faith once for all delivered to the saints"* (cf. Jude1:3) or indeed anything like it, or *someone* whose writing has survived from the 2nd/3rd century would have alluded to such concepts, but they are nowhere to be found. Not being a philosopher, my primary business has been to show that such self-acknowledged paradoxes are opposed to Scripture. But in terms of rationality, it is surely absurd to assert that everything that God does appears evil from a human perspective (#4); that acts of kindness and compassion towards those in need are effectively mortal sins (#2); that the response of a good conscience is "evil self-security" rather than the reciprocation of an innately provided faculty (#8); that doing what one believes to be right and just could ever be a mortal sin (#7); more generally that the vast majority who have failed to interpret the "Good News" in such a way are condemned to Hell. For as we have just illustrated, few if any *Christians* in the first millennium interpreted the Gospel in such a way, let alone the rest of humanity, to whom God also wishes to impart His saving truth so that the World He loves might ultimately be reconciled to Himself.

The instigator of this travesty delighted in the Apostle Paul's writings, so had he not considered this:

*If we or an angel from Heaven preach another gospel to you than that which we have preached to you, let him be accursed. As we have said before so now **I say again**, if anyone preaches another gospel to you than that which you have received, let him be accursed (Gal1:8,9 New King James Version)*

266

Yes, Paul, I think we have got the message, or have we? I remember this passage with its extraordinary reiteration very well for it was the text of my first sermon during a short-lived vocation as a Baptist minister. I asked the congregation (there weren't many), what would be the key word or phrase in the text? I can't remember their response or mine, but I know what it should have been from a contemporary perspective: "*if anyone preaches another gospel to you than that which **YOU** have received, let him be accursed*". Obviously the "you" Paul was referring to in the first instance will have been the recipients of his pastoral letter in Galatia, being one of the churches founded by him and led by men of whom he will have approved such as Apollos in the case of the Corinthian Church (1Cor3:6). Can it possibly be the case that all the leaders of these churches fifty to a hundred years later became accursed distorters of the gospel? *All of them*, I ask? - that is quite impossible. Then how can it be that none of the writings of the late first and second century Church witnesses most notably Justin Martyr, Irenaeus, Ignatius and Polycarp, the latter two known to be fellow-disciples under the apostle John understood the gospel in the way the Reformers or for that matter 4th-5th century Augustine came to interpret it? Luther himself affirms the matter - none of these Apostolic Fathers had understood the gospel in terms of "faith alone", "resting in the mercy of Christ" from the starting point of a condemned humanity incapable by nature of willing and doing anything pleasing to God. That is why this Augustinian monk came to regard them as being in "great darkness". In all good conscience how can such a position be defended any longer? The scenario that I had once relied upon in my own mind as an Evangelical was that the medieval Church in East and West had lost sight of the true gospel and that Luther & Co were somehow recovering it. Given that these issues pertained to the very nature of human salvation and the historical mission of the Church these could never have been truths that were progressively to be revealed, but heretical teachings resulting in the severing of the Body of Christ, hatred between sincere Christian believers and decades of warfare.

The key to determining the truth of these matters is to get a grip on exactly how the teaching of the apostles was disseminated through their successors to the newly established churches throughout the world. This is set out in Tertullian's "Prescription against Heretics" (chapters 20-28), easily accessible on the internet. Origen concurs but he adds that the apostles when handing on the Faith to the early Church expressed themselves *"with utmost clarity concerning the essentials"* whilst on other subjects *"they merely stated the fact that things were so, keeping silence as to the manner or origin of their existence, clearly in order that their successors who should be lovers of wisdom might have a subject of exercise on which to display the fruit of their talents"*[5]. So those who take the time to examine the Ante-Nicene writings will discern that all were in agreement concerning certain essentials that have subsequently been the cause of schism, whilst other issues including those being dealt with in this book such as God's dealings with those outside the Church and the nature of the age to come were not agreed amongst the Fathers for they contained mysteries the solution for which did not form a part of the "Faith once and for all delivered to the Church" but were data to be subjected to progressive revelation.

A re-united Church enriched by plurality

As we will explore more fully in chapter seven, God never directly initiates but does permit certain evils, even the partial dissolution of His Church when He knows that in so doing the outcome will be better for the participants through the experience or "grist" it provides to them. Through progressive revelation the Catholic Church has (at last) come better to appreciate the ecclesiological reality and contribution of those churches separated from her for the last five hundred years. As she had to acknowledge: *"There is no real precedent in official Church teaching"* for so doing [*Unitatis Redintegratio 1964 intro*]. As I have had ample opportunity to observe in the past within the separated churches and more recently within the Anglican Communion where I still occasionally worship, the Spirit of enlightenment has been at work in the Protestant churches and there is much to be admired in her traditions of worship, music, ministry and her historical social influence for good; also, plenty to be gleaned from her on-going biblical scholarship, some of which I have utilized. And how the Catholic and Orthodox churches could benefit from the enthusiastic worship, devotion to Scripture, stimulating preaching, effective outreach and individual commitment to Christian service of many from the independent Evangelical churches, aspects of which I still miss to this day. Evangelicals are unashamedly conversionist: most emphasize the need for a radical change of life to back up their profession of faith whilst many are as individuals devoted to Christ in a way that might put a good number within other churches to shame. Most are in church on a Sunday because they want to be not simply because they have been told they ought to be. I would look forward to the sermon as the heart of the service: its skilful construction, impassioned delivery and the challenge it presented to live up to the faith (as I then understood it) in the coming week. As a Roman Catholic, noticeably less so in that area, although even in the last few years I have noticed that more effort and attention has been paid by many priests to the homily, for since moving to my current location a few years ago I recognize that the Spirit has prevented me from settling or becoming known and established within a particular parish or at least a specific church – now I understand why. It was necessary for this work to be carried out in virtual isolation without any consultation with the Church until after its release, for it would never have been encouraged, let alone approved. So having attended masses at various churches I have noticed more emphasis being given to preaching although it would still be judged as weak by Evangelical standards in terms of preparation, structure and delivery if not content. For many years now there has also been encouragement from the top for Catholics to become more devoted to the Scriptures. (Be careful what you wish for).

A partial darkening and some internal corruption was foretold for the Church (initially for the Temple) in prophecy and occurred at its appointed time, resulting in apostasy and the fragmentation of the Western Church along with the development of some fatally flawed theology, desolate in its effect towards the healing of the human soul and aberrant in the way it portrayed both the Creator and those made in His image

(2Thes2:11). Clearly the Lord could have prevented this and easily brought matters to a halt: one powerful angel or vernacular writing in the sky *"You should all join the Methodists"* or whatever. That is not God's way, for offences have come, and woe to those by whom they have come. That applies to the world and the Church – *"for there must be sects among you, that those who are approved might be recognized among you* (1Cor11:19). But now there needs to be unity among us before the Good News of the Kingdom can be preached *coherently* as a witness to the un-churched before the end comes. The Catholic and Orthodox churches must be open to the Spirit of Truth, and therefore to new enlightenment regarding issues not directly challenging the Creed or Deposit but entirely relating to scriptural interpretation; something in which modern Protestant scholars often excel; and unlike the controversy of the middle-ages, these do not necessarily challenge ecclesiological integrity, although they may well challenge some established doctrines as does this disclosure. For as the Catholic Church acknowledges:

*There is a **hierarchy of truths** since not all truths of the Catholic doctrine are equally **connected with the foundation** of the Christian faith [Unitatis Redintegratio 21st Nov 1964 – para 11]*

Hypothetically speaking, if the Spirit were to encounter intransigence in one quarter, He might very well turn to another to spearhead the process and so put the former to shame. At the end of the day, home must be where the heart is, yet others could become instrumental in leading the way. The Head of the fractured Body may of course call upon whomsoever He pleases to enlighten the Church -because He is ineffable, His ways are inscrutable, and He clearly has a sense of humour (cf. Mt11:25). Determining whether this revelation is a "progression" or a deception requires the reader to have a very open mind indeed. Most readers will have access to excellent websites containing most Bible versions, Greek text and word search facilities. Holy Scripture was intended to be *"useful for teaching, rebuking, correcting and training in righteous living so as fully to equip the believer's faith"* (2Tim3:16-17), so may it be used to correct and perfect the understanding of the churches. For whilst the

Bible was never intended to be exclusively relied upon for the formation of Christian doctrine, neither may its teaching, where that is clear and explicit, be contradicted by any church.

A willingness to acknowledge the possibility of *personal* error is the starting point for everyone, as I have now had to do twice in my Christian life; once on conversion to the Catholic Church after for twenty-eight years regarding her along with one of my former heroes Charles Spurgeon as "the devil's masterpiece", and her leader in Rome as anti-Christ. Now a further eighteen years later, through this encounter I am expounding concepts, some of which are nearly as radical and new to my understanding as they are bound to be to the reader's. For before the summer of 2013, I would myself have failed to comprehend and regarded as heretical (bordering on the hysterical) a fair deal of what is written here, such as the dual fulfilment of prophecy concept (DPP) and everything else pertaining to Paul's fellowship of the secret; anthropological dualism, the planting of souls, the concept of the final "Elijah" or messenger who had still to come; the existence of the book of Enoch as a valid and inspired subsidiary reference source, or any significant doctrinal problems within the Catholic Church. Nor did I perceive the need, still less the feasibility of ever re-establishing full visible unity amongst all the baptized. All these are a direct result of a personal revelation from a spiritual source during an eighteen-month period, many focussed within a frenzied ten-day period of enlightenment. The origins of that spiritual source some are bound to question: for this private, usually inoffensive soul has been called upon to disturb many sincere and devoted Christians as, I believe, part of the process of clearing the path for the realization of God's Kingdom in its fullness, for which at least a measure of ecclesiological re-integration becomes a necessity for the sake of the final gospel witness to the unchurched world. Outright scepticism is an entirely healthy starting point for the reader, more especially if they are Catholic/Orthodox Christian. If so, this writing is more a matter for the Church's hierarchy to consider. Yet if you are a fellow layman and it grabs your interest, but you think I am a heretic (or worse), *obey the Church*; or if you are open to the idea that my writing might be prophetic, *obey the Church*. Those who

271

heed the Magisterium defer to Christ; those who wilfully reject it had better have a good reason. Thankfully for most outside the Catholic Church, a genuinely clear conscience provides exemption, at least whilst that conviction is sustained. As still a member I needed to be quite certain that this commission is from Christ; it is assuredly not my own unaided work, I simply don't have the capacity. There is of course another possibility; but why should the devil's party (who I indicated earlier have been in touch) dare countenance the idea of a Church united and empowered to preach a unified gospel relating in part to their own demise? Why should the Wicked One wish the need for personal holiness to be asserted or God's loving, magnanimous and equitable providence to be affirmed? Why should the accuser of the brethren wish the underlying goodness of the human spirit to be defended, or the one destined for desolation want to be outlining the glorious prospects of the faithful? There has also been an interior witness; a personally unprecedented love and joy in the Lord, together with various phenomena that have helped validate this commission albeit only at the personal level to date. If such could be easily verified it would undermine the principle of faith (Mk8:12), nor could it be relied upon (Mt24:24). Yet what has been presented here is potentially verifiable, and suitably gifted Bible-believing Christians should relish such endeavour, if not its outcome.

Enlightenment through Protestant scholarship

Recent scholarly interest in studying the Bible in the context of other ancient texts, aided by the discovery of the Dead Sea scrolls has thrown new light on the various forms of Judaism that prevailed in the first century, resulting in a new perspective or rather various new perspectives on Paul's teaching arising within Protestant academia. These have considerably reshaped the understanding of justification by faith in the apostle's thought in the minds of many biblical scholars, although the development has had much less impact at ground level within independent Evangelical churches, certainly in the UK. If the agreed aspects of these new perspectives[6] is broadly right then Augustine and the medieval Reformers who later built their theology on his virtual *sola gratia* emphasis have all substantially misunderstood St Paul's teaching concerning law, grace and righteousness. Protestant theologians were also at the forefront of reviewing what Paul intended on the occasions he used the phrase "*dia pistoes iesou christou*", also considered in the previous chapter.

Summarizing the stages of progressive revelation in chronological order since the Fall:

a) Natural law and human reason – observing God's greatness and goodness in what has been created and in His kindly intentions towards humanity. Linked to that, the witness and controlling influence of the conscience regarding God's requirements for human behaviour and the benefit of virtue;

b) The Law, the Prophets and JHWE's personal presence amongst His people of the Old Covenant; intended also to be an enlightenment for the Gentile nations;

c) The short-lived presence, ministry and teaching of the incarnate Son of God to His disciples and others privileged to experience it; largely restricted to Jews and those who lived amongst them;

d) Detailed teaching of gospel salvation through the Church established by the apostles on a foundation which cannot be supplanted;

e) Century by century deepening of the Church's understanding concerning matters not essential to what is required for gospel salvation but nevertheless important in their historical context, such as arose at Vatican II;

f) Fulfilment of Jesus's promise that the Spirit of Truth would finally "*lead the Church into all truth and tell her of the things to come*" (Jn16:13); her sagacity having been perfected through a more complete understanding of Holy Scripture, the Church having "*come to the unity of the Faith to a perfect Man to the measure of the stature of the fullness of Christ*" (Eph4:13).

Yet what all Christians particularly in the West need to keep in mind is that progression to the fullness of Truth will not have

273

been a steady upward path, for the Faith was not handed down to the Church in the form of a Book that was progressively to be unravelled, but by a depository of faith preserved and transmitted in written and verbal form:

*Therefore, brethren stand fast and hold the traditions which you were taught, **whether by word or our epistle** (2Thes2:15 New King James Version).*

Holy Scripture was a vital part of that depository, but it was Scripture that had ***already been explained to the churches receiving it***, or at least those aspects vital to their salvation: such essentials were not to be unpacked through the centuries, let alone fifteen centuries later. So although Church historians necessarily point out that very little indeed is known about the Church's development in the critical late first century period, the second and third century Christian writers that we know of did have a reasonably uniform understanding of the essentials of the Faith, which is surely what one would expect given that they had been tutored by the various apostles or the men nurtured by them. There is therefore a strong case for regarding the ante-Nicene teaching and praxis as normative *for matters essential to gospel salvation,* allowance being made for a progressive deepening and maturing of the Faith over time through the action of the Holy Spirit and *sensus fidelium* (collective sense of the faithful). But the latter cannot pertain to the essence of the Gospel: its means of initiation, the nature of saving faith and the provisions for ongoing sanctification. Given that it was not until the fourth or fifth century that theology was moulded into any precision and doctrines were systematised utilizing a relatively recently agreed plenary canon of Scripture, the particular interpretations that Late Antiquity exegetes came to when interpreting the abstruse pastoral letters of St Paul needed to have been tested against the universal witness of the immediate post-apostolic Fathers, for the latter had not been entirely reliant upon the precarious business of biblical exegesis using texts written in a language with which the Latin Fathers in particular were unfamiliar. The fact that few if any of the very early Fathers had provided biblical commentaries on Paul's letters is hardly the point; the Faith "once for all delivered to the saints" had been received by them either from the apostles themselves or their direct appointees. What had been passed on to them must have incorporated *all of Paul's teaching that was essential to the practice of the Faith*. I beg the reader carefully to think through the implications of this for it follows that there can be nothing essential to gospel salvation that could be discovered or recovered by Augustine or any of his successors four or more centuries later. It is quite impossible that the second and third century churches could have been uniformly in error concerning such matters as the nature of repentance (that it pertained to moral reform, not acknowledging oneself to be morally bankrupt and "relying on God's mercy in Christ") or the economy of grace (that God had provided certain spiritual faculties to fallen man: natural precepts by which he had effectual free will to desire and do some good such as exercise compassion and practice justice, albeit not to be raised to eternal life apart from gospel grace). It will have been necessary to understand these matters to discern the true essence of human nature and the *disposition required* for saving faith. In many of these considerations, especially those pertaining to natural law as well as how the Christian and Jew should regard God's Law, Augustine came to an understanding markedly different from the teaching of those who had been personally trained by the apostles and their immediate successors. And so, I have concluded, he deformed the living tradition of the Church, which some in the East have dared to assert yet he never received any conciliar condemnation, even from the Greek Church. Review my comments in chapter one under "the mystery of Augustine" which Evangelicals will regard as a virtual inversion of the gospel as they have understood it. Yet my conclusions regarding such matters as free will, innate human enlightenment/natural law and God's intelligible justice are not contradicted by the ancient Church, quite the contrary. That is because some of the distortions derived from flawed exegesis became embedded in the doctrines formulated by the Western Church; these were later reinforced by those who separated from her in the middle ages. It is therefore no surprise to me that once the Bible is unravelled, the outcome is to be much closer to the understanding of the very early Fathers than it is to Augustine, still less the

275

"Reformers", especially in those areas that were heavily dependent upon an understanding of the Pauline epistles.

I do not however claim or expect entirely *to match* the teaching of those earliest Christian witnesses, partly in view of authentic development and partly because this writing incorporates concepts that I have come to understand from Scripture were not intended to be grasped until the very end, the most fundamental being that the benefits of the Saviour of the World's atonement avail *at the forensic level* for the world as whole, not just those who have been called out from her to be the human agents of her healing and reconciliation:

*"He gave Himself as a ransom **for all**; (a fact) to be testified in due time" (1Tim2:6).*

Through the cultural and religious developments that God permitted if not positively decreed should develop through history, He well knew many would not give consideration to the Christian message or have an accurate idea of its content. In contrast to the tradition in which I first came to faith in Jesus Christ, the Catholic Church recognizes the many things that are true, virtuous and holy in other religions as well as in all "people of good will". She nevertheless teaches to all who will receive it that only in Jesus Christ is to be found the fullness of Life and Truth, and the only Way by which we can experience cognisant divine fellowship in the present age or indeed can ever have *intimate* communion with the One True God. Yet all who have conformed to the divine precepts known to them through spiritual revelation or natural law are deemed to fear God. They have hearts that will readily accept the Good News of Jesus Christ's Lordship and His saving work on their behalf when these things are made manifest to all. For God has willed that all demonstrating the essence of true humanity are ultimately be reconciled to Himself and thereby come at last to share eternal life. But such divine benevolence does not extend to the human grouping featured in the next chapter.

276

Notes: CHAPTER FIVE

1. The first apology of Justin Martyr chap. 46

2. The second apology of Justin Martyr chap. 2

3. Augustine "Of the morals of the Catholic Church" chap. 20

4. Enoch1 chap. 1 v1

5. Origen de Principiis   - Preface paras 2 and 3

6. The New Perspectives on Paul are sketchily reviewed in wikipedia

Chapter Six

The Mystery of Evil

and the defaulters from the Universal Covenant of life

*If you (Cain) do well, will you not be accepted? But if you
do not do well, the Sinful One is crouching at the portal
and desires to have you: you must master him (Gen4:7
from Masoretic text)*

I made the point at the start of the previous chapter that the Bible
does not set out God's plans for His whole creation but concerns
His redemptive strategy for humanity and the key players within
that plan: Himself, His Son and Spirit, Israel and the Church.
Believe it or not the devil has a role too or else he would have
been destroyed or shut away long since, for God is sovereign.
Satan has no autonomous right to continue existing, let alone
exercise any authority in the world, and yet He does so at God's
behest. It has been made clear to me why that is the case and it is
explained in more detail in the final chapter. We can learn very
little about either the angelic or satanic realm from Scripture;
indeed, even God's plans for men and women outside Israel and
the Church have been obscured, hence (I believe) such a
disclosure at this time. In terms of the realm of evil and the
numerous legends pertaining to it, this brief chapter will only
consider those aspects which are at least alluded to in Scripture,
and with a specific aim in mind: to complete the jigsaw
regarding the eluded Universal Covenant of life; in this case
considering those who default from it.

We reviewed the above verse from Genesis in chapter two in the context of that covenant. Because it has been eluded by the churches, so too have been its defaulters; they have been lumped together with the "unsaved", being those outside the New and Old Testament's Covenants of Promise. In terms of the Church and its mission that has not essentially mattered for she is to preach the Good News of Jesus as Lord and Saviour, practice justice and offer compassion to all in the world, regardless of how deserving or otherwise the recipients may be. The sun has shone on the righteous and ungodly and so has the gospel along with the blessings that have flowed and sometimes ebbed from the Church to the world. The churches have generally understood there to be one covenant for each testament period and an exclusive one at that. We have hopefully already indicated why such a concept should be repudiated, firstly by the reality of Abel and others declared righteous before the Abrahamic Covenant was established; still more so by the story of Ishmael. He had been circumcised, *blessed by God* and by his father Abraham, sent on his way in peace yet he was excluded from the covenant initiated through his father, for the seed of his union with Sarah were to be the children of promise, and such is the Church in the current dispensation (Gal4:28). Yet through Abraham, all nations were to be blessed, and that included the twelve that would spring from the seed of his son Ishmael, yet not necessarily through incorporation into an exclusive covenant as we have been at pains to point out. So now we need to consider how the other eluded grouping (defaulters from the Universal Covenant) may be identified, not necessarily by us, for Christians are not to attempt to make any such distinctions in their witnessing or charity, but by God, their Judge and ultimate Avenger. Along with the powerful spirit that becomes their adoptive master these defaulters from the Universal Covenant play a mysterious role in God's strategic plan to raise up the children of Adam, ultimately to divinity.

Whilst *we* are to make no distinctions, the fault-line between those outside the Church who have been "planted by God" and those who are satanic (*ek tou diabolou*) is more pronounced than that between those of God's seed who are being saved through the gospel and those who are not currently "in Christ". This is clearly reflected in their behaviour when one knows what to look for, and to a still greater degree in their future destiny, as far ahead as Scripture permits us to discern it. As with other aspects of natural law, these mysteries concerning the broader scheme of things have lain almost imperceptibly beneath the pages of Scripture, yet references are made there to this grouping, but as already indicated they have been understood by most to be referring to non-Christians:

*This is what distinguishes the children of God from the children of the devil; whoever does not live uprightly and does not love his brother is **not from God**... Do not be **like Cain** who was **from the evil one** and murdered his brother (1Jn3:10,12 New Jerusalem Bible)*

*Let us love one another since love is from God and everyone who loves is a child of God and knows God. **Whoever fails to love does not know God** because God is love (1Jn4:7,8 New Jerusalem Bible)*

Those who can "love" but do not possess "*agape*"

It is necessary in this context to distinguish between *agape* and other forms of love, for those of the devil's party can exhibit the one but not the other. Those devoid of *agape* may love in a romantic way and to form friendships but it will always revolve around themselves. They may show fondness towards an individual, but it will always be on the basis that if that person were removed from their life, their happiness would be diminished. That is an entirely valid emotion that a saint would share, but it isn't *agape*. For *agape* is *ek tou theou* (1Jn4:7) so a child of the devil will not possess it. Augustine was entirely logical in his insistence that only a Christian can truly exercise compassion or genuinely care for another human being; if there were only two categories and every non-Christian were a child of the devil as he believed, such would be the case; but it is neither the observable reality, nor is it scriptural. Most Old Testament Gentiles and present day non-Christians are assuredly not satanic or evil (*ek tou ponerou*) but they do *inhabit* the sphere of darkness still controlled by that prince and are yet to be delivered from it (Col1:13 cf. Greek). Most evidently possess *agape* which pertains to compassion and empathy; an internal urge to show kindness to a fellow human being which extends to any living creature in need, regardless of whether there is any benefit to the benefactor. Its impetus arises from the motions of the spirit (inner man); the response is the essence of being human and the justifying marker for the Covenant of life. *Agape* is the love of God (in the sense of a genitive of origin), imparted to the human spirit, being a key part of His blueprint for humanity. It operates through natural precepts - the workings of the conscience that Satan's assignees no longer reference or indeed retain (1Tim4:2).

Retaining God's image: retaining the seed

John also tells us that:

*Whoever is born of God does not (habitually practice) sin for **his seed remains** in him; and he cannot (habitually practice) sin because he has been born of God (1Jn3:9 from Greek)*

Note his seed has *remained*; it is not referring to something that is either accredited or infused through spiritual regeneration but to that which has been present there since birth:

*"That the working of the Father and the Son operates both in saints and sinners is manifest from this, that all who are rational beings are partakers of the Word, i.e. of reason, and by this means bear certain seeds implanted within them of wisdom and justice, **which is Christ**" [Origen][1]*

This third century theologian believed that St Paul was confirming as much in the passage where he writes *"Say not in in thine heart, who shall ascend into Heaven (to bring Christ down from above) or who shall ascend into the deep (to bring Christ up from the dead). But what sayeth Scripture? The Word is nigh thee even in thy mouth and in thy heart"* (Rom10:6-8), by which, Origen believed, *"he means that Christ is **in the heart of all** in respect of his **being the Word or reason**."*[2] Referring back to John's verse, the apostle well knew that even the children of God commit sin but he is saying is that those in whom God's

281

seed remains do not consistently practice it. That is because they are restrained by God's implanted law in their heart (cf. Rom2:15) which is evident from the subsequent verse. Those who are of God maintain sound reason and exercise restraint; they do not consistently practice unrighteousness; the children of the devil do (it is or rather has become all they know), and they also fail to love (1Jn3:10). When one who is of God sins grievously, he hurts others but also grieves himself. Unless he is a masochist he will not consistently practice such wickedness, or if he does he will be thoroughly miserable. When a child of the devil causes hurt by his actions or his deception, he is simply being himself and feels quite content or even exhilarated; he will gleefully boast of his exploits in the courtroom when hopefully he is apprehended. This positive delight in evil practice is what motivates serial killers to offend repeatedly; it is within the nature of godlessness. Frequent reference is made in the Bible's Wisdom literature to those who effectively go in the way of Cain by "*leaving the paths of uprightness to walk in the way of darkness*" (Prov2:13 Masoretic Text) as opposed to those who continue to "*walk in the way of good men and who keep the paths of the righteous*" (v20); for according to Solomon (or whoever) the day shall come when "*the upright shall dwell on the Earth and those who are perfected will have pre-eminence in it whereas the wicked shall be cut off from the Earth and the treacherous ones rooted out of it*" (vv21,22). Of course, if all had been born in a state of depravity none would be in a position to "leave the paths of righteousness" for they could never have been on them in the first place. The reason they leave is because they no longer are in any way directed by the precepts God provides to those who are made in His own image. In a sense these people cease to be fully human for a reflection of God's image is what defines the human being from other creatures. Those who are heading for perdition are not those who have failed to apprehend the grace and healing of Christ as it is offered through the gospel, for contrary to the teaching of Arminius and the wishful thinking of many modern-day Christians, man has no innate ability to respond to the grace of Christ (Jn6:44; Rom8:29,30). The "damned" are rather those who irrevocably reject the Word's interior witness, in other words not those who have failed to come but those who have departed. Unlike agnostics and those of other faiths rejecting the gospel, they are without excuse for all have such an enlightening deposit in their nature, at least to start with, so those who turn their back on it, evidenced by the misery, despair and often destruction such people cause to their fellows, will be afflicted with appropriately severe punishment after their death. This will be seen to be right and just to those who do possess sound reason, as it was to most of the earliest Fathers who commented on the matter[3].

The evil of ensnarement

The Greek verb used by John for "sinning" is *hamarto* - literally missing the mark, for evil always pertains to what is lacking or missing. It can be translated sin or transgress or offend as it is in Acts25:8 though *skandalizo* is more often used to denote offending. *Skandalizo*, meaning to offend, ensnare or cause to stumble, is generally a stronger verb than *harmato*. Similarly with the noun *scandalon*:

Woe to the world because of offences (skandalon) for offences must come, but woe to that man by whom those offences come (Mat18:7)

This statement followed Jesus's earlier warning concerning those who offend children, or alternatively cause them to sin. It is instructive to observe how firstly, the King James Version and then the New King James Version handle the translation:

But whoso shall offend one of these little ones which believe in me, it were better for him that a millstone were hung about his neck and that he were drowned in the depths of the sea (Mat18:6 King James Version)

Whereas the New King James Version takes Jesus to mean something rather different:

Whoever causes any one of these little ones who believe in me to sin, it were better ...etc (New King James Version)

The King James Version is envisaging child abuse whilst according to the NJKV it is the children who will be ensnared into sin. This is an example of the problems faced when translating from the Greek, where a word may have a wide semantic range or as in this case the word order is ambiguous. Neither translation is "wrong" whereas obviously Jesus (or Matthew) will have intended one rather than the other. What both interpretations agree about is that whilst sinning is bad and none can avoid it completely, encouraging others to sin is radically worse, positively wicked in fact. It is a key characteristic of the children of the devil. Their father set the trend back in the Garden of Eden. It was his act of ensnarement toward our first parents that resulted in the Fall. God's seed is said to remain in those who are "of God" (1Jn3:9) referring to the fact that His divine image has been retained within the spirit. That image cannot so much be referring to our invisible Creator's form as His moral nature and nobility.

God fulfils his wondrous purposes for the ultimate deification[4] of frail children of dust by permitting certain souls to succumb to the control of the devil. The Cain and Abel story is again important in identifying the instrumentality of human free will within that process, in which the elder brother chose a course of evil so as to be later classified in Scripture as *"ek tou ponerou"*: derived from the Evil One (1Jn3:12).

The children of the devil are variously described in Scripture as:

i) Twice dead, plucked up by the roots (Jude12)

ii) Having names missing from the Book of Life (e.g. Rev20:15)

iii) Devoured by Satan (1Pet5:8, cf. Gen4:7)

iv) Having forfeited their soul (Mat16:26)

v) Having gone in the way of Cain (Jude11) (cf. 1Jn3:12) or departed from the path of righteousness (just considered)

vi) "Goats" – humans devoid of compassion (Mt25)

vii) Not having retained God's seed or image (1Jn3:9)

viii) Those who destroy the Earth – the ones to be destroyed at final judgement (Rev11:18)

ix) Those who cause or encourage others to sin: the ensnarers (just considered)

x) Having had their conscience seared (i.e. withered away) (1Tim4:2)

xi) Devoid of truth (cf. Jn8:44)

xii) Belonging to Satan (Jn8:44)

xiii) Planted by Satan (Mt13:39; 15:13)

xiv) Messengers or agents (not "angels") of Satan (Mt25:41)

xv) The desolate ones (Dan9:27)

xvi) The servants of Satan (2Cor11:15)

Cain as a type

Adam and Eve were the progenitors of fallen humanity (1Cor15:22). Their disobedience put a temporary end to the prospect of eternal life for all humanity, although the apostle Paul doesn't place a great deal of weight on Adam's sin (1Tim2:14). Nevertheless, he says that -

*As through one transgression there resulted condemnation to **all men**, even so through one act of righteousness, there resulted justification of life to **all men** (Rom5:18 New American Standard Bible)*

Adam is the type and federal head of fallen humanity that lives under the reign of death. Cain who was in a literal sense the firstborn of fallen creation can be regarded as the type of individual reprobates, being those who become rejected by themselves rejecting the interior witness of Christ in their "hearts". In his short epistle, Jude warns against false teachers who would come into the Church, whom he describes as deluded, defiled, disregarders of authority and blasphemers of the glories, both barren and uprooted so "twice dead" (v12). He adds:

Woe to them for they have gone in the way of Cain (Jude v11a New King James Version)

Cain was a murderer, not a false teacher, yet he is referred to in type: the human first-plant and the first man to be cursed by God and given over to the devil who according to the Genesis account he was potentially capable of mastering (Gen4:7). Scripture affirms Cain to be wicked, satanic and the type of those devoid of moral restraint or compassionate love – psychopathic, inhumane and heartless:

*For this is the message that you heard from the beginning, that we should love one another; not as Cain who was **of the wicked one** and murdered his brother. And why did he murder him because his works were evil and his brother's righteous (1Jn3:11,12 New King James Version)*

Cain's parents had been banished from the Paradise garden and the source of eternal life (Gen3:24). However, they and their offspring were not entirely banished from JHWE's benign presence (cf. Gen4:1,3,4 and especially Gen4:14,16). They will have continued to worship and bring offerings to God, or else why should Cain and Abel do so (especially Cain)? But after the elder son's astonishing defiance in rejecting God's personal plea to him to resist sin (or the Sinful One) crouching at the portal of his soul (Gen4:7 King James Version), after slaughtering his righteous brother a further degree of banishment from God's presence was established in his case:

*My punishment is more than I can bear; surely you have driven me out **this day** from the face of the ground; I shall be hidden from your face (Gen4:13,14a New King James Version)*

Cain - the first defaulter from the Universal Covenant of life

Those within the Covenant of life are those whose names remain in the Book of life having demonstrated they are "of God" (cf. Rev20:15; Mt15:13). Cain defaulted from this covenant for wilfully defying the God who had pleaded with him and failing to do what he was perfectly capable of doing: maintain his integrity and thereby not permit the Evil One to get the better of him by slaughtering his brother and showing His contempt for His Maker. Having defaulted, he becomes alienated from the rest of humanity ("whoever finds me will kill me") and also from God altogether ("from TODAY I will be hidden from Your face"). Cain then might also be described as the type of those who become entirely alienated from God (the godless), having rejected and subsequently lost the witness of the divine will for human behaviour reflected in the conscience. Externally such will still be aware of standards of acceptable behaviour and will maintain it to a degree to be accepted in society; so even they do not usually exhibit "absolute depravity". As for such who operate within the Church to pervert doctrine or bring about schisms, a still higher degree of subtlety and sophistication is required if an agent of Satan is to be transformed into an agent of light (cf. 2Cor11:13-14). To appear the spiritual master, apart from being erudite and voluminous he must incorporate *much that is seemingly sound* within the poison he is peddling if a sufficient number of the faithful are to be deceived; most likely those with itching ears who ache for an easier path than the arduous Way afforded to those who would be the true disciples of Christ (2Tim4:3). By their character and legacy may such deceitful apostles be discerned but by then it can be too late; the damage has been done and must be repaired.

Satan and his seed to be bruised

Referring back to the proto-evangelium (Gen3:15), Satan and his seed were cursed: their heads will be crushed under the feet of Christ with His Church (Rom16:20). By opting to leave the paths of uprightness (cf. 2Pet2:15) upheld by all who defer to conscience, they opt out of the benefits of the atonement which brings justification *of* life (Rom5:18); just as those incorporated into Christ through baptism who fall away from the faith deprive themselves of the benefits of the Christian faithful, which is justification *and* life of an eternal quality.

287

The twofold praxis of unrighteousness

For here is another mystery: God through His only begotten Son created all things including the human soul, but they were not all planted by Him (cf. Rom9:21,22 & Mt15:13). The precise arrangement has not been elucidated but who was planted by or assigned to whom will be determined by the outcome (whether they are rooted up Mt15:13), but from a human perspective it will have been a matter of free will. Similarly, "the elect" are those who from a human perspective respond to the gospel and persevere in the faith, even if from God's perspective they are foreknown and were divinely enabled to apprehend Christ. All God's children sin to a degree and those outside the Church do not have the means to be healed in their souls, made whole, delivered from the corrupting influence of the body or "saved" as the Bible refers to the matter. The twofold praxis of unrighteousness arises from, at the one level the activities of those who remain within the universal Covenant but of course are still inclined to sin, and at the second level to those which default that covenant and practice wickedness in accordance with the will and whims of the spirit who has mastered them and gained a hold over them. "Defaulting covenant" is also referred to in the New Testament as becoming reprobate (*adokimoi* – disqualified) or being removed from the book of life. No names are ever added to these books, only removed, reflecting the outworking of an inclusive covenant. The non-defaulters being enlightened by natural precepts endeavour to live upright lives for the sake of their own peace of mind and self-respect. Their acts of kindness and civility are therefore not entirely altruistic, nevertheless they are sufficient evidence of "faith", for faith (and conscience) senses that virtue is rewarded (Heb11:6). They are accepted in the Matthew 25 (final judgement) context, since such people demonstrate the possession of compassionate love (*agape*) which determines whether they are "of God" and destined to play a part in His Kingdom (Mt25:34).

The counter-Church

The "*adokimoi*", being the disqualified or reprobates are the
darnel or tares in the parable to be considered shortly, and they
seek to poison the minds of others and lead them astray. Unlike
"lost sheep", the "goats" are only ever restrained by external
motivations to conform, succeed or be admired; and where these
are no longer a concern as in the case of some notorious
criminals, by nothing at all. In one sense they are free spirits,
oblivious to any obligation to take heed to the law that has
universally been engrained in the human heart to guide and
restrain. These who go in the "way of Cain" are in effect an
inverted image of that other vocational group *(ekklesia* or
Church) called out from the world to go in the "Way of Christ".
Like Christians, the godless are also no longer their own; they
are in the ownership and service of another (1Jn3:12); they too
are spiritually directed and empowered through the effectual
working of their lord (Eph2:2 Greek); they too are no longer one
of the lost: the "sheep without a shepherd" upon whom Christ
will have compassion (Mt9:36). These are no sheep at all and are
not lost for they have found their herdsman or rather he has
found them. He had been prowling around seeking whom he
may devour (1Pet5:8); he had crouched at the portal of their
souls desiring to possess them. It looked promising, and so he
had been granted permission to sift them as wheat to see if there
be any trace of "faith" left in them (Lk22:31,32). Some will
regard such an analysis and the texts to adduce it as obscure and
arcane: so be it, for it pertains to the mystery of evil; by far the
most intriguing aspect of divine providence required to unlock
"*to musterion tou theou*".

The elect: planted by God, assigned to Christ

The elect are planted by God and earmarked for Christ, as is
indicated in Christ's high-priestly prayer:

*I have revealed You to those whom You gave Me out of this
world. **They were Yours – You gave them to Me** and they have
obeyed Your word (Jn17:6 New International Version)*

Note how our Lord prays: "they were Yours". Surely everything is God's, but He means they were of God and not of Satan, like Cain who was of the wicked one (1Jn3:11). The genitive (of Satan) cannot pertain to creation or indeed procreation but to ownership, assignment and party.

The wheat and darnel: inseparable within the gospel age

The two planters of souls are figured in the parable of the wheat and darnel (Mt13:24:30), which has particular relevance to this chapter, as well as providing a broad indicator for the age to come. Whilst it is only a parable, it is helpfully explained by Jesus Himself on this occasion. It will not do to try to restrict it to the Church as Augustine and many others have attempted. Of course, it is analogous to the visible Church and the invisible wheat within her, for those in Christ who bare no fruit will be rejected (Jn15:2), but Jesus explicitly tells us it pertains to the world and everyone in it (Mt13:38). (The parable suited to the Church is Paul's concerning the "great house" and the vessels of honour and dishonour within it (2Tim2:19-21)). In Jesus's parable, the wheat represents all men and women who are planted by God in the sense described above. The darnel represents human seed planted by Satan (Mt15:13). Jesus characterises them as distinguishable by their own wickedness and the fact they ensnare others into sin (Mt13:41), just as darnel (tares) can damage and poison the wheat. As the darnel is gathered together and burnt, a similar fate awaits the satanic seed, but not until the end of this age. Keep in mind, we have not been pondering a theory about the meaning of a parable but outlining Jesus's own explanation. Keeping also in mind God's undoubted sovereignty and the fact that Christ has already triumphed over these evil powers, their continued presence must be by divine prerogative; likewise, the "planting" or assigning arrangement. Further background information to this mystery is provided by Paul, for the seed planted by Satan equates to the instruments of God's retribution created for destruction to whom he refers (Rom9:22). In the same chapter, he mentions "instruments of His mercy" which he makes clear (v24) exclusively refer to elect Jews and Christians. It is therefore assumed by many there are two groups whereas in fact there are three. The third are the bulk of humanity who are neither destined to be co-inheritors with Christ, nor the ones "*created only to be captured and destroyed*" (Rom9:22; 2Pet2:12); the souls who according to Paul have been adjusted or adapted (Greek: *katertismina*), being foreknown and destined for satanic use to fulfil God's wondrous purposes, such as having His own Son betrayed and executed for the salvation of mankind and the ultimate defeat of His arch-enemy. This is typified in the example Paul himself provides in Romans nine to explain the purpose of such instruments: the exaltation, hardening of heart and final humiliation of the Egyptian Pharaoh to display JHWE's power to save and deliver His people from their oppressors (v17). Given that evil is not a substance but a deficiency it cannot be created. An innate sense of God's law and the ability to empathize with other humans pertain to common grace, which is a benevolent gift which God commonly provides, yet He is not duty-bound to do so any more than He is to provide the special grace needed to apprehend Christ (Jn6:44). When the common variety is withheld or diminished it will be for a good purpose, which is hinted at in Romans9 and will be enlarged upon in my last chapter. Grace of the common variety is made available to all, most of whom choose to co-operate with it, whilst celestial grace is provided to those God has appointed to it. As a result, there are three broad categories of people: in terms of morality some are incapable of any good for their consciences are defiled and therefore they are guided and motivated only by the needs of the flesh and the will of Satan; others (the majority), although they cannot meet the standard of holiness and purity required to be in communion with the Son and Spirit (which requires spiritual rebirth), they can do good and be a blessing for the rest of humanity: "for I was hungry and you fed Me, etc." The Matthew 25 "sheep" did not need to be religious, holy or perfectly fulfil a law to show compassion, for they were justified by utilizing the quality they possess through being human; "faith" working through love. They had utilized the moral compass with which they were provided, deferred to conscience and so acted like decent human beings. The third group who have been sanctified by the Word, the Spirit and the blood do good and must *be* good by walking not according to the flesh but to the spirit if they are to be joint inheritors with their Master. In terms of eschatology, there are likewise three outcomes which are evident in Scripture old and new: In God's Revelation to Jesus Christ relayed through John, the largest eschatological group are pictured as the *"nations of those who are saved"*, whose kings bring their treasures to the City in which Christ is enthroned with His elect who are privileged to see Him face to face (Rev21:22-27; 22:4). In Isaiah, they would have been (under "Plan A") the survivors of the nations who from Sabbath to Sabbath would come to the holy city and bow in the Lord's presence, *"and on their way out they will see the corpses of those who rebelled against Me"* (the wicked and godless) who will be an abhorrence to all humanity (Is66:23,24). In the Gospels they are the sheep of Matthew 25; the elect having already been gathered to Christ so as to be spared the climax of tribulation (Mt 24 vv31,40,41). In Romans 8 they are those of the human creation longing to be liberated as children of God who do not have the first-fruits of the Spirit (v21,22) waiting for the revelation of the sons of God who already do (v23). For God's special blessings and curses are applied to a small proportion of the human family, as we saw regarding the populating of the postdiluvian world. The Book of Enoch (chapter 50) clarifies the distinction between the "holy and elect" on the one hand who will be honoured at His coming, and others who will not be honoured but having repented will be "saved in His Name" for "His compassion is great" (v3). As always, there is a third group who will be unwilling or unable to repent or bow the knee and they will not be spared (v4).

Many may struggle with Romans chapter 9 and the concept of souls (vessels for the spirit) adapted for destruction in terms of God's justice. As Paul writes, it is not for His own pleasure that God long-sufferingly endures these people's abhorrent ways, but for the ultimate benefit of those He would bring to glory (v22,23). One also needs to keep in mind that these are instruments that are being utilized by Satan, who functions in the present age as the "prince of the power of the air", the spirit that now works in the children of intransigence, being the ones who will never respond to God's light or truth. Since Satan does not waste his limited resources and by tradition looks after his own, these may become persons of renown (cf. Gen6:4) who enjoy wealth, power and prestige in the world such as the example of Pharaoh given in Romans 9. They are likely to be influential in politics, industry or religion (for sure) and be greatly esteemed and respected even by the good; as were some Pharisees in Jesus's time and as recently as the last century, a democratically elected Chancellor of Germany. For often being respectable they will not be easy to spot, for only God and on occasions those filled with His Spirit may gaze into the window of their souls and discern the emptiness there (Acts13:9,10), for the desolate ones are not to be defined by what they possess and practice but by what they have lost and so fail to practice (*agape*). Any such people leading the Jewish community in Jesus's day could not fool the Saviour, who declared quite plainly: "*You are of your father the devil*" (e.g. Jn8:44). That was **not** the way Jesus generally addressed or approached "sinners"; the multitudes whom He loved and regarded as sheep without a Shepherd (Mt9:36). Others within the devil's party more readily display their affiliation, such as those thankfully few criminals who abuse, dehumanize or destroy others without mercy or remorse and have a great time doing it. The behaviour of such can be so appallingly inhumane as to be genuinely beyond the comprehension of ordinary people as is evident in the cases of certain classes of criminals that I have made a point of researching. Two traits become very evident in such people and one hardly needs to be a theologian to discern them: an absence of conscience (thus no shame or remorse) and a total absence of empathy or compassion for their victims. This is the common observation of judges, juries and victims when such people are brought to human justice. The nature of their crimes and their attitude concerning them genuinely mystifies many ordinary people; by now it should be evident why such behaviour occurs and that it is assuredly not the common stock of humanity, Christian or otherwise. If the divine light provided to the mind's "eye" of natural man still leaves him somewhat in the dark and in need of spiritual healing, how deep will a man's darkness be if the "eye" itself is darkened; or as Jesus expressed the matter (though it is invariably mistranslated), "if the light that is in thee is darkness, how great is the darkness (that is in thee)" - Mt6:23). Thankfully, the majority demonstrate by their moral restraint and empathy that they have a working conscience (their mind's eye is enlightened) but they will continue in a measure of darkness until they are finally liberated from the bondage of corruption into which they were born (cf. Rom8:21) or encounter the grace of the gospel in the meantime. Once it is understood that those who become disqualified (reprobate) from the universal Covenant are deployed by the devil, it should be no surprise that a good number end up in the churches to wreak havoc, pervert doctrine and damage her reputation, so undermining the Good News of God's love for humanity. The Mother Church is an obvious target for Satan to deploy his limited resources, whereas wherever for example the "prosperity gospel" is being preached he scarcely needs to bother. That does not excuse but may help explain why the Catholic Church has experienced the scandals it has over the years. What is quite intolerable and has grieved the hearts of ordinary Catholics has been deception and cover-up, but it is widely acknowledged that the current Pope is working hard to get to grips with these problems. His predecessor openly acknowledged the evil that had crept into the Church; one suspects he eventually became overwhelmed by it:

"How much filth there is in the (Roman Catholic) Church, and even among those who, in the priesthood, ought to belong entirely to him! How much pride, how much self-complacency! What little respect we pay to the Sacrament of Reconciliation, where he waits for us, ready to raise us up whenever we fall! ... ... Lord, your Church often seems like a boat about to sink, a boat taking in water on every side. In your field we see more weeds than wheat. The soiled garments and face of your Church throw us into confusion. Yet it is we ourselves who have soiled them! It is we who betray you time and time again, after all our lofty words and grand gestures. Have mercy on your Church; within her too, Adam continues to fall."[5].

Thus spoke Joseph Ratzinger (currently Pope Emeritus) weeks before his papal election in 2005. Such is surely a fitting confession for a Church earnestly seeking renewal. And such should be the response of us all, once we grasp the extent of our faults and failings.

Indifference to truth

There is another feature common to the human category we are focusing on regardless of whether they are outwardly respectable or plainly criminal, and as always it pertains to a deficiency: they are indifferent to truth for they are not of the truth (Jn18:37b). Their adoptive father was described by Jesus as the "father of lying" (Jn8:44) and so those he masters are pathological in that trait. Having no working conscience, they will only speak the truth if it is convenient for the purpose in hand: there will be no other incentive. Anyone who is of God may lie but will never feel entirely comfortable about it unless, perhaps, it is a "white lie" to avoid hurting another, which on at least one occasion is commended in Scripture (Jam2:25 cf. Josh2:1-5). The means is sometimes justified by the end; that would appear to be a divine principle (next chapter). Those who are indwelt by the Spirit and already united to Christ will be highly sensitized in this area, wishing to avoid even so much as a hint of exaggeration. For truthfulness is integral to holiness; which is why the promises of God are so dependable even if He fulfils them in the most surprising ways. The wicked are having their consolation in this age and will pay a fair and just penalty for their crimes against God and humanity in the next. Like Judas they may appear to fulfil Satan's purposes of destruction in the immediate sense but actually fulfil God's inscrutable designs in the ultimate sense. If as Romans 9 implies these souls are innately deficient, such will be taken into account at judgement, for no-one is judged for that of which they are ignorant or incapable. "*To whom much is given much is required*" and the converse equally applies regarding the severity of punishment (Lk12:48). Some will nevertheless struggle with the whole concept of human instruments adapted for dishonour (Rom9:22), for God's *modus operandi* can be extraordinary, none more so than in the sphere we are currently reviewing.

Children of the devil in Jesus's ministry

What is striking as one reads carefully through the gospel accounts is Jesus's starkly contrasting attitude to the people he encountered, all of whom were to one degree or another sinful. It will be surprising to some that in calling his disciples there is little if any reference to their sinfulness. These were ordinary working men: Simon Peter was conscious of his own unworthiness when he became aware of his Lord's divinity (Lk5:8), but Jesus's only recorded comment concerning the moral state of His new recruits was a positive one regarding Nathanael: "*Behold, an Israelite indeed in whom there is no guile*" (Jn1:47). This cynical joker was not perfect (Jn1:46) but those who *are* perfect such as the incarnate Word, look for the good in people and love them for it (Mk10:19-23). Judas was another matter: Jesus knew He was recruiting a devil (Jn6:70). This was not a term he employed when addressing the majority who had fallen short of the glory of God, i.e. sinners as opposed to "children of the devil". He did not ask His disciples to "acknowledge their lost estate", simply to follow Him (Mt4:19). Unscrupulous tax collectors on the other hand were required to turn their lives around (repent) and make restitution. Note this tree-clambering penitent's childlike exuberance:

*Zacchaeus stood up and said to the Lord: "**Look Lord!** Here and now I give half my possessions to the poor, and if I have cheated anybody out of anything, I will pay back four times the amount". Jesus said to him, "**Today salvation has come to this house** because this man too is a son of Abraham" (Lk19:8,9 New International Version)*

The Man who has been appointed to judge the world was remarkably tolerant towards the human weakness of His disciples and ate and drank congenially with tax collectors and sinners, much to the contempt of certain religious leaders (Mt9:11). Consider His gracious dealings with the woman accused of adultery. Having challenged her accusers with "*Let he who is without sin among you cast the first stone*", He asks the woman: "*Did no one condemn you? Neither do I condemn you. Go and offend no more*". (Jn8:11). However, when faced with wickedness and hypocrisy amongst religious leaders, the tone sharpened noticeably:

Serpents, brood of Vipers! How can you escape the condemnation of Hell? (Mt23:33)

Jesus was addressing certain scribes and Pharisees who are confirmed as "occupying the seat of Moses" (Mt23:2); in view of which, He said, they should continue to be obeyed by His followers (Mt23:3). Their position of authority was one reason Jesus was so scathing: they of all people were without excuse. As He told them:

If you were blind, you would not be guilty*, but since you say, "we can see", your guilt remains (Jn9:41)*

These wicked tenants of God's vineyard had refused John's baptism unlike the majority who had acknowledged him to be the "prophet of the Most High" (Lk1:76) and an "esteemed preacher of righteousness" (Mt21:25,26,32). In so doing, these leaders had in the Bible's words thwarted God's plan for them (Lk7:30). If they had been good tenants, teaching and pasturing God's people in the ways of righteousness, these erudite and revered religious leaders would have been the ones to support the Lord and take the work of the Kingdom forward. Yet in rejecting these leaders of His people, Jesus did not there and then "turn to the Gentiles"; that was to be Paul (Acts13:46); that was to be later; that would be the fellowship of the secret. The inauguration of "the Kingdom" remained a strictly Jewish affair: Jesus appointed a motley crew of small businessmen, fishermen, a physician and a tax official (exclusively Jewish) for His immediate circle and prepared them to build the Kingdom of God in His temporary absence. Those more established leaders who had expected to be the princes of God's Kingdom rejected Jesus and all He stood for. It was largely through their influence (Mk15:11) that many of the palm-waving crowds that had been heralding King Jesus as He triumphantly entered Jerusalem would become a baying mob calling on the Messiah's crucifixion a short time later. For it is in the nature of lost sheep easily to be led astray. Jesus was handed over to Pilate "*because*

297

of envy" (Mt27:18): ordinary Jewish folk were hardly envious of Jesus but their religious leaders were, because their flock were looking to Him rather than to them, and under Jesus they knew they were to be axed (Mt21:41). In their teaching these blind guides were "straining out gnats and swallowing camels"; neglecting to teach or practice the weightier matters of the Law – justice, mercy and faithfulness (Mt23:23). There was a stark contrast between the attitude of these Jewish leaders and many of the people they led. It is typified in this verse concerning Jesus's daily preaching in the Temple:

*Every day He was teaching at the temple. But the chief priests, the teachers of the Law and the leaders among the people were **trying to kill Him**. Yet they could not find any way to do it because all **the people hung on His words** (Lk19:47,48 New International Version).*

Most people Jesus encountered were excited by His ministry, and not only the miracles, but as Luke describes above they hung on His every word of teaching. This reality needs to be grasped: had they not been so cajoled by their leaders, the Jewish people might very well have welcomed Jesus as their messianic King, whereas many of those leaders whom gospel writer John unhelpfully labels "the Jews" (e.g. Jn19:38) wanted Him dead, and since that was in accordance with the divine plan, they soon got their wish (cf. Lk24:20). Little did these leaders realize they were being used; for through divine ingenuity the satanic seed were playing into God's hands as they always do. For religious leaders who conspired against the Messiah incorporated the devil's children (who are always strategically employed), and as is their wont they went on to ensnare a sufficient number of the people who looked up to them to bring about, humanly speaking, the most perverse injustice in human history, enacted at the place of the skull. Their Victim was aware of these leaders' origins:

You are of your father the devil, and the desires of your father you want to do. He was a murderer from the beginning and does not stand in the truth, because there is no truth in him (Jn8:44NKJ).

He also told them, *"If God were your Father, you would love Me since I originate from God"* (v42). Yet Jesus received respect, love and honour from a good number of Jewish people He encountered during His ministry as Luke had reported:

Jesus increased in wisdom and stature and in favour with God and man (Lk2:52).

The majority were of God; desiring a Good Shepherd to lead them but easily deceived and led astray; as were many such people including a good number within the Christian churches nineteen hundred years later, adoring and cheering their political messiah in Germany who went on to leave much of Europe in ruins. *"God has at last given the German people a pious and faithful ruler in the person of Adolf Hitler"* affirmed the Protestant group calling themselves "the German Christians" in the 1930s; and Catholics weren't immune from such error either. Such had failed to grasp what we have just been saying about the Jewish people as a whole. The Pharisees had also acknowledged: "The whole world has gone after (Jesus)" (Jn12:19). That was an exaggeration for He predominantly ministered to the Jews. His fame and favour came despite the fact that for the earlier part of His ministry Jesus did not want the general public to know He was the Messiah or Son of God (e.g. Lk9:21) for He had another "baptism" to undergo first (Lk12:49,50). So, as Ignatius observed[6], if it were not for the devil working in the minds and hearts of those he controls (the sons of intransigence - Eph2:2 cf. Greek) inciting the Jewish people against their true Messiah (Mk15:11), and a devilish disciple betraying Him, Jesus could never have been crucified (cf. Lk24:20).

But then God's perfect plan for humanity would not have been fulfilled, for the crucifixion was according to "the definite plan and foreknowledge of God" (Acts2:23) and Satan's seed were an essential part of it. For it was necessary that not only the Son of God should die for mankind's sin sometime in history, but that He died when He did and how He did within the narrative of the Israel project and its subsequent transmutation into the Church project. The children of the devil had unwittingly played their part to bring about the ultimate Victory of God assured through the cross, and they continue to play their part in the world including the churches, mosques, synagogues and temples, especially keen to pervert religion and the meaning of holy writ for their own destructive ends – *"for offences must come, but woe to the ones by whom they come"* (Mt18:7). The reason such offences must continue for a little longer is outlined in the final chapter.

Notes: CHAPTER SIX

1. Origen De Principiis Book 1 chap. 3 para 6

2. Ibid

3. e.g. First epistle of Clement chap. 11

4. Deification as a term and concept was quite widely understood amongst the early Fathers in the context of Christian salvation and is prevalent today more particularly within Eastern Orthodoxy. In the West, Thomas Aquinas (13th Century) denoted deification to be the end purpose of human existence.

5. Joseph Ratzinger, "Meditations on the Way of the cross," Good Friday, 2005,

6. Epistle of Ignatius to the Philippians (spurious) Chap. IV

Chapter Seven

The Theodicy

*It was fitting for (Jesus), for whom are all things and by whom are all things, in bringing many sons to glory, to make the captain of their salvation **perfect through suffering** (Heb2:10 New King James Version)*

If *I* ruled the world, every day would be the first day of spring; every heart would have a new song to sing and we'd sing of the joy every morning would bring. My world would be a beautiful place where we would weave such wonderful dreams... I could go on, but it has all been sung before[1]. For the Christian, the spiritual dimension that has been the focus of our consideration in this book transcends the sentiments of that song from "Pickwick", but one should acknowledge that it does depict a better world in terms of actual human experience than exists at present or has ever existed since the Eden incident. Christians will hasten to explain that the cruelty, injustice, broken relations, sickness and death that has become an inescapable aspect of life on Earth was the result of that one act of disobedience by the first human couple. Non-Christians presented with such a concept are inclined to regard it as facile and frankly I cannot blame them, for it is only a third of the story when understood from a more enlightened Christian perspective such as that possessed by the thirteenth apostle (cf. Rom8:20,21). But before we come to the providential dimension hinted at in those verses of Paul we must recognize also that there exists a realm of evil that is extraneous to humanity which took the lead in that initial catastrophe; a sophisticated principality of wickedness that endures as a force in the world to the present day:

For we wrestle not against flesh and blood, but against principalities, against powers, against the rulers of the darkness of this world, against spiritual wickedness in high places (Eph6:12 New King James Version).

The verse is addressed to Christian believers, but the One who remembers the needs of the sparrows is aware that the activity and influence of this evil realm impinges upon the whole human family and all created life that falls under His care. For there is a third reason apart from humanity's initial disobedience and Satan's treachery for things having to be as they are in the World, and that will be unravelled as we progress through the chapter. In terms of the realm of evil that confronts mankind, it might appear that we *are* wrestling against flesh and blood for the diabolical activity that St Paul was referring to is normally exercised through the human agencies under its control. These are the human seed that we considered in the previous chapter – they are the darnel poisoning the wheat that must remain until harvest. Of course, the rest of humanity sins and causes plenty of trouble as well, the more so for being led astray and corrupted by Satan who deceives the world through the people he controls. So, God holds Satan rather than mankind personally accountable for the world being in the state it is; he will pay by far the greater price, as will his delegates, messengers or agents. What is more difficult to explain is why these wicked beings continue to thrive, influence and offend. As one traces events back to the Fall, one should discern that it is not entirely a matter of "free will" that resulted in wickedness being retained on the Earth but a deliberate aspect of divine providence. Yet the evil does originate from a malign exercise of the free will that the Creator is bound to give to any being to whom He wishes intimately to relate, starting with the angelic realm. However, and here lies the problem for many, it must be acknowledged that the extent to which a created being having chosen a course of evil is then permitted to continue practicing it and hurting others is entirely a matter of divine prerogative (or else impotence or indifference which is not the case here). Being one who since rejecting the theology of the Reformers has come to perceive the Creator to be holy and loving *in the sense that that these qualities are*

303

defined in Scripture (1Cor13:4-5), this whole area had been hard to reconcile until recently.

Adam and Eve had been warned that if they disobeyed God they would die that very day. I explained earlier that the warning did not refer to physical death (they continued for centuries) or what would happen to their souls after they died, but to the disruption in their relationship with God whilst they were in the body. Yet this pair could have been eliminated there and then; the Adam project could have been rebooted, feasibly with a better outcome for humanity, for the two had been created pure in soul and body and unlike fallen man were potentially capable of full obedience. God was not obliged to establish His human creation through such corrupted progenitors; He well knew the outcome for His creation, Himself and His Son when He chose to reject what might appear to human minds to have been the logical rebooting option. Yet as hinted earlier, this incident in the paradise Garden and the inscrutable way that God chose to handle it is in fact the most staggering aspect of His love for humanity in view of the personal cost to Himself and especially His Son. In terms of the consequences for His earthly creation, many were now to be subjected to a life that was frustrating, vain and unfulfilled (*mataiotes* - Rom8:20). For the majority that has been the case: their life has certainly not been without purpose and sometimes joy, yet the primary intent for which they had been created was not accomplished during their earthly lifetime – that had been to know God; that had been Life of an eternal quality. Very shortly after the incident in Eden the divine prerogative was exercised again with the first man to be born of woman. Cain had become entirely alienated from God (Gen4:14), yet He still ensured that this murderer and his seed survived. Again, he could have been wiped out there and then for his fratricide and insolence towards God but instead was provided with a mark for his protection (Gen4:15) such that he and his accursed seed would continue up to the time of the flood. The book of Enoch relates how the spirit of Abel petitioned God for Cain's seed to be annihilated, which duly occurred through the worldwide Flood. This clarifies Gen4:10 and especially Heb12:24 concerning the reference to Christ's blood speaking better things than Abel. This inspired book also expands on Gen6:1,2 also alluded to in Jude1:6

304

concerning angelic or rather satanic union with women and the irretrievable corruption it caused, even extending to the animal Kingdom through bestiality. But what cannot be perceived without reference to the book of Enoch yet is needed to understand the rationale behind the universal Flood is that these satanic collaborators had imparted knowledge to humanity that the Lord had intended mankind gradually to discover over many centuries. As with Adam and Eve and the forbidden fruit from the tree of knowledge, humanity in its infancy was not ready for the knowledge they provided which would lead to their destruction, yet could never be unlearnt, hence the need for a radical universal cleansing by water. Enoch19:1 explains that these rebellious sons of God who left their appointed place (cf. Jud1:6) and were responsible for the global contamination and the thwarting of God's plans for mankind's development were able to assume different forms to carry out their illicit unions (re: objections raised by Mt22:30). Through God's mercy, the bulk of humanity who ignored Noah's warning and perished in the Flood has subsequently had the Good News preached to them by Jesus Himself (1Pet3:19,20), as, the apostle indicates, do all the dead have opportunity to hear the Good News so that although having been punished in the flesh "*they might live according to God in the spirit*" (1Pet4:6). Some struggle with that concept believing it to undermine the relevance of the gospel. It becomes far more intelligible once one understands the context of gospel salvation within God's broader reconciliatory plans. These imprisoned spirits were given the opportunity to repent and acknowledge Christ's lordship; they were not to be betrothed as His eternal Bride, nor did they escape punishment for they had been imprisoned for centuries. The very early Christian writers including Irenaeus confirm my understanding that Adam's physical death, though partly a punishment, was in effect a concession by which once freed of the body he could be freed from sin so that he could begin again "to live for God"[2]. He was equally clear that the spirits of those who died in Old Testament times had the gospel preached to them by Jesus after His crucifixion and were given the chance to place their faith in Him[3]

As we saw earlier, although all who came off the ark were blessed by God, one of the sixteen seeds stemming from Noah's sons was cursed, leading to the wickedness of Sodom, Gomorrah and the Canaanite territories resulting in their partial annihilation. Of course, wickedness continued through till the time of Christ and until the present day, and that is not surprising in view of the role Satan himself had been permitted:

*Then the devil taking (Jesus) up on a high mountain showed Him all the kingdoms of the world in a moment of time. And the devil said to him, all this authority I will give you and their glory for this has been **delivered to me** and I give it to whomever I wish; therefore, if You will worship before me all will be yours (Lk4:5-7 New King James Version)*

Satan was a liar, but he could hardly hope to deceive the Son of God on such a matter, nor did Jesus deny Satan's claim to have been given authority over the world's kingdoms. Jesus goes on to describe him as the "prince of this world", or "leader of the world order" (*archon tou kosmou*), whilst Paul refers to him as the "prince of the power of the air" (Eph2:2) and "a crafty schemer" (2Cor2:11); St Peter as a prowling lion (1Pet5:8), and St John as holding the whole world under his control (1Jn5:19). Unlike the coming age of the Kingdom of Christ (cf. 2Tim4:1), Satan is not currently prevented from deceiving the world (Rev12:9) but in spite of the salt and light provided by the worldwide churches and many people of good will outside them, he continues to preside over a principality of wickedness that impacts upon nations and their governance, greatly adding to people's suffering. This prince had not been cast out after the resurrection of Christ (cf. Jn12:31) – it looked initially as though that was being indicated by the short-lived witness of expelled demons and miraculous healings, but the Adversary's final ignominy has been deferred. Yet if, as is indeed the case, Christ has done everything necessary to achieve Satan's demise, why should that be? Or were the apostles Peter, Paul and John mistaken on the matter of his continued authority on Earth? One only has to review the events of the century just past to recognize not only that they were right, but that that influence has scarcely been eroded nineteen centuries into the Christian era. Was there ever a conflict as grim as the Great War whose centenary is currently being commemorated; or a deception so insidious and activity so heinous as that practiced by the German Nazi Party in the war that followed it? It is as if suffering were an essential part of God's purposes for humanity. Whilst He does not initiate it, He certainly has the power to end it for He is sovereign, and his Son has already been victorious over Evil.

Now that I am clear why these things must be, I would not wish it any other way for truly God is Love personified and does know best. Suffering is no accident: "*I form the light and create darkness; I make peace and create calamity. I the Lord do all these things*" (cf. Is45:7). Spiritual masters in the past have put forward various philosophical arguments for the need for such suffering within God's economy. We have already touched upon "free will" as the instrumental cause of evil's introduction into God's good creation. But that doesn't of itself explain why evil beings have been permitted to prosper or have been granted ongoing major spheres of operation and influence. Thomas Aquinas provided a partial solution to this mystery in his epic Summa Theologica when he stated quite succinctly that "*God permits evil so as to bring out of it a greater good*". More specifically he proposed that "*diverse grades of goodness occur in things, many of which would be lacking if no evil existed; indeed, the good of patience could not exist without the evil of persecution*"[4]. In other words, without evil and the dysfunctional practices associated with it, there would be no place for virtue, or at least it would not so clearly be seen to be virtuous and something to delight in; not only in human affairs but in the worshipful admiration of God Himself. If Satan had not been permitted his little triumphs, there would have been no glorious victory for God and His Christ, for there had been nothing to conquer. How could God have demonstrated the staggering extent of His love and grace if He could have spared His only Son? If Adam had not sinned or the humanity project rebooted, there would have been no Saviour, and what a Saviour: *O felix culpa, quae talem ac tantum meruit habere Redemptorum*[5].

307

The ultimate purpose for human suffering

But this is only a part of the story, although I think we can already dispense with comic writer Woody Allen's proposal that the existence of evil indicates that "God is at best an under-achiever". Such a case could be made if evil existed to the degree that it does and yet God was unable to overcome it or had no real use for it, but neither is the case, for it is a temporary yet essential ingredient within the plan of human destiny. Suffering is neither a result of divine impotence nor a miscalculation; as well as being the backdrop to highlight the beauty and loveliness of the good and therefore of God Himself, its principle purpose is to prepare humanity for the next phase in her development. Neither is that merely a philosophical speculation, it is a biblical reality that again has been historically eluded through a failure to grasp both the context of gospel salvation within broader providence and the nature of the ages to come. Human beings currently possessing bodies originating from dust (cf. Gen2:7) are destined for glory and service at least as splendid as that of the angels of Heaven (cf. Heb1:14). Suffering, and consequently the existence of evil is a necessary part of the process of deification which requires human beings to be, as it were, "stretched" or go beyond themselves in order to be fitted for such glory and responsibility. The Son of Man set the pattern: He tasted death for every man for our salvation, but there is something else we are told about His death:

*Looking unto Jesus, the author and finisher of our faith, **who for the joy that was set before Him**, endured the cross and despised the shame, and has sat down at the right hand of the throne of God (Heb12:2 New King James Version)*

The highlighted phrase is hardly the one on which one would normally focus - this is something you may have noticed within this presentation. The Godhead's love for all humanity (Jn3:16) and the Son of God's obedience and suffering to deal with our sin are rightly the focal points. But Jesus's awareness of the joy and glory awaiting Him is nevertheless referred to and it hints at what is to be adduced in this chapter: the divine principal that suffering is beneficial, indeed necessary for those who are to be

308

glorified. Jesus might appear to be the exception, for He is worthy of glory through divine birth-right. Nevertheless:

*It was fitting for Him, for whom are all things and by whom are all things, in **bringing many sons to glory**, to make the captain of their salvation **perfect through suffering**, for both He who sanctifies and those who are being sanctified are **all of one**, for which reason He is not ashamed to call them brethren (Heb2:10,11 New King James Version)*

So even the Son of Man was made perfect through suffering (confirmed also in Heb5:8,9). In His case it had nothing to do with being made sinless, for He always was sinless. It pertained to His personal capacity and Office, especially that of High Priest:

*Therefore, in all things (Jesus) **had to be made like His brethren**, that He might be a merciful and faithful High Priest in things pertaining to God, to make a propitiation for the sins of the people, for that He himself has suffered, being tempted, He is able to aid those who are tempted. (Heb2:17,18 New King James Version)*

His awareness and personal experience of human suffering also prepares Him for His role as a merciful Supreme Judge of humanity. It set a pattern and example for those who as co-heirs must support Him as priests, kings and judges; they are to share in Christ's glory but must firstly share His suffering:

*Now if we are children, then we are heirs: heirs of God and co-heirs with Christ; **if indeed we share in His sufferings in order that we may also share in His glory** (Rom8:17 New International Version)*

But what advantage could human beings have had over the angels of Heaven? – a personal day-to-day experience of sin and suffering. Is that really an advantage? – Not if our destiny were to be a spiritual, albeit blissful stasis, beholding the vision of God's glory, wonderful though that currently is for those who have "fallen asleep" as Scripture describes the temporary separation of body and spirit in Heaven. But the emphasis from the Old Testament prophesies, the gospels, the epistles and

Revelation as far as the next age is concerned is for the elect to be *"the children of the resurrection"* (Lk20:36). For the believer's destiny once resurrected does not merely consist in beholding but *supporting* God in His activity in eternal union with His Son. But as with any marriage, *howsoever* the Bridegroom may relate to His Father through eternity so must His Bride for they are now in union; and *whatsoever* His Son's activity and domain, so shall His co-heirs share in it (cf. Dan7:18). Clearly the spouse concept is mystical in the sense of the "wife" (cf. Rev19:7) being a corporate identity, but so is Christ's bride-in-waiting the Church, which functions as His Militant Body on Earth; each person playing his or her role as a member of that spiritually directed administration. St Paul also affirms that eternity will comprise numerous ages (e.g. Eph2:7 cf. Greek) and, if the title-subject of this book is anything to go by, God is full of surprises. If the Church thinks she can be clear about the precise nature and procession of eternity, she should surely think again. For this few millennia of human history on this pin-prick we call Earth is in terms of time and space a grain of sand within the desert of eternity. Who knows what plans God has for the limitless theatre that is His universe? For God's Word became flesh; Jesus being from two natures (human and divine) yet essentially one subsistent nature as the incarnate Word of God. Humanity has therefore been permanently incorporated into the Godhead, indicating future physicality and terrestrial activity as well as delighting in the prospect of beholding the divine Glory that historically has tended to be the focus and expression of the Christian's future hope. Yet none shall be disappointed, for being in eternal union with the One *"in whom dwells the fullness of the Godhead bodily; the Head of all principalities and powers"*, **we shall be complete in Him** (Col2:9,10).

Yet it is *all* humanity that suffers in the present: having encouraged believers to stand fast against their Adversary who is prowling the Earth like a roaring lion, the apostle Peter adds this: *"knowing that the same sufferings are to be completed in your brotherhood who are in the world"* (1Pet5:9 cf. Greek). It is unlikely Peter here was alluding to their sister churches, he is surely referring to the human family. They also are suffering

310

through the devil's malevolence, and for a purpose, for all the scattered seed of God will in due time enjoy future communion with the divine glory; it is a question of staging, the faithful of the Church being the first-fruits. For when Jesus comes again:

*He shall be glorified **in His saints** and admired by those that believe on that day, for (after all), our testimony **among you** was believed (2Thes1:10).*

This is re-affirmed in Paul's letter to the Corinthians:

*For as in Adam all die, even so in Christ shall all be made alive; but everyone in **his own class**: Christ the first-fruits; afterwards those who are Christ's at His coming (1Cor15;22,23).*

Where profundity lurks

"Christ the first-fruits" could refer to the Church *a.k.a.* the Body of Christ, *a.k.a.* Christ (e.g. 1Cor12:12). Christians are the "first-fruits of creation" (Jam1:18). Jesus is also described as the First-fruits but He was never "dead in Adam" in the Pauline sense for He Himself was the Second Adam; and He cannot be a "class of those in Christ" (*hekastos de en to idio tagmati*) for He is the Christ. Likewise, Christians are no longer "dead in Adam", they are alive in Christ now, so it cannot be they who are spiritually made alive at His coming, rather those who receive and acknowledge Him when He appears. The verse is unlikely to be referring to resurrection, partly because the context is the consequence of original sin (dead in Adam, made alive in Christ) apart from which it would hardly be necessary to inform the Church that Christ arose from the dead before they will. The apostle never states the blindingly obvious any more than he was likely ever to have been absurdly tautological (e.g. Gal2:16 earlier translations): such instances are where profundity or mystery lurks. As with the passage referring to the fellowship of the secret (Eph3:6-9) in which Paul takes three verses, a pulsating build-up and three references to "a mystery" to inform us that the Church is not Jewish, something has to be amiss in our understanding or in the translation, or there is something we are simply not perceiving.

311

St Paul's verses quoted above align with Old Testament prophecy that all who shall call on the name of the Lord will be saved from perdition. Logically and fairly, the same principle would be expected to apply to those who have died having never had the opportunity to know the Saviour, and that is substantiated on two occasions in the first epistle of Peter (3:18-20 & 4:6). On the other hand, those alive at His coming who are not of God and refuse to obey the gospel of Christ will in Paul's language be set ablaze (2Thes1:8) however literally one chooses to take that; they will certainly be removed from His presence and everyone else's (v9). By "not obeying the gospel" is meant refusing to acknowledge the Lordship of Christ even after His identity has been manifested. For one can only obey or refuse to obey what has been clearly understood; so when Christ re-appears on Earth and indeed wherever He has presented Himself in person (cf. 1Pet3:18,19; 1Pet4:6; Jn15:22) there can be no excuse for those who reject Him. Likewise, if a universally agreed announcement of the coming Kingdom of Christ were presented to the world from a re-unified Church it would be a clarion call that would seriously need to be heeded (cf. Mt24:14). And such would be the roll-call: *Who is on the Lord's side; who will serve the King?*

The apostle Paul regarded the earthly creation as being in labour during the current age (Rom8:22), waiting for the revelation of the sons of God in the regeneration. When Christ is glorified in His saints the birth-pangs having at that time reached their crescendo will be over, and, the apostle indicates, the whole Earth can be healed and renewed. Then:

He must reign until He has put all enemies under His feet (1Cor15:25)

The Church as the Kingdom of Christ on Earth is involved in a spiritual battle with satanic forces yet cannot eradicate them. It may have appeared to fourth century Christians that things were heading that way in the wake of Emperor Constantine's conversion to Christianity such that Romans16:20 concerning the future crushing of Satan under the Church's feet would be achieved through a progressive ascendancy of the Church. Sixteen centuries later it should be obvious that could never have been what was intended: world peace and Christian dominion cannot occur in this age. Apart from which Jesus had stated quite categorically: the darnel will grow till the end of the age, then the reapers (His angels not the Church) will remove it and destroy it (Mt13:30). As for the a-millennial perspective I had once favoured, either Revelation 20 is entirely meaningless (a very dangerous position to assert in view of the epilogue (ch22:18-19)), or else the elect are in some sense already ruling with Christ on Earth. I think not: the Pilgrim Church was never even metaphorically intended to be in the business of "ruling the nations with a rod of iron" (Rev2:27 & 12:5). That could hardly be further removed from the Biblical depiction of the assemblies of Christ in the late first century and how their apostolic founders had instructed them to relate to the world and its authorities. It refers to what is to be done in the next age such that when at the end of the "Day", all earthly authorities have been subjected to the Arbitrator (cf. Is2:4), His Kingdom will be handed over to His Father for whatever subsequent ages may hold in store within a new Heaven and Earth (cf. 1Cor15:27-29).

Caesar is king of the world and Jesus isn't (yet)

I would like to be able to re-echo the aforementioned Professor N T Wright's frequent mantra that Jesus is King of the world and Caesar isn't, but alas not just yet. It is true that all authority in Heaven and on Earth has already been given to Jesus Christ by the Father (Mt28:18), but as is obvious as one looks out of the window, He does not in any constitutional or executive sense function as King of the World in the current age, nor is He referred to as such in the New Testament. The messianic role *prophesied* for Jesus according to the Old Testament is another matter but in view of "the fellowship of the secret" that more pertains to the age to come. The Holy Virgin's child was declared to be the King of Israel and King of the Jews by the astrologers, and later rode into Jerusalem on a donkey prefiguring such a Kingship; for that is what the prophets expected would be the Jewish messiah's imminent destiny:

For unto us a child is born, unto us a son is given: and the government shall be upon his shoulder, and his name shall be called: Wonderful, Counsellor, the mighty God, the everlasting Father, the Prince of Peace (Is9:6 King James Version)

And through the same prophet:

*How beautiful on the mountains are the feet of the messenger who announces peace, who brings Good News, who announces salvation, who says unto Zion, **"your God reigns!"** (Is52:7).*

But notice how St Paul when quoting this prophecy in his letter to the Romans (10:15) subtly subverts it: the single messenger (intended to be John/Elijah) is replaced with "those" (i.e. the preachers of the gospel), whilst the bit about "your God reigning (on Earth)", which after all was Isaiah's central message, is omitted. Christ is only once alluded to as King of the World in Matthew25 (v34) when He takes His seat to judge the nations at the *close* of the age. His first act will be to remove the godless and loveless resulting in peace and reconciliation for all people of good will, such that the Church will in its fullest sense be able to proclaim: our God reigns! But for now, darkness still invades the Earth and gross darkness the people, but the Lord shall arise over His restored Church and His glory shall be seen upon her; then the un-churched shall come to her light and kings to the brightness of her rising (cf. Is60:2,3).

Exploring this theme a little further, there are essential elements of a meaningful global reign which are entirely lacking in the current age: not just a physical Presence but any designated vice-regent or institution to carry out regal functions on the King's behalf such as to regulate government or appoint and if necessary admonish those in high office. The Bishop of Rome is Christ's vicar (substitute) on Earth but though he may be intended to have universal authority in the spiritual realm, his secular constitutional authority is restricted to the hundred or so acres of Vatican City. Neither is there a globally recognized Charter of Authority or Constitution, nor any mechanism for dealing with those who usurp the Sovereign's authority to rule. That is as intended for the Kingdom of God on Earth is currently confined within the universal Church. As such she will supplicate and endeavour to inculcate good governance but has no mandate to regulate in secular matters for she is neither a dictatorship nor constitutionally elected. The kingdoms of this world have not yet become the kingdoms of our Lord (cf. Rev11:15) in any meaningful sense, nor can they do so in the current age. The darnel is poisoning the wheat: it is not being neutralised by the Church but will be removed and incinerated in a single divine act (Mt13:24-30). That is the unmistakable and uncompromising teaching of the parable.

The news the messenger on the mountain which we noted St Paul omitting from his recounting of it was, as Handel's Messiah joyfully expresses it: *"Thy God reign-eth; break forth into joy; glad tidings, glad tidings!"* Of course, JHWE had always reigned and always will: the point of that publication was that through Emmanuel, God with us, the Anointed One was expected to reign *on Earth*; as a result of which Zion would have been liberated, evil eradicated and world peace initiated (Is2:4; Mic4:3). That's what great kings achieve, especially ones with a divine prerogative. It didn't happen as and when the prophets had expected, and we cannot look to the Church for such achievements. For now, she *reflects* the light of Christ to the world just as the moon seeks to regulate the night by reflecting the sun. But in that moonlight the creatures of the night may still comfortably creep about. But when the sun herself arises, that which is wholly evil will be set ablaze. Then shall our God, being Overlord of the Church truly reign on Earth with the whole Israel of God.

Christian submission to earthly authority

The Christian gospel was not intended to be subversive in terms of its adherents' approach to earthly authority. Jesus is Lord of the Church and King of the believer's heart, but the Christian is to have no earthly king but "Caesar" or his equivalent and is to render him or her what is due, otherwise he is denying the faith (Mk12:17). Of course, if "Caesar" requires the Christian to worship him as a god or directly oppose the teaching of Christ then to render to God what is God's, the faithful disciple may potentially be called upon to pay the ultimate price in martyrdom. For most Christians that is not the reality, though of course it hasn't always been the case. Yet even St Paul lived happily in Roman lodgings for two years teaching and evangelising *"without hindrance from anyone"* (Acts28:30). That would unlikely to have been the case if he had gone around asserting in mid-first century Rome that *"Jesus is King and Caesar isn't"*. His principal opponents and the instigators of his frequent imprisonments were more often unbelieving Jewish leaders than the civic authorities. Likewise, he instructed the churches to respect and pray for those in authority over them, as these were established by God for their good (Rom13:4-6).

Clearly the structure and composition of the earthly authorities is not as a reigning King Jesus would establish them for the personal qualities required for those participating in any administration of His would be quite different; more in accordance with His predecessor David: people after His own heart. For what *is* entirely subverted by the Christian gospel is how authority is to be exercised – both now in the Church where he who leads becomes the servant of servants, and in the future where it will not be the militarily powerful who inherit the Earth but the gentle and the peacemakers (cf. Mt5:5); for even the Son of Man did not come to be served but to serve and give His life as a ransom for many. So here is perhaps the most obvious flaw in NT Wright's thesis that Jesus in any meaningful sense became King of the world at His resurrection: under the present arrangements the gentle, the merciful, the pure of heart and the peacemakers are the people *least likely* to be running the *kosmos* (world system); nor have they ever been throughout the gospel age; nor can they be because of the continuing presence and influence of Satan and his seed. For when Jesus is King, Ephesians2:2 would not apply: Satan and his hold over people, death and sickness will have decisively been dealt with, not merely assured for the future. On the other hand, that same professor's related emphasis on what the Church should be doing in the meantime: renewing humanity by establishing Kingdom principles here on Earth such that God's Will is increasingly seen to be done *"on Earth as it is in Heaven"* is right on the money. That is something the Protestant Evangelical world especially needs to hear, for not untypically I had scarcely a notion of such a socio-political aspect of mission during my quarter-century as an Evangelical, whereas it has always been more to the forefront in Catholic thought and mission. But such renewal can only be in the context of preparing the ground for Emmanuel meaningfully to tabernacle with His people that together they may rule the world (cf. Rev5:10). Spiritual renewal of individuals through the centuries within the Church has been our Mother's other vital function in order that elect people from every nation and age, the chosen and faithful will have been prepared to participate within God's realized Kingdom at their resurrection together with those alive at His coming.

So for the current age, as the apostle Paul refers to the matter: God has placed all things under Christ's feet, but as ultimate Victor and Overseer rather than reigning Monarch, albeit that He really is Head over all *to the Church* (Eph1:22). The kings of the Earth are inferior to Christ and answerable to Him in final judgement, but they do not currently take their orders from Him more's the pity; He does not act as their overlord, and most of them would not recognize Him as such. That is why the Christian's citizenship is said to be in Heaven for that is where His ultimate allegiance lies, where His Lord is currently located and his spiritual treasures are being deposited. The Old Testament prophets on the other hand expected the promised messiah to be based in Jerusalem, enthroned as king of Israel and thereby king of the world, acting as Great High Priest for His Jewish nation who in turn were to function as a Kingdom of priests and monarchs for the world (Ex19:6). Instead, *"He has to remain in Heaven until the time comes for restoring everything"* (Acts3:21).

The Messianic Kingdom

The Catholic Church has long rejected pre-millenarianism as an approved doctrine, although it was the predominant view of the ante-Nicene Church Fathers including Justin Martyr, Irenaeus, Hippolytus of Rome, Tertullian, Cyprian, Barnabas and Lactantius and by deduction others whom they had instructed or

317

by whom they had been instructed but had not made their position clear in the writings available. Such were supported initially by Augustine of Hippo together with a good number of his contemporaries inside as well as some breakaway groups outside the Church. It was initially Marcion who challenged the consensus in the second century; he was later clearly shown to be a heretic. The other key influences being Augustine (who changed his mind) and Origen of Alexandria (who was inclined to a Platonic spiritualism); these colossi of the Western and Eastern Church ensuring that Millenarian views came to be rejected by the fourth century, reinforced one suspects by the conversion of Roman Emperor Constantine which transformed the Church's perspective with regard to its relationships with the political structures of the world. The Eastern Orthodox Church has regarded the Revelation of Jesus Christ via John as very much a mystery and is predominantly a-millennial. For an outline of why pre-millennial views had largely been abandoned by the middle ages, Wikipedia proves useful background[6]; the consensus is that the influence of Augustine was the key factor. Yet such is God's wisdom, for the vague and predominantly spiritualized eschatological understanding that the Apostolic churches in East and West have held for centuries has been perfectly suited to the recruitment process for Kingdom. Unlike chiliasm, particularly in its perverted hedonistic form, the predominant Church teaching since the beginning of the middle ages will have held little attraction to vain, faithless, materialistic glory-seekers and such are not the people the Lord has wished to recruit in His service. That was evident at His first visit, where the superior and erudite of the religious establishment were bi-passed and the Good News of the Kingdom was announced to shepherds on a hillside. Its propagation was spearheaded by an apprentice carpenter from Nazareth (of all places - Jn1:46) who turned out to be the promised Messiah; He in turn had recruited uneducated fishermen and the like to support Him and they would go on to turn the world upside down. It is only now as the end of the age approaches that those who think of it as the millennial age depicted in Revelation are liable to become discouraged and be unprepared for the lead-up to what is to follow. But in terms of timeframe and structure, the Bible does not lend itself to dogmatism in this area: a "day" with the Lord can be as a thousand years (2Pet3:8), and "judgement" is not restricted to the act of condemning or acquitting but to sorting everything out as we saw with the Old Testament prophecies 2Peter3 implies a destruction of the Heavens and Earth at the time of Christ's coming; the "Day" argument could still apply, apart from which the apostle was in no doubt that a new Heaven and Earth would be created (v13). Others such as NT Wright believe Peter's reference to the vanishing sky and burnt-up Earth to be a typical use of cosmic language to denote a cataclysmic event within the time-space universe, a hypothesis supported by extra-biblical writing of that period. Paul, John and Enoch all of whom were physically or spiritually transported to Heaven and back to glimpse the future indicate that the Son of Man is coming to restore and liberate creation, although that will be a devastating and destructive event for those who continue to resist the Good News of His Kingship once that is clarified (2Thess1:8). Most accept that the Earth and certainly the *kosmos* (world order) will be radically altered after Christ's coming, though quite how different the former will be is uncertain. If Scripture is unclear or ambiguous about the matter then so must I be; there have always been certain data the Lord would not supply to anyone, even those who were about to establish His Church (Acts1:7).

The Enoch perspective

Although ex-canonical, the Book of Enoch is regarded by many as inspired, valid for reference and according to its introduction written for the express benefit of those living at the very end of the current age (cf. 1En1:1). It envisages a Messianic rule on Earth together with the "elect and holy", whilst at the same time envisaging an entirely new Heaven and Earth that will be created or prepared for the time of the General Resurrection and Universal Judgement of mankind and the angelic realm. It provides more detail on the physical means by which human life and wellbeing are to be sustained prior to that. Politically, the whole "structure of unrighteousness would be removed" (En91:5); those not of God, having made their irrevocable choice for destruction are necessarily culled and a righteous rule established. It distinguishes more clearly between the "righteous" or what John describes as the "nations of those who are saved" (cf. Rev21:24) as distinct from the "elect who hang on the Elect One" (En40:5). Describing the respective fates of the *three* main categories of people at the end of this age, Enoch foretells:

__The righteous__ shall be victorious in the name of the Lord of Spirits and He will cause __the others__ to witness this that they may repent and forgo the works of their hands. They shall __have no honour through the name of the Lord of Spirits yet through His name they shall be saved__, and the Lord of Spirits shall have compassion on them, for His compassion is great. And He is righteous also in His judgement, and in the presence of His glory unrighteousness shall also not maintain itself: at His judgement the __unrepentant shall perish__ before Him.

The sequence of events according to Enoch is set out in chapter 91. As the end of the age approaches, wickedness, violence, uncleanness and apostasy will have increased. The first universal judgement had been by flood, the last (on the current Earth) would be in the presence of the Lord, when the roots of unrighteousness and idolatry will be removed from under Heaven (v9) and the righteous (only) would be raised from the dead (v10). This initiates the Messianic Kingdom which would be a period of righteousness in which "sinners would be delivered into the hands of the righteous" (v12 cf. Rom16:20), after which the righteous (according to Enoch) "would acquire houses through their righteousness whilst a house will be built for the great King in glory" (v13). At its conclusion comes the great white throne judgement when all the dead are raised, the world having been written down for destruction after which all mankind shall look to the path of uprightness (v14) within a new Heaven and Earth. Then, "all shall be in goodness and righteousness, and sin shall no more be mentioned for ever" (v17). In essence this goes beyond but doesn't contradict the Revelation account and re-affirms an age or "day" to follow this one in which the wicked are removed and the elect support Jesus Christ as He "subjects all things to Himself".

The fall of Babylon

"MYSTERY: Babylon the Great, Mother of all prostitutes and all filthy practices on Earth" (Rev17:5), the "great city that has authority over all the rulers on Earth" (17:18), by whom all the ship owners and merchants have been made wealthy (chapter 18) and who has been responsible for all the blood ever shed on Earth (18:24). Given the universality of its impact, this "city" can only refer to a mystical entity, for no one country, city or institution could be responsible for all corrupt practices on Earth or all its slaughter. It is referring to the "structure of unrighteousness" referred to in Enoch, or more generally "the wicked" of Old Testament prophecy; it is the devil's party. The two key points for those inclined to dismiss a period of messianic rule on Earth to note is that "Babylon" is to be destroyed in order that the spiritual and political framework of evil *can no longer function in the world.* Currently, wrote John, *"we are of God (but) the whole world lies under the sway of the wicked one"* (1Jn5:19). The fall of Babylon cannot pertain to the end of the time-space universe for the people of the world subsequently mourn over her demise. The rich and powerful are distraught at its downfall whilst God's chosen people celebrate. Clearly even "Babylon" cannot be directly responsible for *all* bloodshed and depravity on Earth but as far as God is concerned she rather than the world is ultimately liable and will bear the punishment of destruction; the second key point then being that Babylon is destroyed *but not the Earth along with her.* It is not always easy to distinguish between past and future events in Revelation but here the sequence at least is clear: not until "Babylon" has been destroyed can "the reign of the Lord God (on Earth) begin" and the "marriage of the Lamb" take place, the wife having at last "made herself ready" (Rev19:6,7). That reflects Old Testament prophecy in which the reign of Christ with His people invariably follows the destruction of their enemies.

Cyrus: a type of Christ

The Neo-Babylonian empire, who under king Nebuchadnezzar had destroyed the first Jewish Temple and brought God's people into exile as slaves in Babylon was defeated by Cyrus the Great – "king of the four corners of the world", being one of his grand titles. God used this enlightened Gentile to liberate His people from Babylon and through his sovereign edict, their temple was rebuilt. He was described by the Prophet Isaiah as "God's anointed one" or messiah (Is45:1). This self-styled "king of the world" destroyed the Babylonian hold over God's people and cleared the path for them to worship JHWE in the city of the great king. This surely prefigures the end-time destruction of Babylon, representative of the mystical, invisible body of satanic evil, currently functioning in the world in opposition to the mystical, visible Body of Christ: the one seeking to bring light, truth, peace and healing, the other moral degradation, greed, deception and destruction. That is the nature of the struggle; it is not the Church versus everyone outside her as depicted in Augustine's "City of God"; it is a two-way battle within the World, not against her. The Church and "Babylon" are both seeking to woo people to themselves but for opposite ends, resulting of course in three outcomes: the saints, the satanic agents and the rest of creation who are to be *"delivered from the bondage of corruption into the glorious liberty of the children of God* (Rom8:21).

According to Paul: "Flesh and blood cannot inherit the Kingdom of God" (1Cor15:50); that inheritance pertaining to when it arrives in its fullness. That is why the apostle was looking to Heaven from whence the Saviour will come *"to change our lowly bodies to be fashioned like His glorious body according to the operation by which He will subject all things to Himself"* (Phi3:21). For those resurrected at that time will have an incorruptible body, which as well as being indestructible will no longer be subject to the corrupting influence of the "body of this death", so they will no longer be inclined to carnality or worldliness but righteousness and peace. Those worthy to attain that age and the resurrection (Lk20:35) will "be like the angels in Heaven" yet still able to relate on Earth to those subjects in corruptible bodies just as the risen Jesus related for a time with His disciples as did angels with the likes of Abraham and Lot. Paul had described the resurrection as being a *"prize he was striving to attain"* (Phil3:11-14) whereas **all** who have died are to be resurrected at some point so Paul cannot have been referring to the general resurrection for he was seeking *to attain a prize.* Two resurrections are also indicated in Paul's first letter to the Thessalonians (4:15-17) in which he states that at Christ's coming, the dead in Christ will be raised before the living elect join them "in the clouds", being the so-called "rapture" so as to be spared the hour of testing when the wicked are ingloriously removed from the Earth by His holy angels (Mt13:41; 2Thes1:7-9; Rev3:10). According to Paul, God brings those who "sleep in Jesus" with Him to Earth; we do not "join them in Heaven" (1Thes4:14). Remaining on Earth throughout will be those who have mourned over their rejection and/or ignorance of Christ (Rev1:7), called upon His name, accepted His Lordship (obeyed the gospel) and accordingly found mercy. If the dead in Christ are to rise before the elect who are alive join Christ in the air then clearly there are two resurrections for logistically there could hardly be a resurrection of all who had lived on Earth before that event. The two resurrections are explicitly set out in the Revelation of God to Jesus Christ (20:5-6) and the principle being applied throughout is to take Scripture at its word unless obvious symbolism is intended, especially in view of the fearsome caveat in Rev22:19. There is no textual justification to treat this datum symbolically particularly as no one has come up with a workable suggestion as to what two resurrections could be intended to symbolize.

The limited infallibility of the Holy Apostolic Church

This writer adheres to the Catholic Church as overseen by the Bishop of Rome whom he would toast and revere, but Conscience first; for neither she nor he is infallible in an unqualified sense, nor do they claim to be. Through what I have experienced there are aspects of my understanding that are more akin to Eastern Orthodoxy than Roman Catholicism, but I have been round the block quite enough. I am not a compulsive denomination sampler, it can be a devastating experience walking around a town where some (not all) of one's former friends regards one as a heretic, reprobate or simply one to be pitied. I now understand the purpose of this extraordinary spiritual journey: it is the current task. The progression has been Spirit-led throughout, for like the majority I don't by nature have the theological nous or audacity to question the heritage in which I first came to faith in Christ, which is no doubt why it took nearly thirty years for me to question my Calvinist beliefs. Apart from which, the Lord has decreed that enough is enough: denominations should be abolished; there can only be one holy, catholic and apostolic Church for *there is only one Body of Christ.* I have emphasized the essential role of the Deposit of Faith, the teaching Magisterium and the validity of Development (living tradition) regarding devotional practices and doctrine that is not intrinsic to the foundation of the Faith, yet within this consummative context my three *priorities* have been Scripture, Scripture and Scripture. A Spirit-directed doctrinal resolution of the Holy Bible should be the final arbiter for Truth, not a pronouncement from any tainted Church. Similar sentiments have been expressed in the past but as I have been at pains to point out *ad nauseam* for it is essential to grasp it in view of the alleged revelations of the sixteenth century which did not meet such a criterion, nothing said here challenges the efficacy of the Apostolic Church's historical soteriological provision or universal mission. Christ has kept His promise: no historical period has existed since His ascension without a saving gospel being proclaimed and a daily Offering in memory of His death perpetuated by the faithful. So whilst no particular Church or Church leader is infallible, the Roman Catholic and complementing Orthodox Catholic churches together with the Assyrian and Oriental Orthodox Church and those assemblies which can legitimately trace their lineage back to the apostles through the process of apostolic succession *do* have a claim to infallibility within certain parameters, namely those essential to Christ fulfilling His promises to His future disciples. That infallibility has to encompass the ability to have sifted through the various alleged inspired first century writings in accordance with the Spirit's editorial direction to form the biblical canon or else we cannot trust the Bible; also, to have provided all essential instruction and sacral provision required for gospel salvation with reference to the apostolic written and oral Tradition or else we cannot trust the promises of Christ pertaining to His Church. It has not however been essential for the churches to have had a thorough understanding or agreed articulation of the mystical mechanics of gospel salvation in order that its benefits are bestowed; and the same would apply to perceiving a broader providence that I have largely been outlining. Infallibility has rather been ensured for the essentialities, such that those who have not separated themselves from the Apostolic churches that administer the means of grace may be saved (soul-healed) and fitted for an inheritance with the saints. Other more arcane issues such as the precise economy of the Godhead, pre-aeonian and incarnational Christology (including what Jesus as Prophet knew and when He knew it) and the nature of the birth of the Mother of God-incarnate are inessential mysteries, not a cause to rupture the body of Christ or perpetuate it with mutual anathematising.

The Filioque clause

This is another example of a subject that I had no intention to revisit, but in view of the reconciliatory aims I must address it briefly (there is plenty of background data on the internet). Many will know it relates to the insertion of the phrase "and (from) the Son" (Latin: *filioque*) with regard to the "procession of the Holy Spirit" within the Nicene Creed that has been a longstanding dispute between Eastern and Western Christianity. I had previously been content with the Roman Church's understanding that the Spirit proceeds from Father and Son, but that at least needs to be qualified. Scripture, indeed Christ Himself is explicit that God the Holy Spirit does *not* proceed or at least has not eternally proceeded (Greek: *ekporouetai*) from Himself but the Father only (Jn15:26) otherwise His statement reported by John would be meaningless. The Son was eternally begotten from the Father whilst the Spirit has eternally proceeded from the Father. Yet *in time,* the Holy Spirit may proceed (Latin: *procedere*) from the Son in the sense that "Jesus breathed on the disciples and said, 'Receive the Holy Spirit'" (Jn20:22). The Son and Spirit are economically subordinate to the Father; that is, they do His will rather than vice versa, yet neither is inferior in nature nor in being. The *filioque* clause tends to understate the Father's monarchical status and limits the role and free course of the Spirit within the mysterious economy of the Godhead. The Son even when He was about to be glorified did not regard Himself as equal in attributes to His Father; He would not tolerate the notion (Jn14:28). Likewise, St Paul: *"I want you to know that the head of every man is Christ; the head of woman is man, and the head of Christ is God"* (1Cor11:3) The one comparison is a profound mystery – as is Christ and the Church (Eph5:32), the other less so: woman is equally human to man and subordinate merely in a relational or operational sense within the context of marriage as Paul taught the matter. To that apostle, in fact all apostles, there is but one God, the Father, *of Whom* are all things, and one Lord Jesus Christ, *by Whom* are all things (1Cor8:6). Many of the ante-Nicene Fathers were later judged to have "tended to subordinationism"; rather they were being faithful to Scripture and reflecting the Tradition that the churches had more recently received in person from the apostles. I have made a point of utilizing only the language of Scripture when referring to God, His Son and Spirit. Those who through a Platonic influence err towards an overly-spiritualized eschatology potentially subordinate the Son, for He assuredly is not pure spirit, yet to know Him and be united to Him must equally be joy unsurpassable and the fulfilment of theosis or else He would not be a part of the Godhead. It is the Son of Man that is to be our eternal Partner in union; not in stasis but abundant activity and royal service; for *"those who are to receive royal power are the saints of the Most High and **their kingship** will be for ever and ever and ever"* (Dan7:18 New Jerusalem Bible). Nevertheless, to be able to grasp the "fellowship of the secret" it is essential that the Father's supreme Monarchy within the Godhead is clearly understood (especially re: Acts1:7 and 1Cor15:28). As we have seen, whenever a heresy occurs (in this case Arianism) there can be a tendency to overcompensate and distort the true equilibrium. Over-reactions to the fatal errors of Pelagius, Manes, Arius and the hedonistic chiliasts, none of which (over-reactions) were themselves fatal to the gospel or the Church's mission have nevertheless served to sustain the mystery of God's broader providence. In terms of the Filioque clause, many great minds and good hearts in East and West have been seeking to reach a consensus controversy: the North American Orthodox-Catholic Theological Consultation (AD2002/3) wisely agreed the two parties should "*recognize the limitations to our ability to make definitive assertions about the inner life of God*". It is not a matter that need divide the Apostolic Church any longer though I am personally persuaded there is a case for the clause being removed and the Creed returned to its original format.

Despite such differences as these, the essential Gospel teaching and provision has been made available through Catholic/Orthodox Christianity in West and East[7] throughout the gospel age in which sense and within which scope they could be regarded as infallible. My findings are in tune with both in terms of what I will call the "inclusive essentials of the Church's historic salvific mission", by which I mean that what is indispensable for that purpose has always been included within what has been deemed to have been indispensable both in the East and West, which unfortunately is not the case for the denominations that have separated themselves. The new doctrinal understanding related in this writing that differs from the teaching of these churches, radical though it appears (not least to the author) relates to matters not directly essential to her salvific mission (in that inclusive sense) but to matters the churches may need enlightenment about in the historical end-age context, particularly pertaining to God's disposition towards broader creation and the general nature of the age to come.

Millennialism had earlier played a role in my own spiritual journey but was a concept which I had largely set aside on joining the Catholic Church. However, the spiritual encounter has reinforced my earlier understanding, albeit not necessarily a literal thousand-year period; for it is only in the context of some period of activity under Christ as King of the Earth that the regal, priestly and juridical roles depicted throughout Scripture with regard to the elect can sensibly be realized in the age to come, for only the priestly aspect currently applies. Some readers may be convinced that as Church members they are currently reigning, ruling and judging; rather I suggest they are learning, serving and enduring in preparation for those more honourable tasks. Those who were meaningfully reigning would surely not be thought of by their subjects as "the scum of the Earth" (1Cor4:13). The main need to review the question of the messianic age arose from the implications of the "fellowship of the secret" to the staging of salvation history; i.e. that the terrestrial aspects of Old Testament prophecy were not currently being fulfilled or "re-envisaged" within the spiritual and religious sphere but have been deferred until "*the fullness of the Gentiles has come in*" (cf. Rom11:25). The establishment of the Church was not to be the climax of the Israel story; rather the latter has been placed on the back-burner until Paul's prophecy is fulfilled:

For if the casting away of (the Jews) be reconciliation for the World, what shall the reception of them be but life from the dead? (Rom11:15).

The other fathers and children

The hopes and expectations of faithful Jews need not be confounded if they are content to share their privileges with faithful Gentile Christians; and so may these fathers be reconciled to their children and all Israel be saved. For when they are, we may anticipate resurrection, even life from the dead (Rom11:15). The First-fruits of this resurrection had indicated that His Father's plans for Israel were not really the Church's business (Acts1:6,7) and this disclosure affirms that Christians have been mistaken in believing the Old Testament prophesies and promises to the Jewish nation were allegories for the current age. Reconciliation could never have been accomplished from a one-sided position of "Told you so" but rather by the acknowledgement of error of all parties. Such also would provide an effectual predisposition for the separated children in the churches to be reconciled with their Catholic/Orthodox Fathers in the Faith, whilst the Fathers *of* the Faith may be reconciled with their Gentile children of the Kingdom who have been grafted in to provoke them to jealousy. Prevarication may prolong what the Church and world have to endure (Mal4:6b) so woe to any who would engender it by their failure to acknowledge error, frustrating the process of reconciliation. With such a warning were the Scriptures of the Old Testament dispensation concluded.

The hierarchical nature of Kingdom

Once wickedness is eradicated and righteousness established there would be less need for certain hierarchical structures, yet Revelation depicts the New Jerusalem coming down from Heaven as "the Bride that the Lamb has married" (21:9). This is currently the "Heavenly Jerusalem" described in Hebrews (12:22), for that is where Christ is installed as King with His angels and saints who are in mystical union with His Pilgrim Church on Earth. This heavenly Jerusalem is described as *"coming down from God to Earth to be married to Christ"* (Rev21:2) and is to be the inhabitation of all the elect, whilst the nations outside will come to its light and the kings of the Earth will bring it their treasures (21:24). So there are to be "principalities and powers" in the next age as well as this (Eph1:21) which Christ will still be heading, the difference being that everyone will know about it and He will, as it were, have a Wife in tow. Given the indubitable physicality, not everyone once resurrected can be seated adjacent to or in intimate communion with the Lord of glory; some must worship from afar. An eternal egalitarianism, apart from being unbiblical could only function within a spiritual environment in which disembodied souls became, as it were, absorbed into God or are in a permanent dream-like state. The latter may be the case for those disembodied spirits currently said to be "sleeping in Christ" or "resting on Abraham's bosom" but it cannot be so after the resurrection, for each will be like the resurrected Jesus before His ascension. For He is the "First-fruits of them that sleep" just as His people are currently a kind of first-fruit of the human creation, most of whom are yet fully to be made alive (Jam1:18; 1Cor15:23). Man is to share in God's divinity yet must remain distinct from God in his essence. He obtains intimate communion with the Godhead through the mediation of the Son. The Christian is already "in the Son" whilst the Son is in the Father and the Father is in the Son (Jn14:10). But in a resurrected reality there will have to be an order as there is in the angelic realm (cf. Lk1:19) yet in due course every soul may be fulfilled in accordance with its established capacity; hence the importance of our life in this body; hence the value of anything by which that capacity might be enlarged; hence the eternal value of temporary human suffering: the grist for glory.

Angelic intrigue

Given the reality of Lucifer, that supreme angel of light who became Satan (Man's Adversary), not all the heavenly host had been happy about God's plans for humankind and some revolted. Surely, thought they, it would be the Godhead with the *princes of the angelic realm* who would oversee the fulfilment of God's plans for His multiverse; why involve a third party, particularly such puny children of dust? Those who were content within their own realm and remained faithful are nevertheless intrigued and desire to look into these matters (1Pet1:12). Little wonder, for the extraordinary transition that is required of fallen human beings to fulfil such a destiny is quite breath-taking, and it is referred to by the writer to the Hebrews:

For He has not put the world to come of which we speak in subjection to angels, but one testified in a certain place saying:

"What is man that You are mindful of him or the son of man that You take care of him? You have made him a little lower than the angels; You have crowned him with glory and honour and set him over the works of your hands; You have put all things under subjection under his feet."

For in that He put all in subjection under him, He left nothing that is not put under him. But now we do not see all things put under him (i.e. mankind). But we see Jesus who was made a little *lower than the angels and **because He suffered death** has been **crowned with glory and honour**, that He, by the grace of God, might taste death for everyone (Heb2:5-9)*

The author of Hebrews obviously writing within the gospel age is referring to the age that follows it as the "*oikoumenen* to come", which indicates an inhabited Earth, not "Heaven". He also states that in the current age we do not see all things subjected to human beings (which is the eventual plan). What Christians *can* see by faith is the Man Christ Jesus already *crowned with glory because of His suffering* (*dia to pathema*) (Heb2:9 cf. Greek), so as to bring many human sons to glory (v10). As all the letters to the Asian churches through John in Revelation make clear (chapters 2&3), this privileged role is ***not for all who have been incorporated into the Church*** through baptism but those relatively few (cf. Rev3:4) within the churches who are found worthy (cf. 2Tim4:7, Lk20:35). God calls many into the Church (*ekklesia* - the called-out ones); of those called only some are chosen as worthy to inherit the promises of Christ (cf. Mt20:16) for they had been called out of the world to be sanctified, requiring their personal co-operation, application and perseverance, which not all provide or have even understood to be the case. It is surely expedient that all who are sincerely seeking to be faithful to Christ within the various churches know what is expected of them in anticipation of His coming.

Scripture is explicit: the suffering that Jesus endured on our behalf also perfected Him for His future Office as well as being an example to those who are to follow Him to glory (cf. 1Pet2:21). How much more necessary must it be for those whose current bodies originated from dust and are tainted by sin to experience suffering to perfect them for the future privilege of sharing their Bridegroom's Life and Domain. For within God's Economy, those called to lead, are to lead through serving and must also be prepared to suffer on behalf of those they are to lead:

*I (Paul) now rejoice in **my sufferings for you**, and fill up in my flesh what is lacking in the afflictions of Christ, for the sake of His body which is the Church (Col1:24NKJ)*

He also told the Corinthian Church that their own salvation was being perfected by their sharing in the apostles' suffering (2Cor1:6). This apostle had received certain revelations concerning future glory, referred to obliquely in 2Cor12:1-6, which is generally accepted as referring to his own experience of being "*caught up into the third Heaven*" (v2). These revelations were so stupendous in nature that they "*cannot and may not be spoken of by any human being*" (v4). To prevent him from bursting with joy or becoming conceited he was given a physical affliction – his thorn in the flesh (v7). God permitted Satan to inflict this physical discomfort on His beloved apostle for his own good, and so that God's strength may be made perfect in Paul's weakness. That would not be the devil's way: he has no time for losers but utilizes his most formidable human agents to do his bidding.

The more one begins to comprehend God's exhilarating plan for humanity, or at least as much of it as has currently been disclosed, the more one should begin to perceive a positive role for human suffering in the present preparatory age. Through Paul's revelation in the heavenly realm, he had an exceptional grasp of this matter such that he positively rejoiced in his own sufferings for the Church (Col1:24), and knew that as the Body of Christ, the Church must suffer for the world:

*For I consider that the sufferings of this present time are not worthy to be compared with the **glory that is to be revealed in us**. For the earnest expectation of creation eagerly awaits for the revelation of the sons of God (Rom8:18-19 New King James Version)*

For the suffering of the elect that anticipates their glory is also a reflection of God's universal justice and sublime equity, being the hallmark of a loving nature:

*(Your tribulations) are a manifest witness of the **righteous judgement of God**, that you may be counted worthy of the Kingdom of God for which **you also suffer** seeing that is a **righteous thing with God to recompense tribulation** to them that trouble you (2Thes1:5,6 King James Version).*

And did not James also write:

*Consider it pure joy, my brothers and sisters whenever you **face trials** of many kinds, because you know the testing of your faith produces perseverance. Let perseverance continue its work so that you may be mature and complete not lacking anything (Ja1:2-4 New International Version)*

Trials incur suffering but help a Christian persevere and spiritually grow towards moral perfection. It is also linked to the need for discipline, which is more readily understood from our experience as children or parents:

God disciplines us for our good in order that we may share in His holiness. No discipline seems pleasant at the time, but painful. Later however it produces a harvest of righteousness and peace for those who have been trained by it (Heb12:10-11)

Suffering endured by creation

But this may be all well and good for the Christian, but the many people who have not heard or heeded the various presentations of the gospel cannot possibly be expected to understand the need for human suffering, for the Church herself has scarcely comprehended the mystery of evil. As this Catechism acknowledges:

*It is a great mystery that **providence should permit diabolical activity**, but we know that in everything God works for good with those who love Him [Catechism of the Catholic Church].*

This brief chapter aims to throw some light on *how* the devil's mischief can work for our good, in which case it will have been achieved with the Spirit's help, for hardly anything written in this context had formed in my mind until the spiritual encounter to which I have testified. But the Church will not perceive or be able to explain the need for human suffering if she does not pay heed to what Scripture testifies are the future roles and responsibilities that the Bride may share with Her Royal Husband within the heavenly and terrestrial plane. And as more and more within the churches are grasping, the rest of human creation is not to be assigned to the cosmic scrap heap; it too is suffering for a purpose. In terms of the elect and those they may come to rule, it is a question of ordering and staging within the process of the enlightenment and deification of humanity so that all might come to share His felicity as the children of God.

It is surely right and just that human beings endure the trials that they do in view of the privileges and responsibilities that await them. All will suffer at some point for everyone has had to be salted (Mk9:49). But it is better to suffer for doing good than for doing evil (1Pet3:17); better to be a miserable beggar like Lazarus and be comforted after death than to live a careless life of ease like Dives who must suffer for much longer. *"Remember that in your lifetime you received good things and likewise Lazarus evil things, so now he is comforted and you are tormented"* (Lk16:25). And the Master again: *"Woe to you who are rich for you have received your consolation now"* (Lk6:24). The fear of God is indeed the beginning of wisdom: those who respect God through religious creed or conscience make the right choices for their eternal welfare. Yet he who would *true valour* see let him come hither, for it is finest of all to suffer for Christ: *"For our light affliction which is but for a moment is working for us a far more exceeding and eternal weight of glory"* (2Cor4:17); and so, every sacrifice must be seasoned with salt.

Being unaware of these matters it is hardly surprising that the world hankers after the kind of potentate and human experience related in the song we quoted from earlier. Those without any religious faith will not realize that life in this world, and particularly life in this fallen "body of death" is entirely a preparation for the next. Christians at least should recognize that life in the present, though not without its blessings, is merely the birth pangs (Rom8:22) leading up to the glories that await those who love God or are capable of doing so once they apprehend His glory. In that same passage, Paul refers to the ***involuntary aspect*** of the human predicament:

For creation was subjected to frustration, not by its own choice but by the will of the one (sic) who subjected it, in hope that the creation itself will be liberated from its bondage and decay and be brought into the glorious freedom of the children of God (Rom8:20,21 New International Version)

As some other translations affirm by their use of capitalised pronouns (e.g. New King James Version), it was in accordance with divine providence that His creation be submitted to frustration and vanity, for Satan would hardly be hoping for its liberation. God well knew the outcome would be even better for all and would demonstrate His glory and grace more fully than if events had taken a different course, and humanity will have been better prepared for the challenges being prepared for them in future ages. Human suffering will not have been wasted; not only will it be compensated for at the individual level but will have been the efficacious means by which the souls of frail children of dust could be disciplined, shaped and "extended" for a future experience that will include for some, not only worship and adoration from afar but an immediate and intimate association with the Lord of Glory (Mt20:23).

Such is the wisdom of God, and such was the role for evil and the realm of darkness; but perhaps spare a thought for its prince. He will have anticipated the direst punishment for his celestial rebellion and what he subsequently inflicted on humanity; but at least, through the human agents he controls he had helped destroy their habitat (Rev11:18b) and surely thwarted God's intentions for the sons of Adam and daughters of Eve to be deified, the plan which Lucifer and his fellow rebels had so resented. But instead the Adversary's mischief has been utilized by God as grist to prepare children of dust for their inheritance. This is the perfect victory for God and His Christ and the ultimate humiliation for the devil and his party. There are related truths that are both observable and borne out by Scripture: the greater the pain, the greater the joy. If every day were the first day of spring as in our song, how diminished it would be if winter had not first been endured. It appears sweeter to regain something that was lost than if it had been there all the time. We see that with the parable of the prodigal: the wayward son returning home to his Father was more cause for celebration than the one who had remained faithful. The angels rejoice more over one sinner that repents than ninety-nine not needing repentance. This is linked to another motif traceable in Scripture: divide to reconcile. Through God's inscrutable providence it applied to man's broken relationship with His Maker, reconciled and

335

restored through Christ. God's first-choice for the Kingdom the Jewish people failed to appreciate the day of their visitation allowing Gentile members into that privileged role; the partition having been broken down between Jew and Gentile through the cross to create one divine assembly. And I trust before too long, the Western Church: divided through internal corruption and a break-away movement; Mother and separated children reconciled, bringing with them the untold wealth contained in Christ's gospel, the full extent of which may yet have remained undiscovered had the Church never divided and gone its separate ways[8]. Through God's wisdom it was deemed fitting that ecclesiological unity be re-established from division and plurality rather than a historically maintained integrity. Likewise, may Western Christianity be re-affiliated with East so that once again the Church may breathe with both lungs; just in time for the greatest reconciliation of all: the whole created order purged, restored and re-united with its Creator. Division always involves suffering for the parties involved, but the joy seems all the sweeter when they are united at last.

The suffering of God

Suffering indeed for all parties: our God is no deistic, impassionate chess master overseeing this wondrous plan. He had been perfectly entitled to enjoy unbroken felicity but for mankind's sake He was prepared to endure the agony of observing His only begotten Son's humiliation and death. If Satan had been barred from planet Earth or Adam and Eve had been erased for their disobedience, Christ need not have died. But He permitted His arch-enemy what appeared to be an extraordinary victory for the sake of what He knew would be the ideal preparation for the beings created in His image to be raised from dust and prepared for a glorious destiny. This is why things have always been as they have been in the world and in the Church. Suffering partnered with essential spiritual healing and progressive enlightenment are the means by which God is drawing man toward his ultimate destiny as exemplified by His Son's own experience. The suffering He had endured was principally (and most would have thought exclusively) to provide for man's redemption; yet it also fulfilled another unexpected function as we have shown from Scripture relating to preparation for Office (cp. Heb2:10,11,17,18) and as an example to those who would come to share in His inheritance. The precise nature of our function through eternity, although hinted at through the various offices and titles applied to those chosen for Christ, *"cannot and may not be spoken of by any human being"* (2Cor12:4). What we have been told in Scripture about our future life with God and His Son (and most have yet to grasp that) pertains to the immediate future in the context of eternity, which is as much as most human minds could currently sustain; to know too much would anyway undermine the principle of faith. God's nature and covenant faithfulness towards those that love Him can and never will change, yet the creative energy of the Universal Deity is incomprehensible, and whatever He has prepared for the future, His divine Son as Agent and Overseer of all that has ever been created or has yet to be established within the universe must be at the centre. His glorified family and joint-Heirs will spearhead that activity supported by all God's redeemable creation. If even one nth degree of this can be grasped, human suffering will have been worth it as it will undoubtedly have enlarged our capacity to enjoy a fuller communion, companionship and participation with the Divine Glory. Such will have been the meaning of life, but who now will discern it?

I (the Lord) have kept silent for a long time; I have kept silent and restrained Myself

Now like a woman in labour I will groan, I will both gasp and pant

I will lead the blind by ways they have not known **along unfamiliar paths I will guide them**

I will turn the darkness into light before them and make the rough places smooth.

These are the things I will do; I will not forsake them (Is42:14,16).

Notes: CHAPTER SEVEN

1."If I ruled the world" – from: Pickwick Composed: Bricusse & Ornadel

2. Irenaeus against heresies Book 3 chap. 23 (6)

3. Irenaeus against heresies Book 4 chap. 27 (2); & Clement (Alexandria) Stromata Book VI chap. 6

4. Thomas Aquinas: De Potentia q3 art.6, ad 4

5. Catholic Easter hymn: "Oh happy fault, which gained for us so great a redeemer!"

6. See Wikipedia under "Church's approach to Pre-millennialism"

7. Along with Eastern Catholic Church that remained in communion with Rome

8. A reflection of Pope John Paul II ("Crossing the threshold of hope") Jonathon Cape p153

Printed in Great Britain
by Amazon